the complete
deep Purple

the complete
deep Purple

Michael Heatley

Reynolds & Hearn Ltd
London

To my sons Drew (vocals, first Purple gig
2002) and Joe (drums). May they continue to
Taste the Band!

First published in 2005 by

Reynolds & Hearn Ltd

61a Priory Road

Kew Gardens

Richmond

Surrey TW9 3DH

A CIP catalogue record for this book is available from the British Library.

ISBN 1 903111 99 4

Designed by James King.

Printed and bound in Great Britain by Biddles Ltd, King's Lynn, Norfolk.

contents

Acknowledgements

The author would like to thank Jerry Bloom, Roy Davies, Nigel Cross,
Allan Heron and Bob Richards for their expert help, advice and
contributions. Also Nephele Headleand, Jo Brooks and Sean Egan.
Finally, respect to Simon Robinson for being the last word on the subject.

The publishers would like to thank Steve Tribe for copy editing, Jo Ware for
the index, Ruth Timmins for picture research and Peri Godbold for working
her magic at the last minute.

Picture Credits

Introduction

Between 1968 and 1976, and from 1984 to the time of writing in 2005, Deep Purple have recorded and released some seventeen studio albums, along with over two dozen live recordings and compilations in various formats throughout the world.

Since their initial demise in the 1970s and then on through the reunion years of the 1980s and beyond, album sales have continued at a buoyant level and currently stand at over 100 million units, consolidating Purple's position as one of the more commercially successful rock bands and holders of one of the most popular back catalogues in rock history. Add to this an extensive and flourishing live bootleg market of recordings from throughout their career and the band clearly occupies an important position within the rock world.

So what is it about Deep Purple that continues to make them special to successive generations of rock fans, nearly four decades after their formation?

Although they were contemporaries of Led Zeppelin and Black Sabbath, Purple were in fact subtly and distinctively different. They were not acclaimed as overnight sensations on release of their debut LP, but prefaced their most productive and commercial work with three studio albums while perfecting their musical direction.

During the late 1960s many groups, early Purple included, jumped from one musical bandwagon to another, ever hopeful of achieving that all-important 'hit single'; at the time the music world was still orientated towards the immediacy of the three-minute single. Yet with the focus shifting to the album as the favoured format for a band to express its creativity, Purple focused their energies on achieving a place in a progressive rock movement where new styles were readily embraced and groundbreaking originality based around virtuosity were commonplace occurrences.

They drew upon individual members' influences – classical, jazz, R&B, rock 'n' roll and (later) funk – and combined their personal strengths to bring together an amalgam of fresh, dramatic and exciting music. Their popularity thereafter grew not by clever hype or overly astute management and market manipulation but through extensive and exhilarating concert performance, their reputation as a live act propagated by word of mouth. This grass-roots popularity generated by their own efforts is why they have maintained such an intensely loyal core of followers over the decades, yet continue to be ignored or dismissed by the critics.

Aggression, virtuosity and live improvisation became bywords for Purple music. Guitar and Hammond organ pushed to the amplified limit vied with driving, deft percussion and soaring vocals to evolve into what became conveniently pigeonholed as Heavy Metal. Though Purple were much more than HM, they developed many of the musical and compositional dynamics that still govern bands of the genre over thirty years later. The influence of these dozen or so musicians of the Purple family is undeniable and incalculable.

Yet by the time the rock world realised the legacy it owed to Deep Purple, the band were no longer performing together. It was left to the various splinter groups formed by the ex-members to give all-too-fleeting glimpses of Purple's former majesty, and to the new bands at the forefront of the New Wave of British Heavy Metal in the early 1980s to pay a more indirect homage. While Zeppelin and Sabbath's contribution to popular music has rightly undergone reappraisal in recent years, Purple remain relatively critically neglected.

Behind the music itself lies a traumatic, confrontational yet fascinating history few bands can rival. In some ways, the artistic and personal conflicts within the band, exemplified by the personality clash between singer Ian Gillan and guitarist Ritchie Blackmore, helped drive Purple to greater heights, and these are also explored within these pages.

Little did I realise when I gazed lovingly on the twelve-inch vinyl sleeve of *Machine Head* as a long-haired sixth-former in 1972 that I would be taking my own teenage son to see four-fifths of the 'classic' Mark II line-up as the next millennium started. For that longevity alone, Deep Purple deserve respect. The fact they still have something to say musically is even more noteworthy: if classic rock exists as a genre, then surely Deep Purple are its embodiment.

PART ONE
The Deep Purple Story
1.Early Purple

When the first line-up of Deep Purple came together in the spring of 1968, the term 'heavy metal' had yet to be invented, while musical genres like 'hard' and 'progressive' rock were barely in their infancy. The aftermath of the now-legendary Summer of Love found the UK in the simultaneous throes of psychedelia and a blues boom, while the Beatles were still far from a spent force and indeed were about to start work on what would become Purple keyboardist-to-be Jon Lord's favourite LP of all time, *The Beatles* (more popularly known as 'The White Album'). It was far from clear that the band then taking its first tentative steps as Roundabout would, alongside the likes of Led Zeppelin, Free and Black Sabbath, go on to pioneer a new style of rock that became hugely popular in the 1970s. But so it would prove.

The impetus for the band's formation came not from a musician but a businessman. Tony Edwards ran a textile business, Alice Edwards Holdings Ltd, in London's West End. But his heart wasn't in the family firm and he'd begun to dabble in the pop world, taking Ayshea Brough, a young singer-turned model, under his wing; she would later shoot to fame in 1970s kids TV series *Lift Off*. Encouraged by this first venture into showbiz, he approached advertising executive John Coletta with the idea of financing and managing a band.

As Edwards later told rock historian Pete Frame: 'We were very green, we knew there was money in the business, but we didn't know how much.' Through publicist Vicki Wickham, Edwards met Chris Curtis. Curtis had been the original drummer with the Searchers – one of the best-loved bands of the Merseybeat era with a string of hits under their belts like 'Needles And Pins' and 'Sweets For My Sweet' – and a man who, noting the changing musical climate of the late 1960s, hankered after fronting his own group. He convinced Edwards he was the man to help him realise his dream. As fate would have it, Curtis had recently moved into Lord's flat and so the keyboardist was naturally approached to join.

Jon Douglas Lord had already been around the block. Born in Leicester on 9 June 1941, he had taken piano lessons as a teenager and later switched to organ when he heard American star Jimmy Smith's classic 'Walk On The Wild Side'. He moved down to London when he was twenty, intending to become an actor, and studied at the Central School of Speech and Drama. However, as he later observed: 'I got good crits, you know, and I did get to play Hamlet, but the criticisms I got were always "a hair's breadth away from being excellent" and that's not good enough. I find it very hard to submerge my feelings and assume others. That's what would always have stood in the way of my being as good an actor as I wanted to be.'

As a starving student, Lord put his musical talents to good use and started playing live, firstly with his own modern jazz sextet then in an R&B/soul band with guitarist Derek Griffiths. The magnificently named Red Bludd's Bluesicians eventually evolved into the Artwoods, led by Art Wood, the brother of Ron, who would later find fame and fortune with the Jeff Beck Group, the Faces and, of course, the Rolling Stones. A fine quintet, the Artwoods cut a series of excellent 45s for the Decca and Parlophone labels but never managed to crack the big time and called it a day in the summer of 1967 right in the midst of the 'flower power' craze.

As Jon recalled in *New Musical Express*: 'I got in a great state of disenchantment with what I was doing, but I didn't know why. I thought, "If I leave, what else can I do?" and there was nothing. It was a dead end. I had had an offer from Eric Burdon to replace Alan Price in the Animals and one from Them which Peter Bardens took, but that was some time before and the offers had ceased. Eventually I said I was going to leave and Art said he wanted to leave anyway; he was married and was fed up with the group life. I was getting into a very cushy way of life. I was lodging with Ronnie Wood and his mother was feeding me and giving me cigarettes. My music was suffering, there was no one making me fight any more and I needed it.'

Lord was soon roped in to work as part of the Flowerpot Men, one of the acts that had cashed in on the Summer of Love with 'Let's Go To San Francisco'. This rode the coattail of 'San Francisco (Flowers In Your Hair)', Scott McKenzie's chart-topping paean to the US hippie ideal and made it all the way to Number 4 in the UK singles chart. The group as such didn't exist – it had been a Tin Pan Alley scam all along – but the song's writers, Carter and Lewis, milked the hit for all it was worth and put together a band which promptly went on the road playing ballrooms, theatres and one-nighters. The other person Edwards and Coletta approached to join their new group was a notorious guitar-player by the name of Ritchie Blackmore.

Born in Weston-super-Mare on 14 April 1945, Blackmore had moved to Heston, near London Heathrow Airport, as a kid and grew up as a talented amateur javelin-thrower with a keen interest in aeroplanes and science. When he left secondary school, Ritchie went into the aircraft industry as a radio mechanic. He'd bought his first electric guitar for £9 when he was thirteen and took lessons from Big Jim Sullivan, a seasoned studio musician living nearby who would later go on to be Tom Jones's guitarist.

By the time he was asked to join the nascent Deep Purple, Blackmore had established himself as something of a veteran player. In May 1962 he got his first professional gig with Screaming Lord Sutch and his backing band, the Savages. Sutch of course was no member of the aristocracy but a plumber's mate from Harrow whose party-piece was running up and down underground trains screaming! In his heyday David Sutch – the king of horror rock – was the Johnny Rotten of his era, the original bad boy of British rock. As was his wont, he gave all his backing musicians nicknames; when Blackmore joined he became 'Bluebell'!

Their live act was second to none – Sutch would be carried on stage in a coffin – and Ritchie quickly learned how to move about and shake some action up there on the boards. It was an object lesson in stagecraft… and, of course, Sutch was a perfect role model for Blackmore's own later bad behaviour. A short stint in Mike Dee and the Jaywalkers followed before Blackmore joined an equally infamous bunch of Brit-rockers named the Outlaws whose singer Mike Berry had just quit. This line-up, which also included bassist Chas Hodges (of later Chas and Dave 'Rabbit' fame), cut four singles in their own right but, more importantly, played on some of the records legendary producer Joe Meek cut during this period – hits by the likes of John Leyton, Heinz and the Tornados, the band that most famously gave Meek his biggest smash in 1962 with the Number 1 instrumental 'Telstar'.

Meek, a true eccentric, was also a pioneer, the first of the true independent pop producers who developed his own recording techniques and was as great in his own way as Phil Spector. Sadly he killed himself in early 1967, turning the shotgun with which he'd just shot his landlady on himself. The Outlaws also acted as backing band for big US rock 'n' roll acts touring Britain such as Gene Vincent and Jerry Lee Lewis. Ritchie graduated from the Outlaws school of rock in April 1964. As he recalled to Pete Frame: 'I left because the group had been ostracised by the business and couldn't get work any more. We were regarded as criminals and got banned all over the place … our humour wasn't appreciated!'

Among these so-called crimes was the band's love of flour bombs, as bassist Hodges later told Frame: 'One day we were driving along and one of us happened to throw a stale cheese roll out of the open door – and it bonked this old geezer. Obviously we found this very funny – so we began to explore the possibility of other missiles. We found that the little half-pound bags of flour were best: if you made a two inch slit in the bag and threw it out – it burst all over the recipient. Ritchie Blackmore was a dead shot – never missed his target!'

A summer season in Rhyl as a member of the Wild Boys (backing Meek protégé Heinz) seemed a much safer proposition, but after six months doing package tours and the like Ritchie again got itchy feet. He flitted around the scene for a while, temporarily rejoined his old boss Sutch, toyed with his own band the Three Musketeers (which lasted just one live gig in Munich, West Germany in the winter of 1965-1966), played with Neil Christian and the Crusaders and even did a tour of Germany with Jerry Lee Lewis. Tony Edwards and Chris Curtis eventually tracked him down in Hamburg, and asked him to join their new project.

As Ritchie later told *Disc & Music Echo*: 'I went back to Germany in 1967. That's where I met my wife. That time I stayed 13 or 14 months and did hardly anything. I used to practise four or five hours a day. I used to hang around the Star Club and the Top 10 and sit in with bands I knew. It's quite interesting to sit in with different groups to see how they think. Then suddenly I got about 300 telegrams from Chris Curtis saying he wanted me to join a group and I came back. That's where I met Jon Lord. There were a few other people in the band. I was just going to be a second guitarist.' But Blackmore, having checked out the situation, decided it wasn't for him and headed back to Germany.

Chris Curtis, who died in 2005, was somewhat eccentric and lived in a bit of a fantasy world, as Lord later remembered in *NME*: 'He was only going to take the good gigs – he had financial backing – and get lots of publicity … Chris said he wanted to sing in the band and he had Justin Hayward of the Moody Blues and Denny Laine in mind to join. He started naming names and we got a bit frightened. He was going to play drums and lead guitar as well. He wanted to play hard [rock] versions of things like "If I Were A Carpenter".'

It must have been a bit of a relief when Curtis, too, decided to drop out and Lord was left to pick up the pieces. Having persuaded Blackmore to change his mind, the next person Jon recruited was a mate from the Flowerpot Men, bassist Nick Simper. Lord and Nick had already spoken about the possibility of making music together outside of the Flowerpot Men. Simper – born on 3 November 1945 in Norwood Green, Southall, Middlesex – had a similar musical background to Ritchie, having cut his teeth in the beat era with bands like Buddy Britten and the Regents before going on to work with the New Pirates (both before and after singer Johnny Kidd died in a car crash in October 1966), Screaming Lord Sutch and then Billie Davis's bands.

The drummer was Bobby Woodman, well known back then in muso circles. Woodman had started out at the dawn of British rock, working at the legendary 2Is coffee bar in Soho's Old Compton Street – where so many acts, from Cliff Richard and the Shadows to Adam Faith, were discovered – as one of Vince Taylor's Playboys. He'd then gone on to work with French singer Johnny Halliday and was the first English sticksman to have a double (bass) drum kit. But his tenure with Purple was shortlived – he was ill at ease with what he called the group's 'circus music' and the management quickly gave him the elbow.

Finding a singer was turning into a difficult process. The band had tried out Dave Curtiss – no relation to the just-departed Chris and former front man with his own group, the Tremors, who'd recorded for Philips – but he failed to make the grade. They also considered Spooky Tooth singer Mike Harrison, and even went to a Jeff Beck gig to watch Rod Stewart but were not impressed!

With the band advertising in *Melody Maker* for a vocalist, hordes of guys applied, thanks to the attractive nature of the advert. Because there were so many they decided to allocate time slots and, as Nick Simper was the only one with a car, he had the job of collecting groups of them from Borehamwood train station and taking them to Deeves Hall, a haunted farmhouse located just off the A1 trunk road north of London where Edwards and Coletta had installed their charges in March.

During these auditions the band started to get tired of the endless process and Nick Simper put forward the name of a fellow West London musician he had seen a few times. The others weren't familiar with him but when Simper contacted the singer in question, he found his target didn't feel this new band would be as successful as he believed his own group, Episode Six, would become. The man who declined the offer? Ian Gillan.

Among the numerous hopefuls auditioned was Rod Evans from the Maze. The band were impressed with him, not least because he had ideas; it was he who suggested they do the Beatles' 'Help' as a heavied-up ballad. Evans, born in Slough on 19 January 1947, had also gone through the usual semi-pro phase, playing in combos like the Horizons and then joined MI5 (the band, not the undercover organisation). Evans not only came up with musical ideas, he also boldly told Blackmore, Lord and Simper that the drummer in his band was better than Woodman.

Blackmore remembered, 'I'd seen Ian Paice in Hamburg in '67 and said I'd phone him if I got a good offer.' Paice, born in Nottingham on 29 June 1948, had started out playing in his father's dance band and then gone semi-pro in Georgie and the Rave Ons, later known as the Shindigs. Quitting his day job in the Civil Service, he joined MI5, who worked mainly on the Continent, and made just one 45, 'You'll Never Stop Me Loving You'. They eventually changed their name to the Maze and cut three singles (including 'Hello Stranger' for Immediate's subsidiary Reaction label) and an EP, but most of the interest in the group was in Italy.

A settled line-up was in place at last and the new group was finally in business. According to Jon Lord, Deep Purple initially modelled themselves on the American band Vanilla Fudge whom he'd seen at the Speakeasy, an infamous music-biz after-hours watering hole, the previous April. 'They'd knocked me out and we were going to be an English Vanilla Fudge, we thought.' Their sound relied heavily on the Hammond organ. So Edwards and Coletta invested in one for Lord: their expenditure on new equipment apparently amounted to a cool £7,000.

The Fudge were signed to Atco and cut five albums for the label. They featured the legendary rhythm section of Tim Bogert and Carmine Appice (who'd later play with guitarist Jeff Beck) and are now best remembered for their heavy organ-fuelled, slowed down makeover of the Supremes' soul classic 'You Keep Me Hangin' On'. The new line-up, briefly dubbed Roundabout by

Tony Edwards, made its debut on 20 April that year at the Vestpoppen in Tastrup, Denmark as part of a short Scandinavian tour, but it was a while before they played live in the UK. By then, they'd ditched their original moniker in favour of Deep Purple, taken from the Nino Tempo/April Stevens classic song of the same name which just happened to be Blackmore's granny's favourite tune. (They'd momentarily also toyed with Concrete Gods and then Fire, until they heard there was already a band with the latter name.)

Work then began on what was to become their first LP, *Shades Of Deep Purple*, cut in an astonishing 18 hours at Pye Studios at Marble Arch on a rudimentary four-track tape machine. It was produced by Derek Lawrence, whom Ritchie Blackmore had known during his Outlaw days; it was he who asked him to take charge for their first major foray in the studio. Lawrence had also worked with Meek and, as he told the Deep Purple Appreciation Society, 'Joe had a large influence on my production style and yes I used a lot of Joe's echo ideas and his in-your-face drum sounds.' He'd go on to work with the first line-up of Deep Purple on all their studio sessions and later stated, 'Much of the form and style that evolved over the first two years, from my point of view, came from Ritchie's unique style. It is my opinion that Ritchie found it hard to copy anything – and that's what made him special.'

Lawrence also got Purple's musicians involved in session work, notably on a single by Boz for UK Columbia – 'I Shall Be Released' b/w 'Down In The Flood' – two Bob Dylan songs on which Lord, Paice and Blackmore played together with Ritchie's old pal Chas Hodges. The singer, real name Raymond Burrell, would go on to fame and fortune as bass player with King Crimson and, in the 1970s, stadium-rockers Bad Company.

Shades Of Deep Purple was put out by a company called Tetragrammaton in the USA and they did an excellent job in promoting it. It helped that the debut waxing spawned a great 45 in 'Hush', a rocked-up version of a tune written by Joe South. It's doubtful the band had ever heard the writer's original country and western version, though Ritchie, who proposed the group should take it on, had heard Billy Joe Royal's shorter, snappier soul/pop treatment in Germany. It proved a great suggestion when 'Hush' quickly rose to the Number 4 slot in the *Billboard* Hot 100 in the summer of 1968.

'Hush' very much typified the quintet's dense early sound, driven by Lord's Hammond flourishes behind the swirling riff and a sizzling 90-second solo. It also had a very catchy chorus, while Evans was a good singer, far smoother than those who came after him. And, of course, Blackmore's wah-wah guitar was all over much of the record. He used a Fender Stratocaster, but would switch to a semi-acoustic Gibson for the second album.

The LP very much set the pattern for all the albums Deep Purple Mark I made – a mixture of group originals, choice cover versions and a medley. As well as 'Hush', *Shades Of Deep Purple* featured a version of the Beatles' 'Help' (Vanilla Fudge having covered 'Eleanor Rigby') and, as part of the LP's centrepiece medley, Skip James's 'I'm So Glad' which had been popularised by the then current 'gods of heavy', Cream.

'When we first started rehearsing, I was just playing the song "Help" on the keyboards, because you cannot play it the same way on the organ like it was on the record,' Jon Lord was to say many years later. 'I was just playing it slowly … they're lovely chords, aren't they? Rod Evans started singing it as a sad but slow song and Ritchie came in and said, "Oh, it sounds good that way," so I did the arrangement for that.'

Last but not least in the covers stakes was 'Hey Joe', which had been the Jimi Hendrix Experience's debut hit single of 1966. Group compositions included the Lord/Evans 'One More Rainy Day', but the real standout was 'Mandrake Root', taking its name in part from what had been a very shortlived Blackmore outfit he'd put together in Germany the previous year. 'Mandrake Root' would eventually be worked up into a live *pièce de résistance* that would end shows amidst blazing strobes, feedback and equipment trashing.

Looking back at this first LP, Ritchie observed in *Disc*, 'I've always been disappointed with our albums. The first one was a good attempt for a first. But people have always said, "It's not you." We've always tried to be too flash on our records.' Bandmate Lord agreed: 'The first Deep Purple album had long-winded classical intros that stuck out like a sore thumb. We didn't have much of a direction in those days.'

Directionless or not, the quintet made its BBC radio debut with a session for John Peel's classic *Top Gear* show in June 1968 and embarked on something of a love/hate relationship with the DJ over the next five or six years, Peel later castigating the 1970s Purple as 'formulaic'. They played 'Hush', 'Help' and 'One More Rainy Day' – and the Radio 1 panel, who could be very difficult about accepting rock bands (they had almost turned Marc Bolan's Tyrannosaurus Rex duo down a few months before), gave them a complete thumbs-up. The consensus was 'enthusiastic, unanimous pass, polished commercial group'.

Confident that things were moving as planned, Edwards and Coletta had by this time been joined by Ron Hire, a salesman from Brighton who entered the fray purely as an investor. By August the company that took the initial letter of all three surnames (hence HEC Enterprises) was in full swing, not only as Purple's management company but also dealing with all the business transactions, including in the lucrative area of music publishing. Within a year, Edwards and Coletta had bought out Hire.

Purple went on to play their debut live British gig at the Red Lion in Warrington on 3 August 1968, pretty much a warm-up for their appearance at the annual blues and jazz festival in Sunbury one week later. This was finally followed by the release of their first LP in Britain in September. When 'Hush' was released it enjoyed a lot of play on Radio 1, but the single failed to match its meteoric ascent in the USA. The success of the later Mark II line-up has always eclipsed the first version of Deep Purple, yet they were a very prolific, creative outfit. They produced three albums and a series of excellent US and UK singles in an unbelievable nine-month period.

For their second long-player, the group switched label, though

not record company. In June 1969 EMI Records, eager to
capitalise on the burgeoning underground scene in Britain,
launched Harvest Records which, in addition to releasing debut
recordings by long-hair outfits like the Edgar Broughton Band,
also became home to the company's more difficult-to-pigeonhole
acts like the Pretty Things and, now, Purple. Though recorded
from August to October 1968 at De Lane Lea Studios in London,
Book Of Taliesyn didn't find release in the UK until early the
following summer. This second LP was a step forward in more
ways than one. Gone was the standard group shot on the front
cover. Instead there was an ornate gatefold complete with sleeve
notes and a mind-bending illustration inspired by King Arthur's Camelot.

Band originals included the stately psychedelic pop of 'The
Shield' and 'Anthem' (with string arrangements by Jon Lord) and
the romping instrumental 'Wring That Neck', boasting some fiery
playing by Blackmore. This was a number that went on to enjoy
more longevity than other stuff on the record and one that marked
the rockier path to come. Known as 'Hard Road' in the States, it
had been put out as the flipside of 'Emmaretta' in February 1969 as
their second UK 45, but the record sadly failed to do business – unlike
their more popular cover of Neil Diamond's 'Kentucky Woman',
which had been a successful American single the previous December.

As on the debut album, there was another medley – this time
'Exposition', an accomplished self-penned prog-rock jam which
segued into Lennon/McCartney's 'We Can Work It Out', featuring
some inspired, snaking runs from Blackmore behind a precise
vocal from Evans. The album closed with an epic reworking
of Ike and Tina Turner's hit 'River Deep Mountain High'.

While Deep Purple struggled to make headway on this side of
the Atlantic, things were very definitely happening for them in the
USA. As Lord later remarked: 'In the States, there are two scenes:
the Underground and the Top 40. We are very lucky because we
seem to bridge the gap between the two. We want to keep this
thing going because the Underground is where the superstars are
made'. When they supported Cream on the latter's farewell tour

over there that winter, Purple went down so well that they found themselves off the tour within three dates.

All that hard work was paying off, and their taskmasters weren't about to let up yet: even before their second album had seen the light of day in England, Edwards and Coletta had Purple back in De Lane Lea in February/March 1969 recording their third long-player in the space of ten months. Simply entitled *Deep Purple*, with its macabre but nonetheless stunning Hieronymous Bosch cover painting, this was released in Britain in November 1969.

The band's third album marked the end of Derek Lawrence's stint as producer and, as he later revealed to the DPAS, 'I was fired – end of story. Actually it occurs to me that they never officially told me I wouldn't be producing them again!' It was, however, an album he still has fond memories of: 'For me those first three albums stand up well for their time – the third is my favourite because the guys had been together longer and were tighter.'

Aside from a radical version of Donovan's beautiful 'Lalena', with its pounding percussion and heavy riffs, this eponymous outing boasted material written by the group. 'Why Didn't Rosemary?' was inspired by Roman Polanski's movie *Rosemary's Baby* which had just come out and continued in the psych-pop style of previous efforts, as did 'Bird Has Flown'. Heavier numbers included 'The Painter' (which they previewed on *Top Gear* as 'Hey Bop A Re Bop') and the hard-driving opener 'Chasing Shadows', with Evans really pouring his heart out.

The crowning moment, however, was the majestic 'April', a twelve-minute epic written by Blackmore and Lord which finished off the record. The piece started with an instrumental band section, which was followed by a second instrumental passage featuring strings and woodwinds (composed and arranged by Lord) before a final section featuring the whole band. Overall, though, you could tell that here was a band – and especially their lead guitarist – which was tugging at the reins to take a heavier, more brutal route.

Sadly Derek Lawrence wasn't the only casualty of this period. Tetragrammaton folded and a lengthy litigation ensued, halting

Purple's assault on the USA after two big tours. And after the recording of album number three, it was the parting of the ways for Rod Evans and Nick Simper too. As Jon Lord recalled in *NME*, 'Ritchie, Ian and I began to get more into the sort of heavy thing, what we were playing was basically rock 'n' roll and we were as interested in the visual as the audio aspect, but to us Rod and Nick weren't doing what we wanted and we had to ask them to leave. That was very traumatic because we were a very close group...'

Indeed, with their bouffant hairdos and clothes that were more Carnaby Street chic than Kensington Market street cred, early Purple did lack that macho rocker look. Rod and Nick were given their marching orders in June 1969. The surviving trio had all agreed that Evans performances had started to dip and he was frequently singing flat, but it may well have been that he had other irons in the fire: He had met a girl in America and was planning to marry her. His girl was from a wealthy family and Evans, bitten by the Hollywood bug, was also considering a career in acting. Maybe this was a natural parting of the ways.

For Nick Simper, things were very different. Although he went on to play with singer Marsha Hunt and then reunited with his old boss Lord Sutch as one of his 'Heavy Friends' in 1970, he felt no justification for his sacking and took legal proceedings against the band. The case was eventually settled three years later with Simper, by then a family man, agreeing a one-off payment in exchange for all future royalties. It was a decision that he would later regret, given the commercial success of subsequent line-ups and the inevitable increase in sales of the Mark I back catalogue.

A gig with Sutch at the Country Club, Haverstock Hill, London on 12 April 1970 saw the bassist sharing a stage with Blackmore for the first time since his sacking from Purple; the band for the evening also included Keith Moon. Sutch later reckoned that Simper, still bitter about his sacking, didn't talk to Blackmore at all. The show was recorded and later released on a highly collectable album, *Hands Of Jack The Ripper*.

After Deep Purple's split, Jon Lord was quite condescending

about the whole affair. 'He won, but what he's got was less than what he would have got if he hadn't sued us, because he wanted some quick money. How can you sue somebody for being fired? The only reason we asked Nicky to leave is because he wasn't right for the band. Isn't that a good enough reason to leave? So his lawyers went "That's wrongful business, so Nicky wants £12,000." So our lawyers did a little calculation and said "Okay, you can have £12,000, if that's what you want." If he had stayed and not sued us, he'd have had £25,000. Nicky did a silly thing and he was very hurt. It's not surprising to me that he was hurt – it's just surprising to me that he'd go to that extremity.'

Simper subsequently formed Warhorse with ex-Bakerloo drummer Mac Poole, which cut two fine albums for the Vertigo label, an eponymous debut and *Red Sea*. In 1978 he put together Fandango and, over the years, has also played with Flying Fox and Quatermass II.

Rod Evans, whose singing Simper once described as 'magic', took his time after Purple, eventually going to the States where he released a promo-only 45 for Capitol, 'Hard To Be Without You'. He then hooked up with ex-Iron Butterfly guitarist Larry 'Rhino' Rhinehart, drummer Bobby Caldwell and bassist Lee Dorman in Captain Beyond – a shortlived project which spawned two albums, *Captain Beyond* and *Sufficiently Breathless*, for the Capricorn label in 1972 and 1973 respectively. The group came to Europe in spring 1972, playing the prestigious Montreux Festival and a set at the Bickershaw Pop Festival, near Wigan, Lancashire, which was recorded though never released. Ultimately Captain Beyond failed to set the world on fire and Rod then underwent a major change of career direction, spending time in medical school with the intention of becoming a doctor.

It wasn't, however, quite the end of his involvement in the Deep Purple story. In 1980 he was enrolled into a bogus Deep Purple line-up assembled by promoter Steve G. who specialised in 'reformed' bands of varying authenticity including a version of West Coast outfit Steppenwolf. Joining up with drummer Dick

Juergens, keyboard player Geoff Emery, bassist Tom de Rivera and guitarist Tony Flynn, Evans was the only one who qualified to have even the remotest connection with any vintage of Deep Purple (Simper apparently having turned down his offer of involvement) and, when the other original members heard about it, there was a brutal court case, which Evans and company lost. He quit the music biz for good thereafter.

Settled in North California and married with kids, Evans now refuses to have anything to do with rock 'n' roll, perhaps burnt from his involvement in this questionable project. Back in 1969, in the first of several slick entrance/exit moves the band would experience over the years, Purple already had Rod's replacement lined up even before the hapless singer knew his employment with the group had been terminated. It was Mick Underwood, former drummer with the Outlaws, who mentioned singer Ian Gillan to Ritchie – 'He looked like Jim Morrison so we said we'll have him,' the guitarist later joked to *Disc*.

Gillan, born on 19 August 1945 in Hounslow, had pretty much taken the time-honoured route most British rockers of the era had chosen, starting to sing in a local band the Moonshiners in 1962 before joining semi-pro outfit the Javelins, who had the fortune to take over the Rolling Stones' residency at Richmond's Station Hotel. His stint with them didn't last long and he went through both the Hickies and Wainwright's Gentlemen (a forerunner of glam-rockers Sweet) before being asked to join Episode Six in May 1965. This sextet, whose stock in trade was melodic ballads and lavish harmony vocals, had been around since 1963 and featured brother and sister Graham and Sheila Carter-Dimmock on guitar and keyboards, lead guitarist Tony Lander and Roger Glover on bass. There had been a series of drummers, the last of whom was the aforementioned Underwood.

Bassist Roger Glover, born on 30 November 1945 in Brecon, had crossed the England-Wales border at a young age and attended Harrow County School where he played in the Madisons and the Lightnings, a combination of whose personnel would eventually form Episode Six. Their career was guided for a time by Helmut Gordon who also managed the Who early on and who got the band a contract with Pye Records.

Soon after Gordon quit, the group's publicist Gloria Bristow took over and, with the arrival of Gillan, helped Episode Six cut six singles for the label. The band played extensively in Germany and in Lebanon and, though they never cracked the UK charts, their records were popular on the pirate station Radio London. Initially their repertoire had consisted almost exclusively of covers of then-current US hits, but Glover then started to write: the first solo composition to get on vinyl was the top side of the single 'I Can See Through You' in 1967, while 'Mr Universe', penned in collaboration with Gillan, was issued as the B-side of a 1968 single for the Chapter One label. The teaming of Gillan and Glover would prove an enduring creative combination.

The group established a reputation as all-round entertainers, one that extended across Europe and beyond. A bizarre club residency in Beirut was recalled in a later song 'Angel Manchenio', for it was there that the Gillan crossed paths with a Spanish gypsy dancer Manchenio. Less than five and a half feet in stature, he was nevertheless possessed of both strength and showmanship, and would climax his act by flinging himself off a balcony some fifteen feet above the stage and landing on his knees before resuming his dancing.

Gillan, no mean performer himself, was understandably impressed. Unfortunately, the pair came to blows when Angel accused Ian of carrying on with his English girlfriend. Ian protested his innocence, and then had to talk his 'rival' out of taking his own life, the gypsy penance for insulting a friend. The honourable solution was for them both to draw blood, then bind the wound together to create blood brothers.

Episode Six had proved a ticket to ride for our pre-Purple pair. But the music scene was changing. Rock credibility was something the pop-tastic Episode Six couldn't buy for love or money. Instead, Gillan and Glover would acquire it overnight when they were transplanted into the ranks of Deep Purple. Gillan's recollection of his first recording session with Episode Six illustrates the attitude towards 'pop' groups at the time, a hangover from the Tin Pan Alley era, and explains graphically why he wanted to transfer to the infinitely more credible rock scene.

'We went to Pye Studios in Cumberland Street to record the A and B-side of a single, a cover of "Put Yourself In My Place", backed with "That's All You Want", a Roger Glover original. Both songs were to be recorded and mixed in three hours. I recall lugging the equipment into the studio and Tony Reeves, the producer [who also later played bass with Colosseum] stopped us and said, "What are you doing?" "Getting the gear in," we said. "Don't be ridiculous," came the retort – "you're not playing on the record!" It didn't affect me directly, as the singer, but I was appalled at the cavalier treatment of musicians.'

Blackmore and Lord had gone along to catch Episode Six playing at Woodford and poached Ian almost on the spot. His first job was to sing on a new Purple single, as Roger Glover later remembered: 'Ian accepted an invitation to join and, of course, there were terrible scenes with Gloria Bristow and the band. Then Ian called me and suggested that I help him write some songs for Purple… I said yes. I mean, we were so broke it was pathetic: the first time Deep Purple saw me they reckoned I looked like a tramp… string holding my threadbare jeans up, tattered sneakers – I was a real mess.

'Anyway I went to Jon Lord's flat and we played him our songs. He didn't like them but asked if I wanted to do a session that evening. Of course I said yes, because I knew it meant money! I did the session and made a few constructive suggestions – and then to my astonishment, they offered me the gig as bass player. I turned it down… which they could not believe! But then I thought about it, realised that Episode Six was on its last legs anyway and decided to look after myself for a change. So I called back and took the job.'

It was just the shot in the arm Purple needed as Lord later told *NME*: 'They had this great affinity with what we wanted to do and

when they joined there was this great upsurge in the group.
I've never known a feeling like it. We were going round with
silly grins on our faces.' Talking to *Disc* about the new additions,
Blackmore was just as glowing: 'Ian is better than the other singer
and Roger has more ideas than the bass player we had before.'
It was a promising start to a relationship that, over time, was
to poison Purple's future in a most pervasive way...

Purple's albums to date had been moderate successes, but
they needed both a heavier edge and more songwriting input. The
success with which Ian and Roger integrated with the instrumental
nucleus can only be hinted at by chart positions and record sales.
When interviewed by the author in 2001, Gillan recalled that when
he and Roger played on the 'Hallelujah!' session, it was almost
like an audition number. 'I was in the band but Roger wasn't at
that point, but he played on the record. They realised they should
start recording the next album... but he turned them down. He felt
that if he left Episode Six they would fold. He felt he owed loyalty
to what had basically started out as a school band. But the writing
was on the wall.'

That first Purple Mark II recording session had taken place at
the De Lane Lea Studios in Kingsway – the song, 'Hallelujah!
(I Am The Preacher)', a commercial effort from the pens of Blue
Mink hit-makers Roger Cook and Roger Greenaway. Gillan recalls
being told 'Sing that, off you go,' the objective being to see how
well the new boys performed it as opposed to Evans and Simper
who had already committed their attempt to tape earlier that very
day. Gillan did well enough, but the song failed to impress the
singer. 'Roger and I thought we could do better than that, so we
started getting into [writing]. The next session, I believe we came
up with "Speed King"...'

'Speed King' would, indeed, herald a new dawn for the band
– but 'Hallelujah!' went nowhere fast when it came out as a 45 in
July 1969. With the charts now forbidden territory, the way was
open for the band to sink its teeth into the heavier fare Blackmore
had been itching to play for so long.

2. In Rock

The band known as Deep Purple Mark II selected Hanwell Community Centre in West London as the rehearsal venue in which to hone their new line-up in the summer of 1969. It was here that the classic Purple line-up would develop the songs and settle on the musical direction that would ultimately secure their place in rock history courtesy of the album *Deep Purple In Rock*.

The Community Centre was the remaining building of what had been a Poor Law school complex. Over the years the other buildings had been demolished leaving only the Community Centre, which had formed the central block of the old school. As a community resource (which it became in 1945), it was possible for bands to rent rooms and play as loud as possible given that there were no immediate neighbours to be sympathetic towards. With the members living nearby, it was an ideal spot for Purple to create their legend.

It would be a full year before *In Rock* hit the racks, but it is undoubtedly the case that the rehearsals at Hanwell, topped by the constant touring over the coming months, were critical to the developing sound of the band that emerged both in live performances and on the album that followed. It allowed them to create their own trademark sound and helped purge them of the somewhat schizophrenic and uncertain music that had formed their first three albums, not helped by the eccentric choice of 'Hallelujah!' as the new line-up's debut single.

The first live gig by Purple Mark II took place on 10 July 1969 at the Speakeasy in London, a familiar venue often played by the former incarnation. At the outset, the set was based largely around two instrumental pieces from their first two albums, 'Mandrake Root' and 'Wring That Neck', which showed off both the band's power and the virtuosity of the individual musicians. This was the first gig where Ian Gillan played congas, having recognised that he needed to do something to occupy himself during the instrumental numbers which were very often stretched to over thirty minutes.

Gillan had also learned some of the older songs, but the sessions at Hanwell were proving so fruitful that new material was being added to the set fairly swiftly. Happily, this allowed the Mark II line-up to develop their own identity more quickly as well as giving the new songs the chance to develop over time through repeated exposure to live performance. The first of the songs to appear on the concert stage was Gillan and Glover's previously mentioned 'Speed King', an up tempo stormer that made its live debut on 24 August at a festival performance in Amsterdam.

The band spent most of the remainder of 1969 on the road nurturing their audience and also fine-tuning the new material that would ultimately make up the next album. Most of the gigs took the form of a series of one-nighters in Britain, but this period also saw some forays into mainland Europe, an area that was to become something of a stronghold in the years ahead.

This pattern of activity was, of course, very different to the previous experience of the band where Britain and Europe had been neglected as Purple looked to build on the early success they had achieved in the USA with 'Hush'. This certainly helped them somewhat when playing on home territory, as they were able to build and develop an audience without too many preconceptions about what to expect from the new line-up of the band. It would equally create some issues for their record company in the USA where, of course, the opposite problem existed. However, that dilemma lay ahead of them.

Despite all the rehearsal activity taking place in Hanwell plus the increased activity on the performance front, Deep Purple had to satisfy the classical cravings that had been slowly fermenting inside Jon Lord's mind since his days with the Artwoods. An offhand remark made by Lord to management during a band meeting expressing his interest in attempting to fuse rock and classical music led to Tony Edwards jumping in feet first and booking both the Royal Albert Hall and the Royal Philharmonic Orchestra. He then instructed Lord, on his return from the final

US tour by the Mark I line up at the beginning of June, to get on with making his dream a reality. Lord was told he had until mid September to come up with something. What he came up with was *Concerto For Group And Orchestra.*

Some members of the band were openly sceptical of the venture, particularly as it seemed to fly in the face of the direction that they were moving in as a result of their rehearsals and gigs. Management ultimately convinced the doubters that it would help to give them much-needed exposure in the UK media. It is worth remembering that, at this point, Purple were no more than an unheralded UK band who had struck it lucky with a hit single in the USA. With the efforts of other bands, most noticeably the Nice led by Keith Emerson, in mind, this foray into 'classic rock' seemed like a risk worth taking, even given the band's recent move from chart-friendly material to heavier fare.

In interviews, Lord tried to make the event considerably less po-faced than it appeared, although declaring that it wasn't an attempt to fuse existing classical pieces with a rock band and that he was writing a full concerto from scratch probably did little to achieve this.

Having said that, Lord did have the background to support his contention that he wasn't jumping aboard any bandwagons. While a member of the Artwoods, Lord had inserted snatches of Tchaikovsky into their version of rock 'n' roll standard 'Shake, Rattle And Roll'. To the band's amazement, these proved popular with the audience and generated a very positive response. Going even further, Lord had wanted to record some tracks with the New Jazz Orchestra in 1966 but the Artwoods' label – the perpetually stodgy and conservative Decca Records, which had once upon a time turned down the Beatles – were unwilling to fund the exercise.

Ironically, the Artwoods were then approached by a German symphony orchestra to write and perform a pop/classical piece, but by the time the plans were mooted the band had all but split up.

Equally, the music recorded by the first incarnation of Purple had not been without evidence of Lord's classical training. Strings had been used on 'Anthem', a track on *Shades Of Deep Purple*, while their eponymous third album featured a multi-part creation called 'April', which included a section written for a small orchestra. Lord clearly had an itch that needed to be scratched more extensively than he had yet managed.

Perhaps the key element in the project was securing the services of conductor and composer Sir Malcolm Arnold. While rooted in the classical traditions, Arnold had composed some pieces using modern techniques and was thus both sympathetic towards what Lord was looking to achieve and equally aware of the difficulties in getting such music played by the extremely conservative-minded musicians who made up the orchestras on whom he would be reliant on performing any of his work sympathetically and well. Arnold also advised Lord over the compositional process.

With the band in the midst of rehearsals and upping the ante with storming live rock gigs, it was always going to be a challenge for Lord to finish the piece in time. However, this was not without inconvenience to Deep Purple and the subsequent discontent of some of his fellow members. Lord had to miss some of the band's rehearsals, and this was a bone of contention – particularly with Blackmore, who was the most committed to the heavier, riff-laden direction that the band were taking.

The piece was performed on 24 September 1969 at the Royal Albert Hall and, to up the stakes still higher, was recorded for future release. The show was also filmed and broadcast by the BBC the following April, just as the band were preparing to release fourth studio album *In Rock*. The aim of increasing the profile of Deep Purple in the UK media was successfully achieved, although some in the band doubted the value of this given the contrast with the music they were performing in their own right.

As Arnold had foreseen, there had been difficulties with the orchestra. As is the case with such things, combined rehearsals were limited to a couple of sessions in advance of the performance. Many of the orchestra were openly dismissive of the whole affair, while the clash of styles between band and orchestra looked as if it might prove insurmountable. This was particularly demonstrable in the area of percussion, where the rock format would have Paice leading the band, while in the classical tradition it would tend to be the other way round. Furthermore, Purple were by now used to playing at ear-crushing volume. However, Arnold was very supportive to the extent that at one point he brought rehearsals to a halt to chastise the orchestra for its disrespectful and incompetent approach to the piece.

The show performed at the Royal Albert Hall was split into two sections. For the first, Deep Purple played a short set which opened with 'Hush', their breakthrough number in America. This was followed by the extended instrumental virtuosity of 'Wring That Neck', while the opening section was brought to a close with 'Child In Time', an impressive new number arising out of the Hanwell rehearsal sessions which would duly take pride of place on *In Rock* in the following year.

The second half was taken up with the three movements of the *Concerto* itself. Lord's trepidation as to how the evening would turn out, understandable given some of the difficulties of the rehearsals, proved to be unfounded and the show was a great success with the audience, the final movement being repeated as an encore. Indeed, many of the difficulties encountered during rehearsals were successfully negotiated and the Second Movement in particular fused the two traditions with considerable effect.

The live album was duly mixed and was released by Tetragrammaton in the USA in December 1969 and in the UK the following month. This contained just the three movements of the *Concerto* but the full show, including the band set and the encore, was issued on double CD in 2002 (a DVD was also made available).

The event succeeded in bringing Deep Purple the higher profile that they sought but it had perhaps been too successful and the aftermath of the show also led to a crisis within the band. From being an outfit trying to establish themselves in their own country with a focus on loud, hard rock, the success of the Royal Albert Hall had reintroduced some of the schizophrenic image the band were trying to avoid. There were even suggestions from within the ranks that the concert had been conceived with aim of furthering Lord's career at the expense of the others. Some people were turning up at concerts to be disappointed at the absence of an orchestra. Indeed, at a gig in Stoke a very apologetic promoter was shamed into telling the band that he had been unable to find an orchestra and hired a brass band instead!

The rifts the *Concerto* created were sufficiently deep that Lord was ready to quit. However, the issues were discussed openly at a band meeting at which Lord confirmed his own personal commitment to Purple and making the new line-up and direction work. There was a commitment to playing the *Concerto* in America and the band agreed that this could proceed. More difficult was the fact that Lord had been commissioned to write another orchestral rock piece. Contractually, it would be difficult to back out of this, so the band reluctantly agreed to go ahead with this – on the understanding that it not be allowed to interfere with more mainstream activities, and that the publicity that attended the *Concerto* should be conspicuous by its absence.

Although a matter of considerable controversy within the band in 1969, it has since been recognised by the individual band members that the *Concerto* did provide Deep Purple with a higher profile than merely continuing to gig would have done. Indeed, the work was played again by Deep Purple in 1999 after the (since lost) score had been recreated by a music-student fan and presented to Jon Lord – though by this time Ritchie Blackmore, a significant dissenter in 1969, was absent. It was also noticeable that orchestras were considerably keener to be involved second time around, as many of them would have been raised in a less conservative environment than previous generations of classical musicians – one where rock music and its various experiments with classical music were viewed in a more positive light.

One final problem remained: the December release of the

Concerto in America, where Purple had become famed for their rock material even though the hit singles were now receding into memory. The potential for confusion was of little consequence, however, as Tetragrammaton was wound up at the end of February 1970. This meant that supplies of the album to shops ceased and the band was owed thousands of dollars in royalties. That this happened was no great surprise to Purple's management as the label had been in increasing difficulties, but the impact was no less severe.

Signs of impending problems had first arisen during the US tour of April 1969 when Tetragrammaton had been unable to get the third album, *Deep Purple*, manufactured in time to coincide with their visit. In truth, the label was already on its last legs financially. Money had been spent lavishly on promotion, but after a couple of years sales of albums were not keeping up with outgoings. In addition to manufacturing difficulties, another issue appeared to be the support provided to the band for this tour. Not only was there no product in the shops, but also Purple had to take measures to save money on hotel bills and the like as the tour progressed.

While Tetragrammaton's demise was therefore far from a shock to Purple and their management, the timing was unhelpful, particularly with a new album being readied for release. Indeed, the arrival of *In Rock* had to be delayed while Purple negotiated the train-wreck of their American label's demise and attempted to find a new outlet. The end result was the purchase of the band's back catalogue by Warner Bros Records, a deal that included a one-off payment of $40,000 which, crucially, was not offset against any future royalties. This went some way to making up for the previously earned money they were now unlikely to see. (It should also be noted that the management had invested heavily in a band that had yet to pay them back to any degree.)

But Warners had, in fact, bought Tetragrammaton's back catalogue as a whole, so there was little real commitment from the label. Indeed, given the focus of the time on singer-songwriters, Deep Purple were very much the odd men out and it was clear that

Warners were not entirely sure what they should be doing with them. This was amply demonstrated by the fact that Warners never reissued the first three Purple albums, simply issuing a compilation (*Purple Passages*) once the Mark II line-up of the band had found success in the States.

The fact it took over a year for *In Rock* to be recorded shouldn't paint a picture of long, self-indulgent sessions of recording and re-recording or of a group of musicians wasting studio time in search of their collective muse. Purple had decided to defer recording any of the new numbers they had already written until after the *Concerto* had been performed. But this endeavour had left them in such debt that they needed to continue their roadwork to ensure a flow of income was being generated. The band was averaging about a dozen shows a month after the *Concerto* gig, and this was maintained right up to the album's release date.

This hectic work rate, along with some crucial BBC sessions, started to build on the publicity generated by the Royal Albert Hall gigs and, accompanied by positive reviews in the music press, starting to provide the crucial momentum for the band in the period leading up to the release of *In Rock*.

Sessions to record their new numbers, most of which were being knocked into shape on the road, were scheduled when they could be fitted in around Purple's touring commitments. These were generally booked at short notice, so the selection of studios was based as much on their ready availability as for any sonic qualities they may have been able to offer. In the end, the album was recorded in three separate studios.

The band's decision to produce their albums themselves with Derek Lawrence now *persona non grata* helped give a level of consistency on the overall sound. Unlike many bands who opt to self-produce, Purple had two very experienced musicians in Blackmore and Lord who also had previous experience as session-men, and therefore possessed more studio savvy than most.

The objective of the sessions was set out by Blackmore in typically blunt fashion early on. The credo was 'If it's not dramatic or exciting, it has no place on the album.' This was reflected both in rehearsals and on stage where the amplifiers were all made to go one louder than the norm – well before *Spinal Tap*. This was also the case in the studio where the VU meters were constantly pushed well into the red as Purple recorded at their by-now customary ear-splitting volume.

Sessions for the album started at IBC's Studio A in Portland Square, central London. They probably had the first session in the third week of October 1969 when 'Kneel And Pray' (which ultimately developed into 'Speed King') and 'Living Wreck' were recorded. Originally, the band felt that 'Living Wreck' was not up to par for the album but changed their minds when reviewing the recordings later on.

The new year started with 'Hard Lovin' Man' being recorded on 1 January in De Lane Lea studios. This session was to be the first one Martin Birch engineered for the band. Birch had worked as understudy to Barry Ainsworth during the recording of *Book of Taliesyn*. At that time, he was basically just the tea-boy with the duty of pushing knobs when instructed to do so but, as Nick Simper recalled, even then he had a great ear for sound. Over the years, Birch would frequently be used for both Purple and their various offshoots and solo projects.

The last track to make it to tape was 'Bloodsucker', recorded at Abbey Road in April. A funkier number than many of the other more straight-ahead rock songs, this would also be re-recorded by the band for 1998's *Abandon* album.

It was during this period that Ritchie was approached by Derek Lawrence to work on a project of rock 'n' roll standards that would eventually materialise as *Green Bullfrog*. Despite Lawrence's disappointment that he had been sacked from the role of Deep Purple producer, he clearly held no grudge towards Blackmore. Ian Paice also went along for the sessions, and Lawrence assembled a talented group of musicians that included Tony Ashton, Blackmore's old friend from the Outlaws, Chas Hodges plus former teacher Big Jim Sullivan and Albert Lee, arguably the two guitarists that Blackmore admired most.

The bulk of the music was recorded at De Lane Lea in two all-day sessions on 20 April and 23 May with Martin Birch engineering. Its release in March 1972 was surprisingly low-key because, for contractual reasons, the artists involved had to go under pseudonyms. This meant that Ritchie had to forego his writing credit on the title track, 'Bullfrog', jointly composed with Lawrence.

One of two new compositions on the album, this was an instrumental guitar workout featuring all three guitarists and very similar to a number Deep Purple had recently done called 'Grabsplatter', played at a BBC session but not released until many years later. Had the public known that two-fifths of Deep Purple was on it, the album would probably have sold in significantly greater numbers.

Deep Purple In Rock was finally released in June 1970 but, while the fruits of the album sessions had been very successful, both record company and management were still looking for a single with which they could promote the band, just as 'Hush' had given them their Stateside break. 'Into The Fire' might have been a contender given its style and relative brevity, but Purple were looking to avoid diluting the album by taking a single off it and were seeking to come up with something else for release.

Sessions were booked in De Lane Lea during May but, having just completed an album, the band were struggling to find the necessary inspiration. However, during a break when the others had retired to the pub, Blackmore and Glover returned to the studio. Blackmore picked his guitar up and started playing a riff which sounded good. However, Glover was less enthusiastic when Blackmore told him it was from Ricky Nelson's 'Summertime'.

It was a riff Nick Simper had introduced to Blackmore a few months earlier. (Nelson was an Elvis follower of the 1950s who had profited when the King went into the US Army, enjoying a string of hits before disappearing from the radar as teen idols do.)

Blackmore pointed out that, as Glover had never heard the 1962 single before, it was unlikely that others would have either, so the borrowed riff became the core of what became 'Black Night'.

When the remainder of the band returned from the pub, the title was chosen (this time purloined from an Arthur Alexander song previously performed by Gillan and Glover as part of Episode Six) and a drunken session ensued trying to come up with suitable words. If you don't think the lyric of the song makes too much sense, then there is a very good reason.

'Black Night' was recorded within three hours – and, while the band attached no particular importance to it, their management recognised it as a potential hit and congratulated them on the birth of their new single. In the absence of any other alternatives, and given the enthusiasm of their management for the song, it was agreed to release this as a single a few weeks in advance of the album it didn't appear on.

To the surprise of the band, 'Black Night' became one of the hits of the summer, being held off the Number 1 slot only by the England football team's anthem 'Back Home' (which is where the then-World Cup holders found themselves rather sooner than expected). More distressingly for Purple, the single opened them up to accusations of selling out, particularly as they appeared on the much-derided *Top Of The Pops* to promote it.

Top Of The Pops was just as contentious a programme for lovers of 'serious' music in 1970 as it has been in recent years. However, unlike the more recent era of declining sales of singles, the art of the 45 was a major influence on the whole perception of both the industry and music fans. In 1970 the singles chart was seen by rock fans as a haven of manufactured bands (e.g. Edison Lighthouse of 'Love Grows' fame), novelty records (Rolf Harris' 'Two Little Boys') or remnants of the British beat boom like the Tremeloes who were trying, usually unsuccessfully, to make a more serious name for themselves with songs like 'Me And My Life'.

For bands like Deep Purple of the post-*Sgt. Pepper* era, the concept of releasing singles in the UK placed them in a dilemma. While their early success in the States with 'Hush' would never be seen as an impediment to future album success, a dalliance with the singles chart at home had the implication of being less than serious at a time when seriousness was at a premium. Nor was it guaranteed that sales success would be accompanied by airplay on Radio 1 which had taken over as the sole national station for pop music following the banning of the pirates in 1967. In these circumstances, these bands would continue to be played on the more esoteric programmes (initially by John Peel but expanded by the creations of the late-night *Sounds Of The Seventies* programmes which also introduced names like Bob Harris and Alan Black to the British public) without feeling that they were selling out.

However, 'Black Night' was insistently commercial with a memorable riff and chorus that belied the drunken chaos in which it was composed, and sailed to Number 2 in the charts. The band agreed to play *Top Of The Pops* but declined to take things too seriously; Ritchie Blackmore, for instance, was clearly seen admiring his nails when he should have been soloing, while Ian Paice seemed to be too scared to actually touch his drums in case they made any noise.

While Led Zeppelin had made a point of not releasing singles in the UK, enjoying increased album sales as a result, the summer of 1970 did prove to be a breakthrough year for many other bands who might otherwise have found a level of discomfort at the situation. Classic songs like Black Sabbath's 'Paranoid', Free's 'All Right Now' and 'The Witches Promise' by Jethro Tull took up high positions in the chart, so Purple's apparent heresy no longer seemed such an insurmountable problem.

Although 'Black Night' was released prior to the *In Rock* album, the long-player was already selling extremely healthily before the single started to take off, so it was not the case that success was being driven solely by the more commercial song. By the time the single charted the album was already high in the charts where it would remain until the release of *Fireball* a year later, although it never went higher than Number 4.

In Rock is now recognised as one of the key rock albums of its era and it undoubtedly confirmed Deep Purple as one of the classic bands of the genre, helping to establish the reputation they still enjoy. The success of the album also impacted on the live shows that the band were playing. The efforts of the past year starting from the rehearsals at Hanwell and the development of new material by constant gigging had produced not only a classic album but had also transformed the band into one of the most powerful live units in the world. The sheer power and energy of *In Rock* was in direct contrast to the three albums that preceded it, and the gigging had built up considerable positive word of mouth which fed into increasing attendances and fees at their gigs and a ready-made audience to buy the album on its release.

The immediate success of their fourth album (though, effectively, a debut) soon found Deep Purple operating at a level that even they would have found hard to believe. As is often the case, the band's gigsheet had been booked in advance of the success of the album and they found themselves with sold-out gigs in venues too small to accommodate their new audience, many disappointed fans finding themselves unable to get into the gig. Most notable was a show scheduled in Glasgow in October which had already been moved to a larger venue, Locarno Ballroom in Sauchiehall Street. This saw about 10,000 fans locked out – a situation which made both the local and national press.

The overall level of performance also moved up a few notches, the gigs reflecting fully the sense of overdrive captured so effectively on the album. Blackmore switched back from his semi-acoustic Gibson ES-335 to the Fender Stratocaster he'd used in the early days of Purple and created additional excitement by starting to trash his guitars. Needless to say, the instruments that were ultimately wrecked were cheap copies and were used many times; any repairs made were intended to ensure that the 'axe' split in the same way each night.

The band travelled to America in August 1970 to meet the long-standing contractual commitment to perform the *Concerto* at the Hollywood Bowl, Warner Bros having reissued the live album more in hope than expectation. The show was played half-heartedly by the band, including Lord; tellingly, it was an edited version of the *Concerto* that was performed that night, allowing for a longer initial set by the 'solo' band unencumbered by the orchestra.

Deep Purple played five other dates while in the USA, but further hoped-for shows never materialised. Warners released *In Rock* not long after the *Concerto* album but failed to appreciate the change in the band and had a different perspective on the dynamics of the new Purple. Warners clearly expected the album to sell on its own account, after which they would provide additional tour support. However, the European experience showed that the success of the album was built on people seeing the band perform live – not vice versa. As a consequence, *In Rock* sold poorly in the States at the outset, reversing the band's earlier position entirely. Having spent two years being fêted in America and ignored in their homeland, the tables were now turned.

Rock audiences weren't the only people taking notice of Deep Purple, as Ian Gillan was shortly to discover. His performance on 'Child In Time' from *In Rock* had impressed Tim Rice and Andrew Lloyd Webber who were then working on their rock musical *Jesus Christ Superstar*. They had been given a pre-release acetate of the song by Tony Edwards when the Purple manager heard they were looking for a singer to play the role of Jesus. The offer of some freelance work proved both flattering and irresistible.

Recording sessions took about three hours, after which it receded into the singer's memory. However, Edwards had also heard some of the other material that Rice and Lloyd Webber had written and was correctly convinced that the project was going to be huge. Thus, once the time came to negotiate a fee, Edwards refused the standard one-off offer of £100 accepted by most of the other musicians who played on the original set and held out for a

royalty for Gillan of two per cent in the UK with the rest of the
world paying one per cent. In some parts of the world, where
Gillan was exclusively contracted to EMI, the record company
agreed to release him in exchange for half of the royalties.

The album was issued by MCA in November 1970 and went on
to sell eight million copies worldwide – a very profitable excursion
for Gillan, and one that gave him both profile and self-esteem
beyond the confines of Deep Purple. Ian was offered a role in the
stage presentation of the show but this could not be accommodated
with the band's increasing touring commitments.

However, having benefited from the *nous* of his manager,
the singer overextended his hand when it came to the film part.
Having impressed Norman Jewison, the director of the film, Gillan
rejected the offer of $1,000 per week during the shoot and pointed
out that, since Purple could earn in excess of that for a single gig,
he was worth rather more. This was too much to take from a
relative unknown, and the offer was withdrawn, denying Gillan the
opportunity to make his big-screen debut.

It remains one of the regrets of his life that he turned down the
chance to play in the movie. 'I told [Jewison] I'd not get out of
bed for less than £250,000,' he recalled in his autobiography, 'and
was soon on my way to the pub to reflect on the fact that I'd just
lost the chance to realise a dream.' In mitigation, he was worried
about leaving his bandmates to kick their heels for three months…

In terms of unfinished business, there remained the obligation
to complete the piece Jon Lord had been commissioned to write
in the aftermath of the success of the *Concerto*. This was entitled
The Gemini Suite and was ready to perform by the autumn of
1970. Lord had attempted to see if this could be performed with
musicians other than Purple but this proved impractical,
particularly given the increased profile that the band now enjoyed.
However, Deep Purple was now a very different band from the
one that had taken the stage at the Royal Albert Hall a year earlier,
being both a more successful unit with a hit album behind them
and also a much more direct and hard-rocking outfit than had been

the case in the early days of the Mark II line-up.

Lord had written the piece in five movements, each representing a member of the band. It was performed at the Royal Festival Hall in London supported by the Orchestra of the Light Music Society conducted, like the *Concerto*, by Sir Malcolm Arnold. Staged with little fanfare and less publicity than its predecessor, the piece was arguably a more successful melding of the different genres than the *Concerto* had been. On the evening of the performance, both Blackmore and Gillan put their very vocal disapproval of the piece to one side and delivered excellent performances for their respective movements.

Lord expressed a desire to record the work in the studio and this eventually appeared in 1973 as a solo project featuring outside musicians, although the ever-dependable Roger Glover and Ian Paice contributed. This version, a 1973 Purple Records release, featured Paice, Glover, Tony Ashton, Yvonne Elliman and Albert Lee, with Malcolm Arnold conducting the London Symphony Orchestra as he had for Purple in 1969. It is the only one of Lord's solo projects yet to emerge on CD, though the Festival Hall performance was issued digitally in 1993 under the auspices of the Deep Purple Appreciation Society.

As the very successful year of 1970 drew to a close, the band made a start on the follow-up to *In Rock*. The album remained high in the charts and continued to sell well, while 'Black Night' was still in evidence. For the first time they had the pressure of having to follow up on success in their own country.

The sessions began in September at De Lane Lea but this time there was no new material readily available and certainly none that had the added benefit of being battered into shape by live performance. Ultimately, the only thing to come out of these sessions was the totally atypical 'Anyone's Daughter'. Future touring commitments limited the amount of time available to be spent in the studio, but the emergence of a country and western-styled song as the first for the new album suggested that keeping the same level of inspiration for a follow-up was going to be an exercise fraught with difficulty.

The remainder of the year was largely spent touring in Europe. It had been necessary to play a gig without Blackmore at Ludenscheid, Germany, owing to illness. Purple had offered to refund the audience's money but they wanted the band to play anyway. A necessarily shortened set was performed which left the band without songs to play when they were called back to the stage. After returning, encore-less, to their hotel, they discovered the audience had continued to demand more music and, in its absence, had proceeded to smash up both the hall and the band's equipment. Blackmore returned for the next gig in Stuttgart, but the authorities were taking no chances and the gig was attended by a unit of the German Army to provide additional security in the event of a recurrence.

Following a foray into France, the group headed on to Scandinavia but the windscreen in their touring van shattered and the journey had to be conducted with the cold north wind blasting through. Each band member took turns to sit in the front seat, but the journey was extremely unpleasant. Notwithstanding the success of their first album together, the Mark II band were still some way of being able to get from gig to gig in reasonable conditions, never mind a higher level of comfort.

It was during this period that the band's key relationship, between Blackmore and Gillan, which was ultimately to prove so ruinous, first started to be put under strain. Blackmore saw the sound of *In Rock* as very much his own and the success of the album as vindication of his ascendancy within the band. Gillan, his increasing self-confidence bolstered by his part in *Jesus Christ Superstar*, failed to accord Ritchie the respect and deference he felt was due. Roger Glover recalls: 'Ian seemed to go off the rails with attitude and drink problems. He and Ritchie were at complete loggerheads, and Ian may have got to the point where he thought "I'm the singer in this band... if Ritchie can behave like that, so can I." So he became just as big an arsehole.'

While the others stayed outside this increasingly argumentative relationship, the continuing time on the road was taking its toll in other ways. Lord started to have recurring difficulties with his back which could be traced back to his days in the Artwoods when he'd had to move his own heavyweight gear from the van onto the stage. Roger Glover also started to have stress-related stomach cramps of such severity that he collapsed on more than one occasion.

These issues, not surprisingly, started to have an impact on the band's performances. The set list had remained stable during 1970, based around the *In Rock* material and 'Black Night', and the band had reached a playing peak that had been maintained for the majority of the year. However, the shows towards the end of the year did not quite have the level of intensity and excitement as had earlier been the case, thanks to these physical and emotional strains.

As if that wasn't enough, the relative failure of the September recording sessions to produce releasable results meant that the need to produce an album's worth of good new material must have added to the other pressures surrounding the band. Purple were also well aware that the stakes had been raised by success, and any follow-up to *In Rock* would be subject to a level of scrutiny and interest which none of their previous albums had generated. While the last eighteen months had seen the band develop by leaps and bounds, as the end of their breakthrough year beckoned the challenges facing Deep Purple loomed large. It remained to be seen how the five musicians would respond.

3. Falling Fireball

While *In Rock* had been recorded over several months between touring commitments, *Fireball* (the fifth studio album under the Deep Purple banner, though only the second Mark II offering) would take even longer to produce. A full nine months was to elapse from the time the band first entered the studio to the point of completion, quite a contrast to the weekend allotted to the first album. And, since Purple had released five albums from September 1968 through to June 1970 – a space of less than two years – this was an unheard-of interval in every respect.

The group had decided to set aside a couple of weeks at the end of 1970 for writing new songs, the plan being to spend January 1971 recording. So in December, after a typically hectic bout of pre-Christmas touring, they locked themselves away for a fortnight in a remote farmhouse in Devon. But little progress was made. The band was exhausted from the recent spate of work and spent most of the time in the local pubs – and, in Blackmore's case, indulging in one of his favourite pastimes, séances. Friction within the band also started to play a part around this time and petty wrangling often disrupted work.

As 1970 drew to a close, bassist Glover commented to one magazine that he hoped the album would be released by the following March. As it turned out, by that time only a handful of tracks had been written. As a stop-gap, and an attempt to capitalise on 'Black Night's still-recent Top 10 entry, a song about a prostitute called 'Strange Kind Of Woman' was released in February while the rest of the album was still waiting to be put together. The single's Number 6 success as the follow-up to 'Black Night' helped reinforce Purple's reputation as a heavy band with commercial potential.

The B-side of the single was the non-album track 'I'm Alone', a song Ian Gillan remembers with some affection. His account of its genesis also provides an insight into how Deep Purple Mark II created their music. 'Roger and I quickly gave up taking finished songs into the studios,' he explained. 'They are brilliant musicians, I'm just a singer and a writer. We play them a song and they look at each other: this can't be much good, they're just playing it on an acoustic guitar! So we devised a weird way of writing. The song comes after the music. That may seem upside down, but "I'm Alone" is the classic example of a song that's written over a jam. It was the same with "Smoke On The Water" and "Child In Time".

'"I'm Alone" was written at Olympic Studios – we have a history of B-sides the band has created in the studio. Usually they'll come up with a riff, and I'll go down the pub, write some lyrics that fit and them come back with 'em. They just crank it out! Jams are often great fun...'

Recording sessions continued to be fitted into Purple's tight schedule as and when possible, at both De Lane Lea and Olympic, just south of the Thames in Barnes. Yet when May 1971 came and went, even the record companies were getting impatient – particularly in America, where the band was scheduled to tour in July. A couple of weeks of solid studio work were set aside for early June, yet still it wasn't complete. Warner Bros desperately needed to have a new album out for the band to promote, so rushed out *Fireball* as soon as they were able, with the hit single 'Strange Kind Of Woman' on board. The LP finally saw the light of day in Europe in September, exactly a year after it had been started.

Fireball today remains a forgotten album within the Purple canon. The fact that the vast majority of the album's tracks were never fully established as concert favourites probably goes some way to explaining this. Whereas *In Rock*'s songs were honed on stage, some of these creations took their time to be played outside the studio walls – if they were played at all.

Opinions within the band were divided over the quality of *Fireball*. 'Compared to *In Rock*, *Fireball* is a contrived album,' said Roger Glover, 'on the whole a bit of a damp squib.' Yet if chart placing is anything to go by, *Fireball* was nothing less than a success. The band had built up a huge following since the release of *In Rock* and from universally positive concert reviews. It was little surprise when *Fireball* reached Number 1 soon after release, pushing the Who's classic *Who's Next* off the chart summit, yet didn't receive the thumbs-up from fans in quite the same way that *In Rock* had.

Perhaps mindful of the time it had taken to finish, the band seemed less than enamoured with it, with the exception of Ian Gillan who, to this day, cites it as his favourite Purple album. After the full-on assault of *In Rock*, *Fireball* was probably something of a surprise to listeners expecting something similar. The opening title track was an out-and-out belter, but the album showed another, more 'progressive' side to Deep Purple's music.

Perhaps the intention was to reaffirm the band's credibility while they were being pushed by management to continue along the hit single road. Certainly, they only had to listen to Black Sabbath's Ozzy Osbourne in the wake of 'Paranoid' going Top 10 in 1970, to find out about the negative effects. 'We opened in Portsmouth with "Paranoid" as usual and suddenly the place went potty. There were kids rushing down the front and girls screaming and grabbing us. We couldn't believe it – it was just like the teenybopper era all over again. We don't need fans like those. But we'll just have to grin and bear them and they'll go away. We're not changing our stage act to please the kids who just bought the single.'

The tendency towards the wilfully uncommercial embodied by *Fireball* is another reason why the album tends to be overlooked today. As already mentioned, little of the material became established in regular concert performance and this has probably helped the album to be overlooked with the passing of time. 'Strange Kind Of Woman' was the only number recorded during the period that became a firm stage favourite, as exemplified on the classic double live set *Made In Japan*. But, America aside, this wasn't strictly a *Fireball* inclusion. Instead, the title track of *Fireball* was extracted on seven-inch plastic in October 1971 and reached Number 15 – Purple's third successive UK Top 20 singles-chart entry.

'The Mule' turned out to be the only album track that became an integral part of the stage act, but it was revamped to become a showcase for Ian Paice's drum solo, replacing 'Paint It Black', the old Rolling Stones number that had been used for the same purpose. The only other piece of music that found its way into the live set on a regular basis was the slow middle section of 'Fools', with Blackmore using his volume-control technique to produce what was described as his 'cello effect'.

While Ian Gillan had vaulted from second division to premier league when he forsook Episode Six for Deep Purple, he now found himself a prisoner of their success. But this didn't stop him making some unexpected solo recordings, with Roger Glover in tow, for a soundtrack album to an animated children's film. The first inkling the public had of *Cherkazoo* – or 'Chez Kazoo', as it was often misspelled – came in the middle of 1971. Ian explained it in an interview as being 'An animal, space, musical travelogue fantasy' that he'd been working on for over two years. 'I'm going to drag it round the film companies,' he said, adding that 'One or two are interested.'

The music bore little relation to Purple, and was more a follow-on from Episode Six: there are parallels, too, with the Hollies, *Sgt. Pepper*-era Beatles, Tomorrow and other practitioners of late-1960s progressive pop. Musicians involved apart from Gillan and Glover are believed to include drummer Pete York, Purple pianist Jon Lord and the string section of ELO (on the 'Walrus'-y 'The Bull Of Birantis').

Had it been released at this time, anyone who thought all Ian Gillan could do was sing (or scream) heavy rock would have had another think coming. Only 'Monster In Paradise' was aired at the time, and that in a version by Hard Stuff, a heavy rock outfit signed to Purple Records whose bassist, John Gustafson, would later crop up in the Ian Gillan Band. The animated series would remain unseen, while the music was liberated from Gillan's garden shed in the 1990s by Simon Robinson of the ever-diligent Deep

Purple Appreciation Society, then in the employ of RPM Records.

Gillan wasn't the only Purple member looking at the possibility of a solo project. When the singer was taken ill with hepatitis in October 1971, causing the cancellation of a US tour and presenting the other four band members with an unscheduled month off, Ritchie Blackmore seized the opportunity to gather an ad hoc group of musicians together to thrash out a few rough ideas. Along with Ian Paice, he requested the presence of Thin Lizzy's Phil Lynott at De Lane Lea studios and the results became known as the 'Babyface' sessions after the proposed band name.

Also a three-piece, Thin Lizzy were at the time awaiting their commercial breakthrough, which would come exactly a year later with the hit single 'Whiskey In The Jar'. Ian Paice had recently caught a gig by the Irish band and been impressed by the black singer-bassist, who was being touted in some quarters as heir apparent to the rock-god crown of recently deceased Jimi Hendrix. Lynott himself probably saw Ritchie's interest as flattering, but Lizzy manager Chris O'Donnell later dismissed the sessions as 'A few rehearsals which had Phil thinking he could live out his Rod Stewart/Faces fantasy.'

According to Lizzy drummer Brian Downey, Blackmore had come to De Lane Lea during the recording of *Shades Of A Blue Orphanage*, the band's second album released in March 1972, plugged in and started jamming. 'We all completely freaked… Phil didn't want to leave Lizzy but he really wanted to work with Ritchie and he was in two minds.' Blackmore revealed some time later that complete recordings of two or three tracks existed that must still be in the vaults. 'They were good but I think it may have been a bit near Hendrix… I was playing that way, and Phil was singing that way.' During the early 1980s, Lynott stated that as many as five tracks were worked up, but the only known reels of master tape found to date proved to contain just three disappointingly rudimentary and incomplete backing tracks.

If Blackmore had cut a solo record at that point, it's likely it would have appeared on a new label as Purple were accorded their own imprint. This was common for the mega-groups of the period as such so-called 'boutique' labels made it look as if they had complete autonomy over their output. It also gave them the chance to get a few of their mates on board, do the odd extracurricular solo project or whatever. The Rolling Stones got Rolling Stones Records, the Moody Blues had Threshold, Led Zeppelin's was Swan Song and Deep Purple... Purple!

The original plan had been for *Fireball* to be released on the new label, but negotiations between managers Edwards and Coletta and EMI (whose Harvest imprint had issued all but the first Purple platter) dragged on too long. Not that the colour of the disc's label – if truth be told a fetching shade of lilac, rather than purple, with a cut-out 'p' (also intended to represent an ear) encircling the spindle hole – would have sold one single extra copy.

A management company called Purple Star had existed since 1970 and been concerned with the *Jesus Christ Superstar* project, in which Ian Gillan had of course sung the lead role. So it was that Mary Magdalene, Hawaiian-born Yvonne Elliman, was signed to the new label, having been whisked from the obscurity of a West London nightclub to play the role (she'd later graduate to Eric 'God' Clapton's right hand, but that's another story).

The first actual Purple member to grace the label was Jon Lord with his previously mentioned *Gemini Suite*, and he would continue his collaboration with Tony Ashton on a low-key level with a film soundtrack (*The Last Rebel*) and a single, 'Celebration'. Later joint projects would include 1974's *First Of The Big Bands*.

The roster quickly grew to encompass US singer-songwriter Buddy Bohn, UK keyboard player and vocalist Rupert Hine (later of Quantum Jump) and duo Curtiss Maldoon. Dave Curtiss, who recorded the album with Clive Maldoon, had, you may recall, been around at the birth of Purple but after failing to snag the vocalist's role, had ended up in Bodast with a pre-Yes Steve Howe. The pair would achieve very belated fame when Madonna, of all people, based her 'Ray Of Light' on the duo's track 'Sepheryn' and paid them the appropriate writing royalty.

Perhaps surprisingly, there was little progressive rock to be found on the Purple label outside of Bullet, a band featuring former Big Three bass-player John Gustafson alongside Atomic Rooster refugees Paul Hammond and John Du Cann. Theirs would be the only non-Purple album released in 1972, a year that saw *Machine Head* and *Made In Japan*, not to mention extensive and rescheduled US touring, take up much of Edwards, Coletta and the band's time.

Having their own label was a sign that Deep Purple had 'made it' – but it was clear that, despite its sales success, *Fireball* had been hard work for band and fans alike. The next step along the path to megastardom needed to be a sure-footed one.

4 Montreux to Japan

Having spent two weeks in hospital after being taken ill in Chicago in October, Ian Gillan returned to his West London flat with a doctor's note advising him to take three months off with absolutely no work at all. But the lure of recording proved too strong and he rejoined the band in Montreux, Switzerland, in December 1971. The resulting album, released a scant four months later, was to be a milestone in Deep Purple's career, giving them a second UK Number 1 and a US Number 7.

The unexpected break from touring had proved a blessing for Roger Glover, who got most of his songwriting ideas for the album during his weeks off, mainly because he was able to relax. The intention with the next album, he explained, was to take things a stage further 'and do a live album – but without the audience'.

The choice of the Casino in Montreux as the recording venue was with this in mind. The decision had been made when they'd played there earlier in the year and had hit it off with the owner, Claude Nobs, who also organised the town's annual jazz festival. After one final gig by Frank Zappa and the Mothers of Invention in early December, the place would be theirs to share with the renovation team that typically carried out running repairs in the off season.

Producer Martin Birch had gone to Montreux early to scout the location and decide which rooms in the casino to use and where to park the mobile recording studio. The group's arrival coincided with the Zappa concert, so they all went down to enjoy it. But during the show an over-excited fan fired a flare gun into the ceiling and the place burnt down.

The group little realised the scene they were observing would provide the inspiration for Deep Purple's most recognisable musical offering, 'Smoke On The Water'. 'The wind was coming off the mountains and taking the smoke and flames across the lake,' relates Gillan. 'The smoke was hanging like a curtain over the water...'

The song title itself came to Glover in a dream one night, about three days after the fire. He woke up sweating all over and admits to having actually uttered the words 'Smoke on the water' to himself. He wrote it down and next day suggested to Ian that they write a song about it... 'Sounds like a drug song,' Ian observed, but he was more than happy to provide the majority of the lyrics.

Not that *Machine Head* would prove a one-song album. 'Highway Star', which would be the band's opening number for many years, was also recorded here. This had its origins on a tour bus going to Portsmouth. A journalist on the bus asked Ritchie how the group wrote songs. Caught in a playful mood, he picked up his guitar, said 'like this...' and started a rhythm. Ian Gillan joined in and ad-libbed lyrics. By the end of the night the seeds had been sown.

The album was done and dusted within a fortnight, returning to the speedy ways of old. No outtakes or other discards would surface on future remastered editions; *Machine Head* (named after the tuning peg of a guitar, and illustrated as such on the sleeve) was straight down the line Purple – no more, no less.

Having finished the tail end of 1971 with an arduous recording session, Deep Purple were only allowed a slight breather over the Christmas and New Year period before a one-off gig in Germany on the fifth day of January preceded the first US tour by Mark II, scheduled to kick off just a week later. It was the start of a year that would culminate in some of the highest and lowest moments in the band's career – twelve months that would see a previously hard-working quintet pushed harder than ever before. And while this resulted in a continued upward curve with regard to popularity and financial success, outside pressures, internal relationships and ill health would continue to dog them in ever-increasing proportions.

The first of an unbelievable six American tours to be scheduled in the calendar year of 1972 started in Florida on 13 January and took in a breakneck sixteen gigs in nineteen days – a perfect example of the strenuous schedules placed upon Purple. There was then a brief and welcome respite on their return to England before four gigs in Germany between 12 and 17 February. There remained just room on the gig sheet to play three UK gigs before jetting off to fulfil Scandinavian dates in late February and early March.

By this time, the group's typical concert fee in the UK exceeded £1,000 – but, upon their return from Scandinavia, they still agreed to do another recording for BBC Radio on 9 March at the Paris Theatre in London for which they received the standard BBC fee of £100. Their reason to commit to such a poorly paid performance in front of an invited audience of approximately 200 was two-fold. On one hand, with most of the year mapped out touring America, it helped keep UK fans happy when the recording was broadcast on *Sounds Of The Seventies* on 18 March. Furthermore, with no less than six of the eight songs performed hailing from the recently recorded *Machine Head*, it was an ideal way of boosting promotion prior to that album's release a couple of months later.

The recording, subsequently issued by EMI, is unique in capturing live renditions of 'Never Before' and 'Maybe I'm A Leo', songs from the album which were soon to be dropped from the set. (The former became Purple Mark II's fourth successive hit single on its March '72 release, but a Number 35 chart placing suggested their Midas touch with 45rpm vinyl was now wearing thin.)

Regular Purple concert-goers would already have been familiar with some of the other *Machine Head* tracks, as both 'Highway Star' and 'Lazy' had been introduced to the live set in late 1971. Two other new numbers were also performed at this show, 'Smoke On The Water' and 'Space Truckin''. The former was to take on a life of its own, becoming one of the most best-known rock songs of all time, while 'Space Truckin'', the four-minute closing track from *Machine Head*, became the band's standard live finale, being regularly stretched to over twenty minutes thanks to instrumental soloing.

Like 'Lazy', 'Space Truckin'' was also initially brought into the set to replace one of the older songs, 'Mandrake Root', which had been in the repertoire since the very first gig in 1968. In essence, 'Space Truckin'' live was very much a welding together of the original studio version with the live structures of 'Mandrake Root'. The song itself was performed very similarly to the studio version, but once that had concluded, as had been the case with 'Mandrake Root', a change of tempo would set down a solid rhythm over which Lord and Blackmore would solo at length in whatever way they desired. A fast flurry of notes, also taken from the *Shades Of Deep Purple* number, was used as Lord's 'check out' which Blackmore would play alongside before taking over soloing duties. Some nights, one of the two might hog the limelight with a lengthier improvisation. Despite the aggressive pounding backbeat laid down by Paice and Glover, the overlaid solos would often veer into very quiet and melancholy passages. As an example of this, Blackmore's volume control technique that, as previously mentioned, formed the central section of 'Fools' on the *Fireball* album, had originally been developed on stage during 'Mandrake Root' and was now, in its turn, incorporated into 'Space Truckin''.

Before the BBC recording was broadcast, Deep Purple were already in the States for another tour, this time kicking off in Kansas City on 17 March and designed to take the band through to 23 April in Honolulu, Hawaii. Towards the end of March, however, Ritchie was taken ill after a couple of gigs in Staten Island, New York. Many years later Jon Lord recalled looking at Ritchie sitting in the airport departure lounge in Flint, Michigan: 'I said, "Are you okay, Blackers?" "I don't know, I feel a bit strange." "Well, you're turning yellow." And he was, in front of our eyes.' Blackmore had a severe bout of hepatitis, the very same illness that had struck down Ian Gillan not six months previously.

With Blackmore now bedridden, there was clearly a lot of pressure on the band to continue the tour, having already been forced to postpone it from the previous year. The clamour from American audiences to see Deep Purple in concert left the band feeling that if another tour was to be cancelled, the building of their popularity in the most lucrative of markets could potentially dwindle – so, with Blackmore in hospital, the band played as a four-piece in Flint, Michigan on 31 March.

With the guitar being such a focal point of any rock band, and Purple being no exception to the rule, they decided to draft in another guitarist to complete the tour. Initially the man earmarked for the job was legendary session player Al Kooper. It was in many ways a surprise choice, not least because he was best-known for his keyboard work, in particular his organ contribution to some of Bob Dylan's classic tracks from the previous decade, such as 'Positively Fourth Street' and the anthemic 'Like A Rolling Stone'.

Kooper had just done a tour with his band Blood, Sweat And Tears, which saw him end up in hospital. He had only been out for three weeks when he received a call from his agent – who was handling the Purple tour – pleading with his client to help him out of a difficult situation. Kooper, who was asked if he would audition with the band at their rehearsal facility the following day, recalled his reaction years later: 'I was dumbfounded. First of all, I was a keyboard player, a fair one at that, who dabbled on guitar. Ritchie Blackmore was a master of the genre he participated in – light years from where I would ever end up. Secondly, I barely knew any of their songs and, most of all, I had just finished a tour that had put me in the hospital.'

Kooper was adamant he didn't want to do the tour but his agent begged him to go to the audition anyway, just to buy him time while he could search for someone capable of handling the gig. A reluctant Al therefore turned up at the rehearsal studio the following day with his Epiphone Wilshire guitar. He knew some of the band from the circuit as their paths had crossed in the past and, after exchanging pleasant hellos, plugged in. 'They started playing something pretty simple,' Kooper later recalled, 'and I joined in.'

Because of his years as a studio musician, he was able to learn things extremely quickly. According to Kooper, the next number they tackled 'was really fast' and he shied away from the guitar solo. The song in question would undoubtedly have been

'Highway Star' from the about to be released *Machine Head* and, Kooper recalled, 'It was simply too fast for me...'

The band seemed confident that it could work and Ian Gillan told Kooper not to worry as Jon Lord could play an organ solo in place of the guitar work. At the end of the audition there were smiles all around as band and crew believed they had found their man. Purple's road manager Rob Cooksey said to Kooper, 'That was great, Al. You passed the ultimate test. The roadies all loved it. And in that first song, you even started the solo on the same note Ritchie does. See ya tomorrow.'

During the cab ride home, Al Kooper considered the situation he found himself in for a full five minutes before deciding he couldn't go through with it. He called his agent, telling him that he had fulfilled his end of the bargain and that he had to inform them he wouldn't be doing it. The agent was in tears on the phone, wondering what he was going to do next, and asked Kooper to at least suggest someone. Kooper suggested one of his favourite guitarists, Randy California from West Coast psychedelic champions Spirit.

Born Randy Wolfe, California was named by Jimi Hendrix with whom he played in New York in 1966 before the Seattle-born axeman flew to England seeking his fortune. When Hendrix headed east, Randy took a westbound flight to reunite with step-dad Ed, who'd previously drummed alongside Ry Cooder with Taj Mahal's Rising Sons. Singer Jay Ferguson and bassist Mark Andes (who'd played with Randy in 1965 folk-rockers the Red Roosters), together with keyboard player John Locke, completed the first and classic Spirit line-up.

Spirit's greatest achievement had come in 1970, two years before his meeting with Purple, in the shape of fourth album *Twelve Dreams Of Dr. Sardonicus*, but a poor review in the influential *Rolling Stone* magazine combined with a disappointing Number 63 chart placing to magnify dissent in the ranks. As his group bar Cassidy split to form Jo Jo Gunne, California came to Britain to link with Hendrix bassist Noel Redding and cut an eccentric, Jimi-influenced solo album *Kapt Kopter And The (Fabulous) Twirly Birds*, which oscillated between inspiration and incoherence. He then tried to end it all by diving off Waterloo Bridge. Ironically, given his eventual end in a surfing accident in 1997, he survived… but while undoubtedly gifted, California did not come across as particularly reliable.

With time not on their side, Deep Purple spent a couple of days at New York's Fillmore East rehearsing with their second choice stand-in. And so it was that, on 6 April in Quebec City, Canada, Randy California performed on stage with Deep Purple for the first and only time. According to recollections from Ian Gillan, the show was well received. Two things that stood out for the vocalist was that Randy California chose to play the solo in 'Child In Time' on slide guitar, and they also played 'When A Blind Man Cries', an outtake from *Machine Head* that would shortly be released as the B-side to the single 'Never Before'. It was to be the only time Deep Purple played the number on stage during the 1970s.

Despite enjoying the experience, Purple clearly realised how important Blackmore was to the band and with much reluctance it was decided to cancel the rest of the tour. Years later Gillan said; 'I don't think it would have been right to carry on without Ritchie. They didn't carry on without me when I was ill (the previous year) and that had a lot to do with the decision to cancel.' Scrapping the rest of the tour meant that in turn, three concerts planned for the band's first visit to Japan between 11 and 16 May were also cancelled. Given that there was growing antagonism between guitarist and singer, it's quite ironic that the group showed such unity.

Personality conflicts exist in any band, and often add an edge to recordings and performances, yet when bands are overworked such schisms can quickly become chasms. If the cancelled US tour of 1971 wasn't enough, the fact that its successor was truncated when Ritchie Blackmore fell ill, and with European and Far Eastern jaunts already inked into the calendar the members of

Deep Purple were spending ever longer periods of time in close proximity with each other. Although it was not yet readily apparent to the audience, friction between band members was steadily increasing, particularly the relationship between Gillan and Blackmore. Lead singers and lead guitarists are invariably the main focal points of any rock band and it's no surprise that the degree of attention they get can have an adverse affect on their personas.

With the huge sales of the new album *Machine Head*, Deep Purple's ever-increasing popularity saw Gillan, the frontman, being rated as highly as anyone else in the business, and rightly so. His voice was as powerful as any other top lead vocalists of the era, perhaps more so. Whether it was Mick Jagger, Roger Daltrey, Robert Plant, Paul Rodgers or anyone else you care to mention, Gillan was on equal footing with the top singers in rock. Likewise Blackmore was established as one of the world's premier six-string performers. His technique, aligned to his showmanship, resulted in many critics and fans considering him to be the top guitarist of the day.

Hendrix was no more, while Clapton had already started to play down his 'God-like' status since the demise of Cream. With the likes of Jeff Beck shunning the spotlight and Free's Paul Kossoff delving deeper into drugs, the combination of theatrics and virtuosity that Blackmore brought to Deep Purple was rapidly increasing his stock among fans of extrovert rock guitar.

The combination of two highly talented performers and writers in Gillan and Blackmore was undoubtedly a major factor in Purple's huge popularity. Inevitably it must have done wonders for their egos and each party started to see his role in the band as more vital than the other's. It was a potential powder keg that could not be relied upon to stay unlit...

Ian Gillan himself has suggested that Blackmore always appeared to have the greater persuasive qualities and as a result invariably got his way with decisions. Ever since the furore surrounding the *Concerto*, Blackmore had almost single-handedly steered Purple in a heavier direction and, rightly or wrongly, was seen as the main driving force within the band. Although all compositions were credited to the whole group, it was by and large Blackmore who came up with the musical ideas. Roger Glover would chip in with a fair degree of composing, while Gillan would invariably write the lyrics, sometimes with the help of Glover.

Gillan was also starting to become disillusioned with what he saw as Purple's reluctance to move forward and expand its musical horizons. Ironically Blackmore tended to share the belief that Purple wasn't moving forward, but for the guitarist it was simply a case of believing that Deep Purple's audience wouldn't allow them to deviate from what was expected from them.

Despite the fact that, in the early days of the band, Blackmore and Gillan would share a room together on tour, they were in essence chalk and cheese. Although on stage Blackmore was as outlandish as anyone, out of the limelight he was quite an introverted and shy character, whereas Gillan embodied the rock 'n' roll lifestyle with his penchant for partying. Something would inevitably have to give.

With Blackmore now recovered from illness, the band once again flew to America for a slightly less strenuous tour, kicking off in Detroit on 25 May and finishing in Anaheim, California on 6 June, eight shows in twelve days. This was followed by a whistle-stop pair of gigs at London's Rainbow Theatre before another Stateside flight. This would then be followed by something Deep Purple were very much looking forward to – their first Japanese dates.

The two gigs played at the Rainbow on 30 June and 1 July became famous for getting the name of Deep Purple into the hallowed pages of the *Guinness Book Of Records* as the loudest band in the world. It's something that to this day is constantly referred to in brief biographies of the band, though of course the volume level that they had been recorded at was to be eclipsed on many occasions thereafter. It wasn't common practice to monitor volume levels then, so in reality the documenting of Deep Purple's

shows as attaining 117 decibels through their 10,000-watt
Marshall PA system was the exception rather than the norm.

That said, the major contributory factor was undoubtedly the
decision to use the same system they had been using in US venues
of five times or more capacity than that of the Finsbury Park
theatre. Also, while it was true that three members of the audience
were rendered unconscious by the volume, most accounts failed to
mention it was because said fans had foolishly decided to put their
heads as close to the speakers as possible.

Six days later Purple were back in the States for tour number
four, ten shows in twelve days. On returning to Europe the rest of
the month was earmarked for recording the follow-up to *Machine
Head*, the band's seventh studio album, *Who Do We Think We Are*.
When the band decamped to a villa on the outskirts of Rome a
long-standing friend of Ritchie Blackmore's, Arvid Anderson,
went with them. Anderson had been in the Three Musketeers
with Blackmore in late 1965/early 1966 and the pair had stayed
in touch over the years. Anderson took an Italian musician friend,
Joe Vescovi, along with him to the villa.

When interviewed for an Italian Purple fan magazine many
years later, Vescovi recalled that, despite the incredibly hot
summer Italy was having, the villa had been turned into a fortress,
surrounded by a host of roadies with doors and windows closed.
As with *Machine Head*, the band once again employed the use of
the Rolling Stones' mobile recording truck but, as it was too big to
get through the archway and into the courtyard, closed-circuit
cameras were set up just as had been the case in Montreux the
previous year.

Blackmore had also started to exert greater control over the band
and Glover, the other major writer in the band, found his ideas
increasingly being ignored by the enigmatic guitarist. 'Ritchie
wanted the band to go his way, and of course the band didn't want
that. I'd come up with loads of ideas and he'd just sit there and
look at me. There was also a rift between Ian and Ritchie on a
technical matter about Ian's singing. Ritchie didn't like the way

Ian did certain things and Ian said "I don't care what you think, I'm doing them my way anyhow." ... This rocking the boat made *Who Do We Think We Are* a very traumatic process, because Ritchie and Ian ended up not talking.'

To compound matters, Glover's approval of some of the ideas that Blackmore played to him was met with responses such as 'I'm saving that for my solo album.' With the combination of exhaustion from the heavy touring schedule and the friction in the band, it was little wonder Purple treated it more as a holiday than a time for writing and recording.

By now the breakdown in the relationship between Blackmore and Gillan had reached the point where the guitarist didn't even want to be in the same room as the singer and consequently spent most of the time working alone or with engineer Martin Birch. As Blackmore has done so many times over his career it was a classic case of cutting off his nose to spite his face, and only two songs were written and recorded in Italy that summer; 'Painted Horse' and 'Woman From Tokyo'. Lyrically, the latter track took its inspiration from the impending tour of Japan.

Having been forced to cancel the first visit in May, the dates had been rearranged for mid August. Two shows at the Koseinenkin in Osaka on 15 and 16 August were followed the next night with a gig at the world-famous Budokan in the capital city of Tokyo. The band's Japanese record label, Warners Pioneer, was keen to mark the special occasion of the band's inaugural visit by recording the shows for a prospective live album. Given Purple's reputation as a live act it seems strange that it took them so long to make such a recording, though the idea had been mooted when the Montreux Casino had been booked for *Machine Head*.

As Roger Glover explained at the time, 'In return for organising the details of our stay in Montreux, and allowing the use of the Casino for nearly a month, we were going to do one concert for Claude [Nobs] towards the end of our stay. We thought it would be a good idea to record the whole thing and possibly get a live album as well as the projected studio album we were about to make.'

With all the problems the band encountered recording *Machine Head* with 'Swiss time' running out, the idea was shelved and the decision to record the Japanese shows would probably never have happened without the initial suggestion of the Japanese record company. Deep Purple live was always a unique experience; the band improvised extensively on every show, and it was largely due to this that they had stayed away from live albums, believing that every gig was unique.

Once Purple had agreed to the idea, they were adamant that it should be done properly. As such, their trustworthy engineer Martin Birch was to be flown out to record the three shows. By this stage in the band's career, Birch had established himself as something of a sixth member and his contribution to the Deep Purple sound should not be overlooked. In testament to this, or more likely in keeping with their lack of interest in live albums, neither Blackmore nor Gillan even bothered to listen to the playbacks.

Only Roger Glover and Ian Paice showed any real interest in the project, and the pair of them were subsequently responsible for mixing the album. The quality of the recordings that Birch had captured was so good it was decided that an album originally planned solely for the Japanese market would be given worldwide release. Unsurprisingly, the decision was not unanimous. Ian Gillan's reservations were backed up by unhappiness with his own performances, having just recovered from a bout of bronchitis. When the album was released, however, listeners would be hard-pushed to find any room for criticism.

Although three consecutive August nights were efficiently committed to recording tape, the capital city's audience were treated to a final show that suffered due to poor acoustics, so it was assumed anything considered for inclusion on the live album would be taken from the two earlier nights. The seven tracks spread over four sides of vinyl were mostly drawn from the second Osaka set, but two tracks, drum solo 'The Mule' and 'Lazy', were taken from the 'unsuitable' Tokyo set and one, 'Smoke On The Water', from the first Osaka performance on 15 August (this because it was the only time Ritchie Blackmore played the trademark intro faultlessly).

Unusually for live albums of the 1970s or indeed any era, virtually no studio trickery was used to improve the results. Jon Lord admitted to only one overdub, where a line from 'Strange Kind Of Woman' was dropped in from another version when Ian Gillan tripped over a mike lead. (Unfortunately, this amusing tale was not substantiated when the concerts were remastered for 1993 release in a three-CD set.)

One by-product of producing a live album was that it deflected audience clamour for the next studio set; with tensions in the band ever growing, the prospect of a double live release at the tail end of the year helped to hide from an eager public the extent of the disharmony in the ranks. From Japan the band flew straight back to America for yet another tour and eventually returned to British soil for the first full UK tour in exactly a year, kicking off at Southampton's Guildhall on 13 September.

The tour helped to cement Deep Purple's popularity in their home country and included one of their biggest UK gigs to date at the Brixton Sundown (now called the Academy). Following a couple of shows in France in mid October, the rest of the month was set aside for the completion of the new studio album and this time the band went to Germany to work in a small studio in the village of Waldorf near Frankfurt. As Glover explained shortly after the recording, 'This time we were in a studio, although still using the Rolling Stones truck. The studio was very rarely used and seemed extremely outdated, but it suited us.' It certainly did and there was far less of the disruption than had been the case in Rome three months earlier. Despite the fact that, in Glover's words, 'Half the band weren't talking to the other half,' they all got on with the job in hand and, as Martin Birch explained, 'knuckled down and got on with it'.

There was no rest for the wicked as November and December

saw the band's sixth North American tour of the year. This was
also the longest and most gruelling to date, kicking off in Quebec
on 6 November and continuing right through to 16 December in
Miami – twenty-five dates in forty days. The tour will always be
remembered for two major incidents, the first the attempted
shooting of Ian Paice by a crazed gunman during the show in
Oklahoma City on 23 November. Two of Purple's road crew saw
the man fire a pistol and called the police. It took six of them to
restrain him. After the show they discovered a bullet hole
just a few feet above Paice's head – a fortunate escape indeed.

The other notable incident occurred on the day after the gig
at the Hara Arena in Dayton, Ohio. Back at the Imperial House
Hotel, Ian Gillan wrote his letter of resignation addressed to
Purple's co-manager, Tony Edwards. Gillan had let it be known
to the management after the recording session in Germany that he
wanted to leave the band and, although they initially kept it under
wraps, at no time did they try and dissuade him, merely asking
him to stay on long enough to fulfil the current commitments.
Gillan agreed to stay for four more US tours, two UK tours and
two European jaunts, stretching off over the horizon to a Japanese
tour lined-up for late June 1973.

In the eloquently written letter Gillan put forward his reasons
and showed his true professionalism by stating that he would
honour their request and see out the commitments for the next
six months. Although not yet released *Who Do We Think We Are*
had, by everyone's admission, been a disappointment. Ian Paice
conceded that the band had struggled to come up with the killer
riffs required and, with the group's reluctance to tinker with the
live set, Gillan felt the band was in the process of going through
the motions and stagnating.

Whether or not this was the case, Gillan was clearly also
exhausted. His batteries had run down and his decision to quit was
to some extent a cry for help. As the singer recalled more than
twenty years later, 'To walk out of the band at that peak would
seem stupid. But I couldn't find any other way to do it. No one

would listen; no one would say shut up. I must have been pretty impossible for no one to come up and actually put an arm around me or say sure, we can work this out.'

Because Deep Purple was by now a major money-making machine, neither of the management team seemed remotely bothered by this and were only concerned with ensuring the brand name continued. Either that or it was an unsuccessful attempt to call the singer's bluff. The rest of the group were told of Gillan's decision immediately. Whether or not this was a wise thing to do is something that time cannot change but it certainly made the remainder of the tour even more fraught.

If all wasn't well within the band, the UK release of *Made In Japan* on Friday 8 December certainly did its bit to enhance Purple's reputation as one of the most exciting bands on the scene. It reached Number 4 in the charts, and, although on the surface that may seem like a step backwards after the Number 1 success of *Machine Head*, it went on to become a bigger money-spinner because the cost of producing the live double was significantly less than any of the studio albums, even though it retailed at a cut-price three pounds ten pence.

Made In Japan was in fact far from the first live recording of Deep Purple Mark II. One of their earlier shows at the 1969 Montreux Jazz Festival had been committed to tape, as were all the acts at that time-honoured event. Later the same year, the band's set at the Royal Albert Hall that acted as a dress rehearsal for the *Concerto* had also been recorded, while a Stockholm radio station had broadcast a show to their local audience.

For many a month, bootleggers had been following the band around and releasing the results. Interestingly, a show in Aachen, Germany in late 1970 was edited and reissued under a number of different titles. The original intention was to create a keepsake for the Japanese market, but the realisation dawned that, by issuing their own 'official bootleg', Purple could diminish the illicit recordings' appeal. 'If we put out our own live set,' said Roger Glover, 'it should kill their market.' As it turned out, it did rather more than that, and in the twenty-first century was still featuring high in polls for the greatest live rock album ever.

As 1973 got under way, the apparently endless touring schedules continued for the first three months with gigs in both mainland Europe and Deep Purple's homeland. Jon Lord also found time for another performance of his *Gemini Suite*, this time in Germany with the Munich Chamber Opera Orchestra at the Munich Concert Hall.

This wasn't the only solo project on the horizon. Although Blackmore might have been expected to have moved to impose his authority on the band further with Gillan's impending departure, he too voiced his intention to seize the opportunity to try something fresh. The guitarist had been showing signs of discontent with the set-up for some time and, having become disillusioned with Gillan's singing style, had expressed his admiration for Free's Paul Rodgers and was keen to progress in a more blues-based direction. The demos Blackmore and Paice had laid down the previous year with Phil Lynott were now seen as a potential stepping-stone for the departure of the guitarist and drummer to a 'Babyface' scenario. Resuscitating the Babyface project as was, though, was now unlikely, since Phil Lynott was now finding greater success with Thin Lizzy. Lucifer's Friend vocalist John Lawton, an acquaintance of Ritchie from his time in Germany in the 1960s, was mooted as singer, but negotiations failed.

With the imminent departure of Gillan, plus the huge financial success the band was now enjoying, the management not surprisingly expressed the importance of keeping Deep Purple together in some form or another – especially as they were breaking into the lucrative American market, where the band would sell 14 million units worldwide during the year. If Paice and Blackmore pursued Babyface, then the only option would have been for Lord and Glover – hardly the faces of the band, even if they constituted the musical backbone – to graft on a new frontman, guitarist and drummer. Hardly a recipe for success.

Jon Lord was the man least impressed by the situation. He'd

already been considering linking up with fellow keyboard-player Tony Ashton, whose claim to fame was having penned and sung the 1971 smash 'Resurrection Shuffle' for one-hit wonders Ashton Gardner and Dyke. That pairing would happen, but some years further down the road.

As it stood, in the summer of 1973, odds were that Lord and Glover would be asked to steer the good ship Purple into calmer waters, their management clearly keen that the golden goose they'd nurtured so long and so expensively should keep laying golden eggs. Talks eventually led to Ian Paice agreeing to remain on board if attempts to persuade Blackmore to stay were successful. And he appears to have lent his weight to that argument. 'I didn't want to get a singer in and carry on where we'd left off,' Blackmore later confessed, 'but Ian Paice said it would be silly to abandon all our efforts.'

Ironically, with ferment going on behind the scenes, the band's American record label, not content with sold-out concert tours and successful album sales, was itching for a hit single. Although Purple had achieved some singles success with the first line-up and a big hit in England with 'Black Night', they had since given far less credence to singles. Though they never went to Led Zeppelin's extent of refusing to release 45s, albums were now the statement as far as Deep Purple was concerned and, by and large, the same applied to their audience.

Warner Bros, trying desperately to get a US hit, had originally taken 'Lazy' from the *Machine Head* LP to release as a single in June 1972. Yet even the inclusion of the non-album B-side, the marvellous blues track 'When A Blind Man Cries', didn't secure a hit. Four months later Warners had another stab with 'Highway Star' and again in April 1973 with 'Woman From Tokyo', far and away the most commercial cut from *Who Do We Think We Are.* That tortuously recorded studio effort from the previous year had finally been released in February 1973, just two months after *Made In Japan,* to a decidedly mixed critical response. Any album, however good, would struggle to escape from the shadow of such an outstanding live set: *Who Do We Think We Are* was nowhere near a Purple highlight.

Blackmore describes *Who Do We Think We Are* as 'a nondescript piece of nothing… I never play it. You hate that, when you're worked to death by the management and they say you've got to record too...' Jon Lord concurs: 'It was a bullshit album apart from two tracks – "Woman from Tokyo" and "Smooth Dancer". They were rather fun. The rest of the album was pretty crappy.' The title of the album had come from a letters page in the music press, Ian Paice suggesting it as a way of having a go back 'as by this time the press hated us'.

While all this was going on, radio stations throughout the States were regularly playing the *Machine Head* album track 'Smoke On The Water'. A month after releasing 'Woman From Tokyo', someone at Warners hit on the idea of a double A-side and coupled the studio version of 'Smoke On The Water' with the live version from 'Made In Japan'. It turned out to be the long-awaited masterstroke and catapulted Deep Purple into the superleague when the single reached Number 4 in the States. Many other countries also released this coupling and world sales topped a staggering 12 million. To think that Purple Records in the UK, didn't decide to follow suit with a release in the band's homeland!

The success of the song took the band as much by surprise as it had the record company. The selection of 'Never Before' as the UK single from *Machine Head* in March 1972 showed that, while Deep Purple could produce great music, they had no idea what made a hit record. The key to the success of 'Smoke On The Water' lay in its simplicity. Though lyrically, the song was to sum up the whole making of the album, it was the opening riff that has made it such an instantly recognisable piece and has gone on to become the bane of any guitar-shop employee who has had to endure endless renditions. The critics also invariably make derogatory remarks about its simplicity.

Blackmore, the originator of one of the most famous riffs of all time, is rightly proud of it and always quick to defend his creation.

In more recent times he has gone on to compare it to the opening notes of Beethoven's Fifth Symphony, after which the critics normally back off. As with Beethoven's piece, 'Smoke On The Water' is equally as enduring and will undoubtedly still be played for hundreds of years to come. It's a great example of Blackmore's knack of producing exciting, memorable music, so often an element that many musicians and composers overlook and despite the talent within the band, 'Smoke On The Water' is a perfect illustration that they were never afraid to come up with something so blatantly simple.

To further capitalise on Purple's huge success, a massive thirty-five-date tour of North America got under way in California on 12 April. The bitterness within the band continued to fester with Gillan, by his own choice, isolating himself from the rest of the group, while Roger Glover was also feeling increasingly in the cold for reasons the bassist couldn't comprehend. The touring atmosphere degenerated further, with less and less communication within the group, and things came to a head on 15 June after a show in Jacksonville, Florida when Glover, suspecting something was afoot, confronted Tony Edwards. After learning that Ritchie would stay in the band only if Glover left, the bassist immediately resigned.

Roger Glover reflected on this unhappy time in his life two decades later. 'I was extremely hurt. I wanted to prove to them that even if they couldn't, at least I'd be a gentleman about it and commit myself through to Japan.' Time clearly hadn't changed the way Glover felt he had been treated, as he also recalled: 'Ritchie didn't say anything to me on that whole tour except right on the very last day and he said, "It's not personal, it's business."'

Many years later Jon Lord recalled the way Blackmore had talked to him about the situation. 'Ritchie said to me: "If Ian's going, why don't we get rid of Rog? We're going to go for a new singer, one who sings more bluesy aren't we? Why not get a bass player who can sing too? Then we can have harmonies."' Lord and Paice, the fellow elder statesmen of the band, went along with

Blackmore's request, and after all the toing and froing the original nucleus of the band remained intact.

Though inexcusably withheld from him for the sake of not jeopardising yet another American tour, the decision to dispense with the bassist had come right out of the blue. Glover had played a vital role in Deep Purple's success and, after Blackmore, was the next major songwriter in the band. If Jon Lord's recollections are accurate then it must simply have been a case that Glover was not ideally suited for the more blues-based direction Blackmore wanted.

Deep Purple Mark II played its final show at the Koseinenkin in Osaka on 29 June 1973. At the end of the gig, amidst a demolished drum kit, with dry ice forming a thick covering across the floor of the stage, Roger Glover stood in front of his amps, with his bass in hand while Ian Gillan made a farewell speech. 'All I want to say to all of you is thank you very much – you are great. Thank you for everything you have given us in Japan and thank you, really, for the representatives of the whole world as far as we are concerned. Thank you and God bless you for everything you have ever given us. And this is the last night, the end. God bless you, thanks a lot.'

5. A New Beginning

When Ian Gillan left Deep Purple he was so disillusioned he effectively left the music business altogether for eighteen months. And there was no shortage of projects demanding his attention. 'I had already got a recording studio, Kingsway in Holborn. My friend was involved in racing motorcycles and I loved that… and I'd always lived in hotels so I reckoned I couldn't live without one! It was great fun putting the design in, as it was a near-derelict building when I got hold of it. I had no plans to go back into music because I didn't see any way I could ever reach the heights I'd reached before.'

The prognosis for the band he'd left was uncertain. Yet though they'd yet to realise it, Lord and Paice had already encountered one of the cornerstones of the rebuilding process that was to end with Purple Mark III when the group circus had passed through Los Angeles the previous April. Dropping by legendary media haunt the Whiskey A Go Go for a post-show spritzer, the pair had been impressed by Trapeze, a band signed to the Moody Blues' Threshold record label. The outfit's original five-piece line-up proved unsuccessful and, shedding two members, the Birmingham band evolved into a hard-rocking trio headed by a young bass player called Glenn Hughes, who also took on lead vocal duties.

This native of Cannock, Staffordshire had emerged from his shell with a vengeance and was now fronting the band – completed by Mel Galley (guitar, vocals) and Dave Holland (drums) – with impressive aplomb. His vocal and bass style were both informed by a deep love of soul music which melded with the trio's heavy rock instrumentation to produce something intriguing and impossible to categorise.

As so often happens in these cases, Trapeze found themselves better accepted in the States than in the rigidly pigeonholed UK scene, hence the fact that they were playing 5,000-seat venues over there and clubs at home. Yet London Records, their US record label, had high hopes of turning them into the next ZZ Top. Third album *You Are The Music... We're Just The Band* was earning rave reviews from every quarter, and it was understandable that Hughes was initially unresponsive to tentative overtures from Purple.

What piqued his interest, though, was the rumour that Paul Rodgers of the recently demised Free was to throw his lot in with Deep Purple as Ian Gillan's replacement. 'I was in awe of the prospect,' Hughes told *Classic Rock*'s Geoff Barton thirty years later. 'Blackmore wanted Paul Rodgers 100 per cent, he wanted him to be the lead singer and to have me as a bass player who could also sing would have been a strong sort of bonus.'

As it happened, Rodgers decided to remain with Free drummer Simon Kirke and, with him, found fast-rising quartet Bad Company. The option of Hughes as lead vocalist was never seriously considered, the objective being more vocal variation than Purple had enjoyed up to this point. The vacancy for lead vocalist was still open. But the arrival of a package postmarked Marske-by-the-Sea, Cleveland containing a demo tape and an old picture of a knock-kneed individual in Boy Scouts' uniform solved that knotty problem.

David Coverdale had been one of hundreds of hopefuls responding to an ad in *Melody Maker*, the weekly music paper then famed for its 'Musicians Wanted' columns in its back pages. Many soon-to-be-famous bands recruited in this way, although few advertised their identity. 'Nobody knew which band,' Ian Paice told Geoff Barton, 'because we didn't say it was Deep Purple, but everyone got a clue from the timing.'

Coverdale was well aware that that Purple were looking for a vocalist, 'but I didn't think about it – every week somebody's looking for a musician. The chick who worked at the boutique I was at was a Purple nut... She took out a copy of *Machine Head* and put it on. Half a dozen guys came into the shop, and one of them said to me "Why don't you go for a job with Purple?" ... and laughed.' This chance remark made the young singer think more deeply about his musical objectives; 'I got really depressed and then violent and thought "I don't want to be regarded as a joke" – it means a lot to me.'

Coverdale was born on 22 September 1951 in Saltburn-on-Sea, Yorkshire. The son of a factory worker turned publican, he grew up in an atmosphere where music and musicians were never far away. He learnt the guitar in his teens but soon graduated to singing. 'I was listening to Alan Freeman's *Pick Of The Pops* and he played a version of "Yesterday" by Ray Charles which had me in tears. I was on my own and I went apeshit. I thought it must be good to have a voice like that and that sort of feel.' David worked on his voice thereafter and learned his craft fronting a string of local semi-pro bands on the flourishing northern England cabaret circuit through the late 1960s and early 1970s.

'I was singing through a Dynatron tape recorder – those were really heady days, it was terrific… we were all very limited. I don't think my voice had broken. That's when I first learnt to sing with my stomach, which sounds silly, but it's totally different from a normal voice.' A job fronting the Fabulosa Brothers provided a steady income. 'With equipment and somebody steering us it could have been as fine as the Average White Band, it was very much that way. We got away with so much because we took established standards and twisted them about a bit.'

If Coverdale's timing was perfect, his tape certainly wasn't. Though never knowingly bootlegged, it has become legendary in hard rock circles, not least because of comments from the unimpressed band members. Ian Paice has likened it to 1960s crooner Scott Walker of 'The Sun Ain't Gonna Shine Anymore' fame – but there was enough in one particular octave jump to tell the drummer that there might be as yet uncharted reservoirs of talent in the twenty-one-year-old unknown whose day job was selling men's clothing at the Stride In Style emporium in Redcar to invite him to the capital.

Initial impressions can hardly have been favourable, not least the fact that Coverdale brought a companion to the audition – a half-finished bottle of spirits! His clothes, haircut, moustache and –

certainly no longer in evidence these days – the suspicion of a weight problem didn't suggest this was Ian Gillan's replacement. Until, that was, he opened his mouth.

'It was supposed to be a two hour audition but we played for hours just blowing like hell. We did a couple of rock things which was embarrassing because I didn't know the words, I wasn't around at the time. I learnt "Smoke On The Water" and "Strange Kind Of Woman" and they didn't play either of those.' His rich, bluesy tone immediately struck Blackmore, who was a big fan of vocalists in the Paul Rodgers style. 'We went through a few rock numbers and then we stopped and Jon Lord went out to listen to it because it was being recorded. He came back and said it sounded good. Ritchie turned to me and said "You can sing rock, let's see what you can do with melody," and we had a go at "Yesterday" and it came out really nice.'

With the rest of the band in agreement, Coverdale was offered the job; it was the proverbial fairy tale come true, the unknown club crooner plucked from obscurity and made singer of one of the world's biggest bands but in his own words he nearly blew it from the off. 'Mr Coletta placed a contract on the table in front of me and told me to sign on the dotted line... Uh-oh... I'd promised my good friend and mentor, Tony Zivanaris, that I wouldn't sign anything 'til he and his lawyers had looked everything over, so, innocently I said okay I'll take them home with me to read through...

'Oh dear, John Coletta very nearly exploded! "What the hell do you mean, look over? This is Deep Purple we're talking about! I could get bloody Mick Jagger... anybody! Who the hell do you think you are? You sign this, or you're out!" I was in total shock. Nobody, but, my father had ever spoken to me like that in my life, this guy's temper was frightening.'

Amazing as it may seem, Deep Purple only needed to audition one singer. And though Blackmore still remained miffed that Paul Rodgers hadn't taken up the offer, the newcomer clearly shared many of Rodgers' formative influences, as well as hailing from the same part of the world, the Bad Company man being a Teessider.

Replacing one of the major frontmen of 1970s rock with a nobody seemed to be a daring decision. Yet bringing in a singer with a reputation and ego to match, as Paul Rodgers undoubtedly was, would doubtless have led to ego conflicts from the off. Both Coverdale, a total unknown, and Hughes, a second-division hopeful, would – in the short term at least – be guaranteed to toe the line, put their shoulders to the wheel and re-establish Purple's upward trajectory, which had been hobbled by Gillan's protracted departure. That was the plan – and it worked.

As Coverdale was soon to discover, Blackmore was the new line-up's principal songwriter and, shortly after his frightening ordeal of signing the contract, he was invited to the guitarist's home in Camberley for a writing session. Blackmore played Coverdale his home demos, which were the blueprints for many of the songs that would end up on the next album, helping to give Coverdale the feel of what was required. He returned to his home in Redcar and was shortly joined by Glenn Hughes, who assisted Coverdale in his writing. Despite Hughes' name being omitted from any writing credits when the album was released he certainly played a part with some of the compositions but, due to a messy publishing contract at the time, couldn't put his name to them.

Coverdale celebrated his twenty-second birthday on 22 September at Clearwell Castle in Gloucestershire, a secluded haunt favoured by supergroups like Bad Company for 'getting their act together in the country' before taking it on the road. The following day saw a press call at which, after a fortnight of writing and rehearsing, he was announced to the world as Ian Gillan's replacement. Glenn Hughes' recruitment inevitably inspired smaller headlines and Trapeze, despite carrying on briefly after his departure, folded without having made the hoped-for breakthrough.

It was David's first time in such an environment and, as he admits, it showed. 'I was so nervous, for three days I never sang. Lordy didn't come down to Clearwell for three days; when he got

there, he asked Ritchie how it was going, and Ritchie said
"Oh, great, but David won't sing!" Jon and me had a drink,
went through a Beatles medley for two hours, and that was fine.
I'd relaxed a lot.'

Jon Lord, ever the facilitator, was unequivocal in his opinions
on the sessions. 'It worked wonderfully at Clearwell. Glenn and
David seemed to have an immediate rapport, and even Ritchie
said it was "not bad" … by anyone else's standards that meant
wonderful! We had a good time recording the album. If David
was overawed to be working with us it only showed when we
were talking between ourselves over a beer – never during the
actual recording… The basic difference was in the use of the
vocals. There was a different approach – much freer and looser,
a progression that's noticeable to us, though I don't know if it
was to the audience.'

With a little time to kill before recording was to commence,
Jon Lord headed off to Germany in early October for another
performance of *The Gemini Suite*, teaming up with the same
orchestra and composer, Eberhard Schoener, that he had worked
with earlier in the year. The concert at Munich's Circus Krone also
premiered a new piece jointly composed by Lord and Schoener
entitled 'Continuo On BACH.' Purple's new bassist provided the
four-string playing at the gig, and Purple Records signing Yvonne
Elliman also appeared, along with Pete York (drums), Ray
Fenwick (guitar) and Roxy Music's Andy MacKay on saxophone.
Even Ritchie Blackmore was in the audience. Thanks to the
Germans' more open-minded attitude to rock and classical
fusions the evening was a great success, prompting German
TV to commission a new composition for the following year.

Recording sessions for the new album, Purple's eighth studio
effort in total, would take place in Montreux, Switzerland in
November 1973 – fireworks thankfully absent this time – and great
progress was made under Martin Birch's expert eye. Wrapping up
the sessions on the Rolling Stones mobile in less than a fortnight,
the band returned to London for mixing at Ian Gillan's studios,

Kingsway in London. The title was to be *Burn*, after a Blackmore riff to which Coverdale had written no fewer than seven sets of prospective lyrics for approval.

In early December, the curtain rose on the Mark III Purple for the very first time at the KB Hallen in Copenhagen, the first of four low-key dates in Europe that would see out a highly eventful year for the band and help to ease Coverdale into his role of frontman. As their live debut approached, David (and the rest of the band) were understandably nervous. 'I went upstairs to a room on my own and had a little discussion with myself – either I would go out there and fall flat on my face or I'd go out there and do it.'

The tour proved a triumph for all concerned, especially Coverdale. Despite the almost iconic status Ian Gillan still retained, the singer coped well, critics and fans alike immediately appreciating his rich tone. 'I never considered myself to be a replacement, it was a new thing. As far as they [Purple] were concerned it was a new band. They just had a reputation to live up to and an excellent one at that.'

One of the things Ian Gillan had constantly moaned about was the group's reluctance to change the set list. Now, with two new members, the set was extensively revamped and, not unsurprisingly, was built largely around the new album. It was a daring move, however, to open with four consecutive cuts from *Burn* – the title track, 'Might Just Take Your Life', 'Lay Down, Stay Down' and the classic 'Mistreated'. The latter was an instant stage success and perfectly illustrated the style of Deep Purple Mark III. It went on to become something of a signature tune for both its composers, and Coverdale and Blackmore would subsequently go on to perform it with their own groups.

The inevitable 'Smoke On The Water' was included and, on initial dates, was preceded by Jon Lord introducing the two new guys to the audience. The song was also extended to allow Glenn Hughes a chance to 'do his thing'. Yet the highlight of the show was another previously unheard track from the new album, 'You Fool No One'. Originally only four minutes on the album, it was transformed into a 15-minute *tour de force* showcasing the instrumental abilities of the three original members, Jon Lord's keyboard introduction being followed by solos from Blackmore and Paice.

The guitarist, in keeping with the band's general shift into a bluesy direction, used his solo to incorporate a wonderful piece that later became known simply as 'Blues', while Paice's solo finished with a revisiting of 'The Mule' that seemed a suitable way to bring the number to a close. 'Space Truckin'' was the only other Mark II song to be played. It proved an even lengthier set closer, being extended way beyond any version the previous line-up had performed, and again this was partly due to Glenn Hughes being given space to show off his vocal and bass skills in a way Roger Glover would never have considered.

For these initial low-key dates, the encore was another *Burn* track, 'What's Goin' On Here', but it was soon to be replaced by the surprise choice of Don Nix's blues classic 'Going Down', popularised to a rock audience a few years earlier by Jeff Beck.

Burn hit the racks in February 1974 to great curiosity, not to mention apprehension, from long-time Purple fans. While it had clear links with the band's past, it equally reflected the more soulful blues influences of the new members. The higher-pitched phrasing of Hughes, coupled with Coverdale's lower timbre, gave the band's characteristic sound a whole new twist. The title track itself, an archetypal Blackmore romp called 'Sail Away' and the well-mannered slow blues of 'Mistreated' were the high moments of a rather underrated album.

'Mistreated' was Coverdale's favourite. 'It has a very heavy blues feel. I had to get right inside it and get myself in the appropriate emotional condition, a very heavy physical thing… I wasn't raised in a shack by the railroad tracks but I've had emotional hassles and that's the only kind of blues I can interpret. That track means so much to me.'

Debate on who actually wrote the song continued for years, with some people questioning Blackmore's involvement. Coverdale maintains that not only did he write the words but also came up with the initial riff on Ritchie's Stratocaster in a rehearsal room. The singer was initially embarrassed, but Blackmore was 'very generous with me and said he had no idea I could play'. Then the guitarist took over and started to shape it into one of the highlights of the Purple Mark III chapter. In stark contrast, Glenn Hughes introduced the song on stage as something that Ritchie had had on his Revox tape recorder for a couple of years, suggesting the idea had been there before Coverdale and Hughes even joined Purple. Maybe we will never get to the bottom of it.

With the album in the shops, the majority of 1974 was set aside for promoting both the new record and line-up, and proving to the world the new band could deliver a powerful live set. After a few European gigs in January, there was to be another enforced lay-off, with Jon Lord hospitalised for three weeks with acute appendicitis. The new Deep Purple was just as much in demand in America as its predecessor, kicking off a twenty-seven-date tour in Michigan on 3 March. By now, the wealth the previous line-ups had built up was starting to filter through, and the result was to be seen in the sleek shape of a Boeing 720 jet airliner. Acquired at a cost of £127,000, it was fully decked out with lounge and beds to make travelling across America more comfortable.

Purple Mark III's debut Stateside tour will always be remembered for one gig – a huge all-day outdoor festival at the Ontario Speedway circuit in California on 6 April. Billed as the California Jam, the line-up of bands read like a who's who of giants from the rock, soul and country fields: Purple's fellow attractions were Earth, Wind and Fire, Rare Earth, Black Oak Arkansas, the Eagles, Seals and Crofts, Black Sabbath and co-headliners Emerson Lake And Palmer. It had been agreed that ELP would close the show with Purple taking the first spot after sundown.

Because the festival actually ran like clockwork, with none of the overrunning typical of such events, by the time the stage was set for Purple's appearance it was still daylight and Ritchie

Blackmore refused to take the stage until the light had dimmed. As the show was being filmed by ABC TV, a representative of the company demanded the group took the stage immediately, but Purple managed to hold out for a further forty-five minutes by employing such delaying tactics as unnecessarily retuning their instruments. By dint of such subterfuge, the band managed to get its way and hit the stage just as the light started to fade.

Deep Purple put on a fine show and, with the gig going down a storm, Blackmore took his revenge on the TV company during his explosive ending to the closing 'Space Truckin''. He had instructed his roadie to pour fuel over the speaker cabinets, causing a massive explosion that, according to Glenn Hughes, nearly set the guitarist alight. Not content with such theatrics, Blackmore then decided to wreck his instrument by aiming it directly into one of the on-stage TV cameras. The pandemonium that ensued had the State police and fire chiefs, as well as the promoters and TV executives, baying for blood. In the event, the management were able to get the guitarist out of the county with the aid of a helicopter before he was arrested.

Back in Blighty later that month, Purple's profile was in need of resurrection. Mark II had largely ignored its homeland over the last year of its life, so the new band determined to make up for this oversight with an extensive twenty-two-date tour that lasted the whole of May 1974. As with America, the trek was a success in both musical and financial terms, and three noteworthy shows in separate London venues gave them a high media profile. At the Lewisham Odeon, Graham Hough – now a BBC cameraman, but at the time a Leeds Polytechnic student – got permission from Purple's management to make a film project as part of his college course, including interviews with all band members. In this, the band members spoke with a refreshing candour about the trials of rock superstardom.

Jon Lord was quick to stress how brief he expected his time at the top to be: 'In terms of longevity you are given anywhere between two and ten years at the maximum. Out of the six,

I would say three have been financially excellent, the other three were getting out of debt, the debt that it cost to start this band. We started this band with one main idea and ideal – that is, that everything we did would be, by our lights, excellent.

'We've never been great lyricists,' he continued, 'and we don't write fantastic melodies or tunes; except for "Child In Time", there aren't that many pretty tunes. We don't construct our songs like Rodgers and Hart used to, or Lennon and McCartney even. "You Fool No One" came from a drum pattern that Ian thought up.'

Lord also commented on one of the prime motivating factors for a rock musician: 'You do seriously feel an immense necessity to be good, and it stems from the fact that you are being paid by a lot of people to excel, to excite them. And if you know you're not doing it I get so brought down.'

Ritchie Blackmore spoke with his usual combination of honesty, astuteness and dry humour. 'We're not brilliant songwriters,' he conceded. 'I write most of the stuff, but I think some of it stinks. We only get away with it because we are so good musically.

'Why we are a little subdued on record is because, when you are recording, you find there [you are playing to] one engineer and a couple of tea boys… it doesn't really inspire you to turn out your best. Whereas when you are on stage, you play to the people and they inspire you. It's an ego thing, really. You like to show off, show them what you know.'

The guitarist explained he had his own dressing room, 'because I like to tune up and I like my solitude before I go on stage. I tend not to get too involved in people because, to be quite honest, I find a lot of people boring. I find myself boring most of the time. I always like to be the opposite; I always was at school, that's why I don't smoke. I used to find everybody at school smoking, rebellious image, so because of that I won't smoke and never had. Mind you I was probably doing other things that were just as bad if not worse.

'I'm still very moody, shy and very honest which a lot of people can't take. The hardest thing in this business is sincerity. Once you can fake that you're laughing.'

Blackmore's final comments betrayed the frustrations building up inside him that would see his departure within the year to steer his own ship. 'There are times when I feel like just saying, let's forget it; let's all go home. We've all got enough money to just say I'll do another LP when I feel like doing it. Because really that's what every group should do, but every group is pressured by the record company, it's only guarding their own interests. Any group only lasts a certain length of time, so they get the most out of them. It doesn't matter if they fold up in five years as long as they've made about ten LPs in the meantime. That really bugs me, going into the studio; "We've got to turn out another LP boys, got to write a song today." It's ridiculous.

'I don't know if I've got the guts but I've often thought… I want to leave, not the band, get out of the business, play when I feel like playing, do a record when I feel like recording. That would be fantastic but you can't have it all your own way.'

Ironically the film closed with a Jon Lord comment that was anything but prophetic when he said, 'It's a history of ten years that will last ten years.'

Ten days later, this time north of the Thames, the Kilburn State Gaumont show was recorded by the BBC for its *Sounds Of The Seventies* programme. All previous recordings done for the BBC had been in their own studios but, since Purple now clearly considered themselves too big to commit to a live performance in front of a couple of hundred people in a studio, capturing the band in its natural environment was the BBC's only option.

The recording was subsequently released in the early 1980s and perfectly illustrated that, while Purple had lost two crucial members, the mainstay of Lord, Blackmore and Paice ensured the band was still a guarantee of first-class heavy rock. Coverdale and Hughes's dual vocals added a new dimension to the Purple sound that generally met with the approval of fans and critics alike. The band also played the Hammersmith Odeon for one night only, with Roger Glover in attendance.

By now, the wealth that Purple was accruing was beginning to have an effect on their unity. The political and economic climate in Britain at the time meant that tax rates for big earners were at an all-time high and the group's accountant advised the individual members to move abroad. Although unforeseen at the time, this move to tax exile ultimately started to fragment the group and management set-up.

The first day of June saw Jon Lord in Germany – not counting his money, but embarking on his concert with the Munich Chamber Opera Orchestra that had been commissioned for Germany's *Eurovision Presentation of Prix Jeunesse*. This was broadcast live throughout mainland Europe to an estimated audience of over 300 million, but won't be remembered as Lord's finest solo work. It was very much a joint collaboration with the German composer and conductor Eberhard Schoener, who'd originally met Jon at the Speakeasy Club in 1971.

The performance comprised of the piece 'Continuo On BACH' that included a revamped version of the vocal movement of Lord's *Gemini Suite*, along with a new and more experimental piece called 'Windows'. Alongside the Orchestra, Jon had assembled a group of rock musicians that once again included Spencer Davis Group guitarist, Ray Fenwick, plus old friend Tony Ashton and the two Deep Purple new boys, Coverdale and Hughes, both of whom came across as being somewhat ill at ease with the rock-meets-classical idiom.

Originally it had been intended to release it on LP in Germany only (where the album was very successful) but the business machine ensured that, via the new Purple label, the album found its way into UK record stores as well – where, it has to be said, it generally stayed! Purple Records was not only an outlet for such solo releases but was also rapidly expanding with many other artistes, though none of them really did much to expand the business empire.

More successful by far was Roger Glover's *Butterfly Ball*, which would be performed at London's Royal Albert Hall in October

1975, though its gestation had begun as early as 1973. The bassist's adaptation of Alan Aldridge's book took him outside the musical parameters with which he was familiar. Pink Floyd had been approached before him, but he was not only willing but also available: it appealed to him as something he would certainly not have had the time to tackle while a full-time band member. 'It was, at the time, a completely different kind of project,' he admitted. 'Why I was given it in the first place, being the bass player of a hard-rock band, was very odd.'

Glover, a one-time student at Hornsey Art School, had first come across Aldridge's paintings in a Sunday newspaper supplement and had been entranced. 'I remember thinking, wow, these are great! A year later I was asked to put the book to music: it was a challenge.' Verse accompanied the illustrations, 'but sadly,' explained Roger, 'the poet William Plomer died just as the book was published and never saw his work.'

Having contacted the artist, Glover was given 'a few records he'd heard he thought I should listen to, all in classical vein: one was Benjamin Britten.' But he had other ideas, and saw a Beatle-esque aspect to the whole thing 'in terms of all-round entertainment', so a more contemporary approach was adopted. Aldridge had also been involved with *The Beatles Illustrated Lyrics* book, so it was no surprise that this suggestion was well received.

Each character in the story had a distinct vocal identity, but the singers selected ranged from professional rock artists to actors and even Roger's then girlfriend. Yet it wasn't a case of choosing from a 'wish list', more a question of dialling up whoever occurred to him as suitable. 'Recording took place over a period of time,' he explains, 'and as I wrote the songs I thought about who I wanted to sing them.' One man who didn't appear was Ian Gillan, though apparently this oversight was 'for no good reason'. Yet the former Purple singer's Kingsway Studios in central London was where *Butterfly Ball* would come together during 1974.

Glover had found post-Purple life difficult to acclimatise to,

recalling that, when *Billboard* magazine announced the band had sold more albums than anyone else, they used the new line-up's photo. 'That hurt very deeply because that was *my* success.'
If such momentary resentment spurred him to greater creative heights, it didn't stop him utilising the vocal talents of new Purple recruits David Coverdale and Glenn Hughes, the latter on the opening 'Get Ready'. 'The song was pitched very high and I had to have someone with a good range: Glenn was the obvious choice. I had no rancour at the fact that he'd replaced me.'

The project's best-remembered track, 'Love Is All', was co-written with singer/keyboardist Eddie Hardin and was selected as the single to announced the album – any resemblance to the Beatles' 'All You Need Is Love' being purely intentional – and has a special place in Glover's heart. 'It summed up the whole project and was the first song we finished. Very melodic.' The song was a major European hit, both in original form and as a cover by Sacha Distel.

The tie-up with Hardin, who'd stepped into Steve Winwood's shoes in the Spencer Davis Group, proved the most creative in terms of songwriting, but Elf – an American band Roger was producing featuring singer Ronnie James Dio and keyboardist Mickey Lee Soule – also played a part. Glover recalls 'Old Blind Mole' coming into his head more or less fully-formed while the duo were staying at his Buckinghamshire home.

Soule, perhaps surprisingly, was also among the vocalists, along with Roger's previously-mentioned girlfriend Judi Kuhl. Both had untrained voices, but that, he explained, was the point. 'I wanted some real voices... naïveté is the hardest thing to find. For some session singers singing is work; it's a whole different matter singing a song from the heart.'

He was also delighted to use John Gustafson, a fellow bassist whom Roger had admired from afar when a member of Liverpool's Big Three. This was, however, in a singing capacity: bass was played by Mo Foster who, with guitarist Ray Fenwick and future Judas Priest drummer Les Binks, provided the instrumental backbone. All had played together in a group called Fancy.

Having made it successfully to vinyl, *Butterfly Ball* was then mooted for a live concert. The idea, Roger recalls, was that of Purple manager Tony Edwards, though the brunt of the organisational work – phenomenal for a one-off concert – fell on Glover's shoulders. And charity, in the shape of Bud Flanagan's Leukaemia Fund and Action Research for the Crippled Child, was to be the beneficiary. Though Roger had rejected thoughts of including the poems from the original *Butterfly Ball* in his recording, preferring to let the illustrations inspire him, he asked veteran horror actor Vincent Price to supply the live between-song narration.

A new track – 'Little Chalk Blue' with vocals from soon-to-be Uriah Heep frontman John Lawton – was recorded and released as a single to promote the concert. Ultimately, the show in October 1975 will be best remembered for offering Ian Gillan a route back to live performance after Ronnie James Dio dropped out of the line-up. Few people could boast the American's vocal range, and Gillan – who had seen the project come together at Kingsway the previous year and admitted 'it reminded me what I had walked away from' – was rewarded with a standing ovation.

Others to share the stage that day included model Twiggy, who sang the closing 'Homeward' in Dio's stead, and Tony Ashton, who reprised his marvellous performance (as a newt!) on 'Together Again'. 'It was a drinking song I wrote especially for him,' Glover admitted – while pointing out that his pal was then enduring a period of medically prescribed abstinence!

A movie was made of the Albert Hall concert which was universally disliked by all concerned – 'It was horrible,' shuddered Glover – while the original concept for an animated TV series never bore fruit thanks to an oil crisis that forced Britain into a three-day working week (and made recording sessions remarkably difficult to schedule). This didn't stop at least one Hollywood production company from approaching Glover, who revealed on the album's CD re-release by Connoisseur in 1999 that he'd been 'tinkering with a screenplay for the past few years'. Whether or not it ever transfers to the screen, *Butterfly Ball* remained his best-regarded post-Purple project a full quarter-century after release.

Purple Records, meanwhile, was an ongoing project, though little success had attended signings unrelated to the parent band. In 1973, Silverhead, a British band fronted by American singer Michael Des Barres, were acclaimed as the bright new hopes. Their act was not a million miles away from the flashy, trashy New York Dolls, who never really broke through either and have only been acclaimed in retrospect. Des Barres, whose wife Pamela achieved more fame than he did with her groupie memoir *I'm With The Band*, would go on to claim a slightly higher profile when he filled Robert Palmer's shoes in Duran Duran spin-offs Power Station (and thereby appeared at Live Aid). Neither of Silverhead's Purple albums, *Silverhead* or *16 And Savaged*, made waves in 1973, however.

Tucky Buzzard were among the label's final recruits, their countrified rock 'n' roll being best remembered for having been produced by Rolling Stone Bill Wyman. Two albums released less than a year apart failed to perform sales-wise, though the Purple link did get the band some support dates with their employers in the States. The lack of direction (or possibly laudable diversity) of the label's output was illustrated by the year's final non-Purple release *Colditz Breakpoint!*, a manufactured-after-the-event souvenir to entice those who'd seen the BBC prison-camp drama series that had won high viewing figures in 1973.

More significant in the story, if not in sales terms, were Elf, the previously mentioned American band that would go on to form the basis of the first incarnation of Ritchie Blackmore's Rainbow. Their 1974 release *Carolina County Ball* was not in fact their debut, Roger Glover and Ian Paice having produced their first, US-only album, after spotting them in New York and being 'blown away. They sounded so raw and exciting. It was hard to believe such an enormous sound could come from such tiny people...

Ronnie Dio had one of the best voices I had ever heard or worked with, before or since. The unusual addition of a piano, played by Mickey Lee Soule, made it very different and they had a solid writing partnership.'

Purple Records would do little after the band's dissolution, apart from issue a stream of compilations from the defunct parent band. John Coletta became Coverdale's manager and started the Sunburst imprint, while Edwards was involved with Safari (one of the leading punk labels with the likes of Toyah, Jayne County and the Boys) and Connoisseur Collection, whose mid-price compilation catalogue occasionally included Purple-related material.

The Purple Records imprint was revived in 1999 under the aegis of superfan Simon Robinson, and in 2004 released 'Purple People', a sampler CD bearing the same title as a 1973 mid-price vinyl compilation designed to showcase the label's roster. The old marketing phrase was revived for the CD's inside cover: 'The new sound for serious listening. From classic rock to progressive underground. And all of it good music.'

Back in 1974, Deep Purple Mark III found that they were to enjoy as little rest as their predecessors. No sooner had the May UK tour closed than they found themselves once again at Clearwell Castle thrashing out ideas for the next studio opus. While tensions within the group had been buried with the adrenaline of a new line-up and a new start, they were now back with a vengeance. This time Ritchie Blackmore was dissatisfied by the funkier aspects of Hughes' proposed contributions for the next album.

The first low-key writing sessions proved no more than a relaxing break and little was completed, but Blackmore's dissatisfaction with the direction and contributions from the other members effectively took the band back to 1972 – same problems, different individuals.

Purple's traditional creative *modus operandi* had seen Ritchie sparking off songs through basic riffs and structures, with other members then turning worthwhile ideas into completed backing

tracks ready for lyrical input. At Clearwell, both Coverdale and
Hughes, now clearly at ease with the band and assured of their
stature, came up with ideas of their own, often rejecting
Blackmore's contributions as a consequence.

The duo's self-confidence was rightly high, and as a
consequence they were now demanding more input of their own.
The funky leanings of Hughes, in particular, began to flavour the
resulting work-in-progress. But whereas Ritchie's dislike of what
he termed 'shoe-shine music' would have previously resulted in
the guitarist's opinion being broadcast in no uncertain terms, he
now seemed grudgingly prepared to concede ground.

Most of the material for the forthcoming Deep Purple album
was composed on the spot during recording in August in Munich.
The new album was initially to be called 'Silence' (mock-ups of
the LP sleeve showed a young girl with her finger to her lips) but
was eventually named *Stormbringer* after one of the tracks.

Released in November 1974, first listens immediately showed
a stark shift in direction from the fiery blues-rock of *Burn* to a
mellower, Adult Oriented Rock (AOR) sound. Though the quality
of the songwriting was well up to standard, the funk of Hughes
runs as a rich theme throughout the album, watering-down Purple's
previous strident attack to the detriment of the more up tempo
songs. Fans and critics were lukewarm over the album, too, the
chart placings reflecting the disappointment many now felt with
the Mark III line-up after such a promising start.

The sessions saw the band start to fragment musically and
compositionally, as each member brought his own agenda to the
creative process. Coverdale now believes *Stormbringer* was too
much of a transition, and the fact it was created in the studio, is
why it lacked 'bollocks'. A Don Quixote-inspired ballad, 'Soldier
Of Fortune', became another late-era classic, though not without
some argument. Jon Lord remembers the recording of this
particular song thanks to an amusing, in retrospect, incident:
'David wanted the right atmosphere for the track and when he was
doing the vocal Stevie Wonder (his all-time hero) came into the

control room with about six other people. David heard the noise but couldn't see who it was and he yelled, "Whoever it is in there fuck off!" When we told him who it was he was shattered.'

The title track itself, 'Soldier Of Fortune' and 'Gypsy' were the few redeeming features of an album far removed from the red-line intensity of previous work. The ultimate effect of *Stormbringer* would be Blackmore abdicating control of the group and his eventual departure.

Having completed the album, August saw Deep Purple once again jetting off to America for a string of large outdoor stadium gigs and the following month the band played six large indoor arenas in Germany and one in Switzerland. The popularity of Purple was apparent at the first gig in Bremen on 18 September where an estimated 12,000 fans turned up at a venue with a capacity of only 4,000. Thankfully it was one of the smallest halls on the tour, as only venues such as the Olympiahalle in Munich were remotely large enough to accommodate demand. The set list remained the same as earlier in the year with the added inclusion of 'Highway Star' as a second encore.

A venture further afield was soon planned, visits to the USA and Australia preceding a second European stint booked for March 1975. As far as Deep Purple was concerned, it was business as usual and, although *Stormbringer* had turned out to be less successful than the previous few albums, it had still hit Number 6 in the UK and made the *Billboard* Top 20. No one could doubt that, despite the changes, the band was still a money-making machine.

Purple's visit to Australia in early 1975 was for a single show – a headline appearance at the Sunbury Festival. The gig is now best remembered for the way in which Deep Purple's set finished some forty minutes later than scheduled. While overrunning is a common occurrence at festival gigs, there were accusations from some quarters that they had done this deliberately. Although they were headlining, it had been agreed that local band AC/DC would conclude the day's entertainment after Purple's set had finished.

Because of the overrun, AC/DC didn't get to perform and this started a feud between the two bands that was to continue for some time. It also probably goes some way to explaining Blackmore's comments some time later when he proclaimed AC/DC to be 'an all-time low in rock 'n' roll'.

The set list from the previous tour was revamped with three new songs included; 'Stormbringer', 'Lady Double Dealer' and 'Gypsy'. While the first two gained a little more fire in live presentation, it was 'Gypsy' that saw the band bring its traditional dynamic and passion to the fore; the Hughes/Coverdale harmonies dovetailed into a Blackmore guitar break that seemed to inspire him even further than on the record.

But Ritchie's mind was now on his own project. This had been brought to the fore with the band's refusal to consider a cover of 'Black Sheep Of The Family', a favourite of Ritchie's from the eponymous debut LP by Quatermass. Recalled Ritchie: 'I brought it to Purple and they rejected it because they hadn't written it. I couldn't believe they turned it down because they wouldn't get a writing credit, but that was the bottom line.' Quatermass were a second-division hard-rock outfit on the Harvest label that featured ex-Episode Six drummer Mick Underwood, still a friend of the band.

So offended was the guitarist by this refusal that he seriously considered recording the song as a solo single. Such side projects were no secret; extracurricular work had been discussed by most Purple musicians in various interviews over the past few years, so solo single talk raised no eyebrows. Yet Ritchie had asked David Coverdale to appear on a solo LP, something the singer thought was a retrograde step ('It's like going back five years... you should go on, or do an instrumental album'). Elf's Ronnie James Dio was, however, glad to accept a one-off £1,000 fee to sing on 'Black Sheep Of The Family'.

While cutting this one-off single in a Tampa Bay studio on 12 December 1974, a free night in Purple's US tour schedule, a rare musical empathy emerged. As the Electric Light Orchestra were also supporting along with Elf, cellist Hugh McDowall was roped in alongside Dio and bandmate Gary Driscoll.

As it transpired, the B-side – 'Sixteenth Century Greensleeves', written with Dio – turned out to be better than the Quatermass cover. What was more, the compositional process had lacked the inevitable argument and compromise that greeted the guitarist's suggestions from his Purple compadrés. 'The way he sang was perfect for what I wanted. I didn't have to tell him – he just sang it,' was the guitarist's view of the man with whom a new writing partnership quickly developed. 'Ritchie told me that we had to go into the studio in a couple of days to lay down a track,' Dio explained, 'and asked me if I could write a lyric for him by the following day! We went up to his room, he played me the chords and I went away having to remember it. I went home and wrote the melody and lyric in my head, and it worked out fine.'

A break after the Australian date gave Blackmore time to slot in work on what was now to be his debut solo album. Ritchie was required for the upcoming Deep Purple tour commencing on 16 March in Yugoslavia, and, with time pressing, used the rest of Elf for recording. Tracks were recorded between 20 February and 14 March 1975 in Munich's Musicland Studios under the familiar guidance of Martin Birch.

The results of the recording sessions finally convinced Ritchie Blackmore he could go it alone. He confided in the Purple management initially, who – with the European tour looming – held the information back from the other members, though they soon sensed something was afoot.

With Purple venturing into virgin territories of the Eastern Bloc for the first time, for the rest of the band the tour had much of a fresh and vibrant enthusiasm about it – at least at first. Audiences in Yugoslavia had been fanatical in their support and the traditional markets of Scandinavia and Germany seemed to prove that, despite *Stormbringer*'s shortcomings, the success of *Burn* and the new line-up live was no passing fad and the band could progress without fear of rejection.

As the dates wore on, however, it became all too obvious that something was amiss with the errant guitarist. Blackmore's stage efforts seemed increasingly detached, with solos introspective, less focused and more experimental, with some of his live work even showcasing themes developed with Elf. (Instrumental passages used in what became 'Man On The Silver Mountain' and his reading of the Yardbirds' 'Still I'm Sad' often turned up in improvisations during 'You Fool No One'.)

David Coverdale was the first to tackle management over this, and the non-committal response he received confirmed his fears. With the financial pragmatism that characterises band management the world over, the Rolling Stones mobile was promptly booked to record the last few shows in anticipation of at least another live album (and another payday) in the future. The Graz, Saarbrucken and Paris shows were taped as a result.

By the time the band played Paris dates in early April, the French press were reporting split rumours as fact, while elsewhere the speculation was considered as just another Purple internal wrangle. And though Ritchie's colleagues officially learned that he was leaving the band at the conclusion of the European tour on 7 April 1975, the official announcement to the press was not made until 21 June. Another chapter of Deep Purple's turbulent story had drawn to a close.

6. Replacing Ritchie

While Blackmore focused on what became Rainbow, the remaining quartet met in Los Angeles to sort out their future – if they had one. The venue was a rehearsal stage called Pirate Sound, run by an engineer used by Purple in the past called Robert Simon. The jury was out: could the band rejuvenate themselves once again, or would Blackmore's departure prove their death knell? Most observers – including Lord and Paice – believed the latter. But Hughes and Coverdale had other ideas.

They were hungry for more success and were anxious to carry on with a suitable replacement. Their view eventually prevailed and a list was drawn up. Jeff Beck, Rory Gallagher and Tommy Bolin made the shortlist of David Coverdale at least. Clem Clempson of Humble Pie and Mick Ronson were others mooted to join.

The plan was to work on new material in LA while checking out a succession of guitarists. It was around this time that Clempson was auditioned. Things didn't really gel: 'He was really good, but he was too much like a Rolling Stones guitarist,' remembered Coverdale. 'We were looking for someone really incredible... we had a high standard to keep up.' After several rather more anonymous candidates were quickly rejected, depression quickly set in. Coverdale then suggested Tommy Bolin, one of his earlier possibilities, who he remembered from his awesome work on Billy Cobham's *Spectrum* album. Coincidentally he was living locally in Malibu, and arrived to jam one morning early in June 1975.

'We all just stood there in amazement!' was how Coverdale described the first few minutes of the audition. It was immediately apparent to all that Bolin fitted right in. Ian Paice 'knew after about ten minutes. In many ways I was the one who relied most on Ritchie, and Tommy and I got on musically straight away.'

Born in Sioux City, Iowa on 1 August 1951, Bolin had first come to people's attention with Zephyr, a Joplin-esque midwest quintet who never broke big commercially but whose three albums at the turn of the decade eventually became cult classics. Relocating to New York in the early 1970s, he formed a jazz-rock outfit called Energy, and it was at this time he guested on the seminal *Spectrum* album. On the strength of his work with Cobham he was then asked to replace legend Joe Walsh in the James Gang, staying with the group for a year and two mildly successful studio albums. A stint in LA putting together another solo band ensued, but money ran out to finance the venture.

From the numerous sessions which he'd contributed to it was clear by now that Tommy's formidable technique not only touched upon many eclectic styles (blues, fusion, funk, reggae and hard rock), but showed that he was able to master them all. Writing for his first solo album was under way when he received the phone call to audition for Purple.

With Bolin agreeing in principle to a deal, a new chapter in the Deep Purple saga was opened. The band remained at Pirate Sound through June and into July to work on ideas for the next album. The quintet spent hours playing around with riffs and grooves, improvising to their hearts' content while Robert Simon handled the mixer desk and taped the more promising creative avenues the band wandered along. (These formed the basis of *Days May Come... the Purple label's archive CD release in 2000.) Without doubt the sheer dynamics and spontaneity of these sessions prove the band were right in carrying on.

Impetus slowed while Jon Lord completed the score for a new solo album and Bolin also started his solo album, *Teaser*. Phil Collins from Genesis added percussion to one track and, although Bolin wanted his new bandmates to feature, contractual reasons prevented all but an uncredited Glenn Hughes cameo. 'Tommy wanted me to sing the whole album,' Hughes recalled many years later. 'I said no; I thought he should sing it, [but] I sang a little bit on the end of "Dreamer".'

Purple then crossed the Atlantic, heading for Munich and Musicland to commence recording what would be their first and last album with Bolin. Ian Paice recalled recently that the band flew in jet-lagged, and a PA had thoughtfully arranged for some strong sleeping pills to be left so the band could get a night's rest before starting work the next day. Tommy came in and, spotting the pills, in one movement swallowed the lot, saying, 'Those were great... what were they?' He slept for forty-eight hours.

Years later, Glenn Hughes recalled that, for him, the album had been nothing more than 'a drug-crazed trip in Germany'. So much so that he had not even played on the album's opening cut, 'Comin' Home', for which Bolin played bass. The first Hughes was even aware of the track was when he played the finished album at his home. Interestingly it's the only album made in his absence Ian Gillan was tempted to listen to. His verdict? 'It wasn't really Deep Purple – it had Jon and Ian on it but it was really Tommy Bolin and Glenn Hughes.'

Come Taste The Band (named after a phrase Tommy had sung in one particularly drunken studio session) was completed in August and proved a strong response to doubters, sounding far more honest and energetic than its predecessor. Bolin's guitar work sounded instinctive and less contrived than the recent, uninterested efforts from Blackmore. All in all, things promised much for the associated tour.

As soon as *Come Taste The Band* was completed, Jon Lord and Martin Birch travelled north from Munich to Oererckenschwick near Düsseldorf and spent three days at the Stadthalle recording Jon's latest solo work. For the recording of *Sarabande*, Jon once again used his friend and conductor Eberhard Schoener along with the Philharmonia Hungarica. Among the rock musicians employed was Andy Summers, an excellent guitarist who had recently worked with Kevin Coyne and later went on to huge success with the Police.

Unlike the previous collaboration with Schoener, this album was entirely Jon's work and was far and away his most accomplished solo recording. As he remarked a couple of years later, 'To me, *Sarabande* is most successful in what it achieved – I'm very proud of that one.' Perhaps mindful of clashing with Purple's new album, *Sarabande* wasn't released until over a year after it was recorded.

With Bolin finishing his album later in September, a return to Pirate Sound in mid October was scheduled to work on the older concert staples before any live dates. It was now that the first forebodings regarding their future came to the surface.

Bolin had professed his ignorance of much of Purple's earlier work, and so would hopefully not be overly intimidated by the legacy of his predecessor. But such was his lack of self-confidence that many of Blackmore's solo parts were to be reproduced note-for-note, robbing the band of much of their unique and exhilarating spontaneity. While this was initially put down to nerves, the assumption being that everything would work out once the band hit the road, other matters also started to arise that threatened to turn the situation sour.

On the one hand, Bolin saw the other four members enjoying the fruits of fame and fortune, and naturally desired the same for himself. However, he had the feeling that he was treated as less than a full member of the band, and that the others regarded him almost as a session player. Conversely, Tommy's interviews in the press had not been shy of promoting his solo album, leading to a suspicion in the Purple organisation that the guitarist was simply using the band as a launch-pad for his own career.

Irrespective of the validity of these views (and there is probably a little truth in each), such feelings were to start the inevitable deterioration of the band into disparate, ego-fuelled factions. Added to this undercurrent was the realisation that Bolin was a frequent dabbler with hard drugs. While this wasn't a problem per se (after all Glenn Hughes regularly used cocaine and hadn't often let it affect the professional side of his life – yet), Tommy's addictive habits were to have a direct effect on Purple and their reputation over the coming months. The inherent problems with the errant guitarist and his lifestyle in hindsight made his predecessor's misdemeanours seem almost tame by comparison.

The tour to promote the new album by Deep Purple Mark IV kicked off in Honolulu in November 1975 and Australasia was visited before Christmas. 'Burn' generally opened the shows, the band performing it much as the earlier line-up had. All ten *Come Taste The Band* songs were featured at one time or another, and bootlegs reveal Purple sounding far more comfortable on these Bolin-led tracks. A listen to the expanded *Last Concert In Japan* and *Foxbat* live CD sets give those who missed the last great line-up fleeting glimpses of their inherent strengths and also their weaknesses. Glenn Hughes' influence on the overall direction w as strikingly evident for all to hear, with a shift in direction away from the purer Purple sound still championed by Lord and Paice.

This improvisational cocktail of funk, hard rock and jazz made the likes of 'Gettin' Tighter' one of the concert highlights, while 'Stormbringer' was the one earlier track Bolin seemed to relate to, giving this a blistering simplicity far more potent than the Mark III version. 'You Keep On Movin'' showcased their melodic sensibilities and assured sense of dynamics.

It was agreed Bolin would have a spot within the show to promote his solo record, and this featured either 'Homeward Strut' or the more occasionally performed 'Wild Dogs', whose wistful lyricism and fragile, delicate vocal prove, in retrospect, particularly poignant. Aspiring drummers could point to takes of 'Drifter' as evidence of Ian Paice's ability at this time to carry the band virtually on his own. Glenn Hughes was also demanding more vocal duties in concert, and the tension between the vocalists often manifested itself on stage.

Low points proved to be the renditions of 'Smoke On The Water' (complete with Glenn Hughes' ritualistic murdering of Ray Charles' 'Georgia On My Mind' as a medley) and the by-now usual strangulation of 'Highway Star'. Before the tour reached Japan, things were not only falling apart on stage but off it as well. Bolin's addictive personality was coming to the fore once again, meaning concerts veered from the explosively sublime (usually when he was sober or clean) to the totally shambolic.

Bolin often teetered on the verge of losing the plot, the American's sparse and often erratic guitar work barely covered by Lord and Paice who desperately tried to knit things together as the performance unravelled elsewhere on stage. Yet, ironically and frustratingly, there were times where Tommy's intuitive flashes of inspiration would suddenly pull everything together with a freshness and latent power that lifted the whole performance to another level.

Minders were appointed to keep Bolin and Hughes away from both drugs and dealers as the tour progressed, but these measures were never completely successful. If things weren't bad enough already, they got far worse in Jakarta, Indonesia. A large stadium gig had been set up via a particularly dodgy promoter who reneged on the agreed concert payments and had also booked a second night without the band's knowledge. A showdown in Purple's hotel after the concert seemed to have smoothed the waters, but soon after Patsy Collins, one of the Purple roadies, was killed after 'falling down a lift-shaft'. Although officially an accident, the incident remains unexplained to this day.

The Jakarta sojourn had one other sad consequence; Tommy Bolin had been unable to score a regular supply of the heroin he needed and had injected himself with inferior-quality drugs, leaving his left arm numb and partially paralysed. Despite frantic medical work, he had not completely recovered in time for the initial Japanese shows, so audiences were treated to the sorry spectacle of Tommy simply barring the basic chords while the long-suffering Jon Lord took all the solos. If Lord, Paice or Coverdale had had the power to do so, the tour (and probably the band) would have come to an end at this sorry low point. As it was, a long set of thirty-odd US dates in January and February still needed to be fulfilled, so the machine rolled on, optimistically hoping things would improve with time or, if they didn't, that further damage to the Deep Purple reputation could be minimised. In the Far East, away from the prying eyes of the rock media, this might have been easier, but when the tour hit the US reviewers were quick to pick up on problems that, by now, were all too evident on stage.

Five dates in the UK, culminating in the infamous Liverpool Empire show in March 1976, ultimately proved to be the swansong of both Mark IV and of Deep Purple as a touring and recording entity. Audiences thus far had welcomed Tommy Bolin's performances with anticipation, curiosity and a measure of good-natured tolerance, prepared to give the new version of the band the benefit of the doubt. In the UK, however, things were going to be far harder. Blackmore was still considered a British rock icon and the presumption that any upstart Yank could fill his shoes was treated with cynicism and scepticism. Catcalls for Ritchie were taken in good nature at first, but with diminishing grace by Tommy as the shows went on. The reception in their homeland proved to be the final nail in the coffin of what the founders now considered a moribund enterprise.

In 1983, Jon Lord told Purple's first biographer Chris Charlesworth, 'At one of the British shows I had to drag Glenn back on-stage to do an encore. I made up my mind that Deep Purple was over. For the first time in my life I was ashamed of being in Deep Purple and it was a disgusting feeling – Ian Paice and I had been in discussions stretching back over several weeks as to what should be done about what we saw as a pale imitation of what Deep Purple ought to be. We had already decided some several days before Liverpool that this was the end. Liverpool just confirmed that; it was a substandard show. We were trying to do our best because the Liverpool audiences had always been marvellous to us. They should have booed us off but they didn't.'

David Coverdale, too, felt the end had come as he walked off stage after the show. Jon Lord: 'In actual fact, when David came into the dressing room that night to see Paicey and myself and say that he was leaving the band, we rather sadly informed him that there was no band to leave.'

Although Deep Purple was effectively finished, nothing was announced to the press until July and, in between the last concert and the announcement, Coverdale, Hughes and Lord got together for one more recording at Gillan's Kingsway Studio for Eddie Hardin's *Wizard's Convention* album. Hardin had long been associated with Purple, and his band with Pete York had supported them on earlier tours. He had also played a significant part in Roger Glover's *Butterfly Ball*. Glover returned the favour by coming along to the sessions and playing bass on one track.

Glenn Hughes, by this time suffering from major drug problems, put in excellent vocal performances on two tracks that were ideally suited to his style. Coverdale also did a fine job on a song he co-wrote with Hardin and Ray Fenwick, although a couple of years later he saw it as a mercenary deed: 'I was a total prostitute. I was living in Munich and I really wanted to go to London for a couple of days and at the same time as I was gonna go, I got this phone call from John Craig… asking if I'd sing on an album. They'd pay for me to come over and all my expenses, so I said "sure". And when I got there I rewrote the words to the song.'

Tommy Bolin's pursued his solo career after Deep Purple split, but drink and drugs would further compromise his prospects. On 4 December 1976 Bolin died of a drug overdose. He was 25 years old.

Debate still rages among Deep Purple fans as to the worth of the Mark IV line-up; the undoubted power and integrity of the *Come Taste The Band* album gave hope to many, while the often erratic nature of their short live tenure meant their potential on stage was never fully realised. Unfocused, apathetic and inconsistent at times, there were nonetheless moments where the quintet meshed together sublimely, contributing in their own unique way to the Purple legend just as the line-ups before them, yet in that very process making that unfulfilled potential all the more painful to bear.

The recordings made at the end of the Mark III era were worked up into *Made In Europe* and released as a single vinyl album in April 1976. Coming principally from the Saarbrucken show of April 1975, this was a less than satisfactory offering, incomplete and heavily edited tracks topped by sampled audience applause, it was emphatically not in the spirit of Deep Purple live releases that had started with *Made In Japan*, but pointed the way to a plethora of live recordings that would attempt to fill a very real gap as, for seven long years, the name of Deep Purple took a well-earned rest.

7. The Wilderness Years

GILLAN

Once Ian Gillan had taken 'a year or two to get everything into perspective', and his hotel and motorcycling sidelines had failed to fulfil expectations, he decided he still had musical ambitions to fulfil. 'It was Roger (Glover) who brought me back with his *Butterfly Ball* concert,' he revealed. 'Somebody dropped out and I stepped in. The reception I got was fantastic, so I went home and wrote a few songs.'

The musicians involved in these songs' demo sessions came fresh from backing Gerry Rafferty and Joe Egan on Stealer's Wheel's second album *Ferguslie Park*. While guitarist Bernie Holland, drummer Andy Steele and bassist Dave Wintour returned to session work, keyboardist Mike Moran would continue his association with Gillan on the singer's solo debut, 1976's *Child In Time*.

The title track of course harked back to Purple days and, when interviewed for a *Radio Times* feature to tie in with the screening of a *Rock Family Trees* series in 1995, Gillan was asked if he'd followed their work without him. 'I've thought of this often (pause)... the nearest I can give you as an analogy is if you split up from your old lady you don't want to know what she's doing with her new husband, do you? I love the band and it was a very passionate thing, a tortuous relationship but to this day I haven't heard the records they made without me.'

The problem facing Gillan, as he'd already correctly identified, was how to top what he'd already achieved. He'd forever be recognised as 'the voice of Purple' by a majority of fans, but he could clearly not hope to rival his former band's unity of purpose and sheer power as a solo singer. Having waited three years to open his solo account, he attacked the problem on two fronts.

Firstly he formed his own outfit (called, not unexpectedly, the Ian Gillan Band) and, to avoid direct comparisons, allowed the music to reflect the individual members' jazzier leanings rather than follow a predictable hard-rock course. To allay fans' doubts as he led them further into the musical unknown, his first album was named after a classic Purple track, while the Ian Gillan Band's live set also revisited past glories.

The musicians involved had been recruited while Ian had been spending a period of tax exile in Paris. Guitarist Ray Fenwick has already cropped up in this story, as has bass player John Gustafson. Gustafson was a volatile character whose route to Gillan's side had been via Purple Records signings Hard Stuff (né Bullet) and Roxy Music, to whose 'Love Is The Drug' he supplied the robust bass line. Gus's off-stage activities were the stuff of legend, but musically he had much more to offer than the standard root-notes. Drummer Mark Nauseef was a former member of Elf. Finally, Mike Moran, who played on *Child In Time* before giving way to Colin Towns, went on to the 1977 Eurovision Song Contest with Lindsey de Paul!

Gillan divorced himself from the Purple organisation after his first solo album and found himself a home from home at Island Records. The label had made its reputation in the 1960s bringing reggae to these shores and were now investing in rock by acquiring proven talents like Gillan and former Uriah Heep singer David Byron. They retained their Caribbean roots, however: Ian would often pass an idle morning playing pool with Bob Marley. This didn't have any discernible effect on the music on Gillan's second album, however.

Released in April 1977, *Clear Air Turbulence* was recorded at Ian's own Kingsway Studios, allowing the band the opportunity to spend as long as they wanted perfecting their music. Hence the presence of just six tracks on this album, none of these falling below the five-minute mark. Little wonder no single was extracted! While the songs were credited to the band as a whole, Gillan took care of his usual lyric-writing duties.

Several points were being made. In his autobiography *Child In Time*, written with David Cohen (Smith Gryphon, 1993), Ian notes that he'd had a go at one of his former managers, Bill Reid.

Though he doesn't name the track in question, one might assume it's 'Money Lender': whatever, Gillan now regrets he did this. 'In truth, I had not a single reason to think badly of the man.' In mitigation, the singer had just been landed with a tax bill for £385,000, so it's hardly surprising he lashed out – even if his aim was off.

Clear Air Turbulence was apparently recorded twice, the first effort not meeting Gillan's demanding standards; a late-1976 tour was cancelled to make time for the re-recording. The next album, *Scarabus*, then appeared in October, just six months after *Turbulence*, as if to show that, after a false start, the band had now gelled very well indeed.

A world tour was high on the agenda after all this recording, and in September 1977 Gillan and band reached Purple's happiest hunting ground, Japan. A show in Tokyo was taped for *Live At The Budokan* – an album that, with act and label parting company in the meanwhile, would remain unreleased in Britain until 1987. This concentrated on *Turbulence* material, with a couple of newer songs and the obligatory pair of Purple anthems thrown in.

Ian had wanted *Clear Air Turbulence* 'to be different to Purple, different even to *Child In Time*, and that came across in the music which was... more jazz-rock than had been expected by some.' He reverted to type with *Scarabus*, which brought the focus back towards shorter, harder-rocking numbers which gave the star of the show his chance to shine. He'd shorn his trademark hair, but lost none of his power. All but one of *Scarabus*'s ten songs clocked in around the three- or four-minute mark. Maybe the new wave, then of course in full flow, had been influential... indeed, Gillan credits punk for showing him the way back to rock.

But the musical agenda was set to change still further, and this would spell the end of the Ian Gillan Band. Shedding all their members except keyboardist Colin Towns, they adopted the snappier name of Gillan, and it was this aggregation which went on to find success in both the singles and the album charts in the 1980s. Looking back, then, *Scarabus* was not only the last Ian

Gillan Band album; it was also a first step in his snappy, retro rock-inspired direction.

Ian doesn't look back that charitably at this period in his career – a time before the New Wave of British Heavy Metal (consisting of groups, ironically, who'd idolised Purple) had put hard rock back on the map, and a period when his commercial stock was at its lowest ebb. In his book *Child In Time*, Gillan says, 'Although I was with fine musicians and great mates, the one thing they did not take seriously was rock 'n' roll... the whole group idea seemed to be about making music in a complicated and tricky way.'

Simplifying matters led to enormous commercial rewards, as *Mr Universe* hit Number 11 in the UK chart. This success enabled him to survive the closure of Acrobat, the indie record label he was on, as he was snapped up by the altogether more influential Virgin concern. With Richard Branson behind him, Gillan became the role model for Phil Collins to follow a few years later as 1980's *Glory Road* and the following year's *Future Shock* peaked at Numbers 3 and 2 respectively – the undisputed highpoints of the singer's post-Purple career. The latter was accompanied by a Top 20 single in 'New Orleans', a supercharged version of Gary US Bonds' 1961 hit.

Though such commercial heights could not be sustained, follow-ups *Double Trouble* (a live effort) and *Magic* performed creditably, hitting Numbers 12 and 17 in 1981 and 1982. But then came a shock that reverberated across the rock world: Ian Gillan opted to succeed Ronnie James Dio as the singer with Black Sabbath.

This unlikely link-up proved to be brief, spanning an album plus European and American tours. It all started to go wrong when the album *Born Again*, recorded in May 1983, was mixed: Gillan was sent his copies of the album and smashed all twenty to pieces in a fit of rage, and this was before the touring even started.

With Sabbath fans demanding word-perfect renditions of the 'classics', Gillan was forced to resort in the short term to a lyric book, which could and did get lost under the clouds of dry ice that flooded the stage. A Stonehenge backdrop straight out of *Spinal*

Tap provided the only laughs around, and October saw him hand in his notice with the US tour (which he fulfilled) to come.

The final irony was the fact that, when Sabbath reconvened in 1986, the next vocalist in line to try on the unfillable shoes of original singer Ozzy Osbourne was… Glenn Hughes. By that time, of course, Gillan had other fish to fry.

PAICE ASHTON LORD

The tried and tested combination of Jon Lord and Tony Ashton had led to many good times and some good music over the years, but rarely anything that was intended for mainstream consumption. The 'supergroup' of Paice Ashton Lord which took its bow in 1977 would, it was reckoned, change all that – but it needed the addition of singer and guitarist Bernie Marsden from Babe Ruth to provide a conventional frontman and songwriter.

His successful audition at Emerson Lake and Palmer's Manticore Studios was sealed when he confessed he didn't know any Deep Purple numbers: having had their ears assailed by countless hopefuls blasting out 'Smoke On The Water', this was music to Lord and Paice's ears and he was swiftly hired. Bass player was the similarly little-known Paul Martinez.

The by-now familiar Musicland Studios in Munich were the new group's first stop, every step of the way being followed by documentary film cameras: the stakes were clearly high. The pressure was on the relatively untried, twenty-six-year-old Marsden to come up with an album's worth of songs, for which he was to be bought a house – the first he'd ever owned. *Malice In Wonderland* was the result, and the band, working with Purple-friendly producer Martin Birch, turned in a competent album.

The touring show was to be an all-singing, all-dancing affair, with a horn section, a pair of girl singers, Lord and Ashton at matching Hammond organs and everything but the kitchen sink thrown at the audience. It wouldn't be Deep Purple – in fact, the repertoire would be totally Purple-free – but it *would* be showbiz. The stakes were high, Lord and Paice having reportedly invested a quarter of a million pounds apiece in staging the extravaganza. UK dates sold out in record time. Such was the confidence of all concerned that the band's first public gig was a BBC *Sight And Sound In Concert* show at Golders Green Studios in March 1977. The documentary film was still being shot, and all looked good for the venture.

But then the sixteen-date European leg of the tour was cancelled. And while the UK shows were well received, the Purple hordes did not flock to the record shop to buy music which was a long way removed from past glories. In short, this was simply too different. A second album was recorded at Musicland with Mack, soon to be immortalised though his work with Queen at the very same studio, at the controls instead of Martin Birch, who was otherwise engaged with Rainbow. While Bernie Marsden had proved a game and youthful frontman, Tony Ashton's erratic behaviour – he'd been knocked spark out at one gig after falling over – had proved difficult for all to cope with.

An injection of new blood was called for, and David Coverdale's visit to Musicland suggested the possibility of a band rejoicing in the acronym CLAP. As it happened, he lived around an hour's drive from the studios and was purely paying a social call. But it would have taken the addition of a charismatic frontman of his magnitude to persuade Purple followers to take the outfit to their collective heart. The songs recorded for the second PAL album remained in the can, Lord and Paice sadly wrote off their investment and the band was no more.

As is detailed elsewhere, Marsden, Paice and Lord would all eventually link with Coverdale, but on his own terms. The legacy of Paice Ashton and Lord is one album (the aforementioned *Malice In Wonderland*), plus the BBC *Sight And Sound* performance which was eventually issued on CD and the memory of some totally over-the-top shows that will live with those who witnessed them.

RAINBOW

Having recorded first album *Ritchie Blackmore's Rainbow* with the re-christened Elf after their May 1974 support tour to Purple had brought the time and opportunity for plans to be hatched and songs composed, Ritchie dispensed with the services of all but singer Ronnie James Dio from the first line-up. Drummer Colin 'Cozy' Powell, formerly with the Jeff Beck Group, made up a triumvirate of charter members, with Jimmy Bain and Tony Carey, on bass and keyboards respectively, completing what many consider the definitive Rainbow incarnation.

An early peak was reached with 1976's *Rising*, a UK Top 20 album whose songs were all cut in two or three takes, Martin Birch's production adding a driving feel. Its raw power was typified by the likes of 'Stargazer', with its trademark Powell drum intro and evocative lyrical imagery from Dio, and 'Tarot Woman'. The following year's *On Stage* reached Number 7 and was much acclaimed, reprising versions of Purple's 'Mistreated' and 'Blues' among newer material.

Long Live Rock 'n' Roll, recorded in a French chateau in the company of some less than friendly ghosts, yielded two UK Top 40 singles – the title track and 'LA Connection'. Kelly Jones of Stereophonics spent much of his youth listening to this album, more melodic than *Rising* but rivalling it as the most fully realised Rainbow offering. Rainbow's 1977 release was the obligatory live double *On Stage*, and proved equally successful sales-wise.

Dio officially took his leave from a turbulent line-up in January 1979. (Cozy Powell: 'They were two very strong characters and something had to give.') Yet, far from falling apart, Rainbow entered a period of commercial success, *Down To Earth* being their most successful LP to date in sales terms thanks to the UK Top 10 singles 'All Night Long' and 'Since You Been Gone'. Its Number 6 success gave Blackmore's band their third successive UK Top 10 album.

Don Airey took on keyboard duties, throwing in classical references like Mars from Holst's *Planets Suite* in 'Eyes Of The

World', while the new vocalist was Graham Bonnet, formerly singer with 1960s duo the Marbles. But the self-confessed 'short-haired yobbo with the Hawaiian shirt on' was too much of a contrast with Dio for some fans. Thus 1981's *Difficult To Cure* would feature a third lead singer, American Joe Lynn Turner, who would, later in the decade, appear in the Purple ranks.

A bigger blow than Bonnet's departure had been the loss of Cozy Powell, unhappy with the band's new US-oriented 'commercial' direction. Having been through the hit single loop already with 1973's 'Dance With The Devil' and found it wanting, he departed for stints with Michael Schenker, Whitesnake, ELP and Black Sabbath. Yet it would take his 1998 death in a road crash to silence whispers that he, Blackmore and Dio were to reform the *Rising* line-up in an attempt to recapture past glories.

Talking of rumours, the 'Purple to reform' whispers that had been circulating since the band's Blackmore-less demise in 1976 grew significantly in volume when Roger Glover boarded the Rainbow train circa *Down To Earth* as bassist and producer. His influence was also apparent in the lyrics of his collaborations with Blackmore, which tended towards matters of the heart rather than the sword and sorcery of yore. 1981's *Difficult To Cure* reached the heady heights of Number 3, fuelled by the similarly successful single 'I Surrender', which had been commissioned from ex-Argent guitarist now songwriter-for-hire Russ Ballard.

There were high hopes that 1982's *Straight Between The Eyes* would bring a US breakthrough, but the album, which made Number 5 in Britain, was deemed a failure Stateside at Number 30, despite its Foreigner-esque feel. Blackmore was frustrated because 'the band's softer phase... died a death in Britain, which hurt a bit... and every time I wanted to play a real hard rock song Joe couldn't really manage it.' The curtain came down on Rainbow in early 1984 after touring *Bent Out Of Shape*, leaving their leader free to take up alternative employment...

WHITESNAKE

David Coverdale's post-Purple career was conducted under the band name of Whitesnake – also the title of his first solo album, released in May 1977. There remained strong Purple connections in that co-manager Jon Coletta took up David's option as a solo artist and Roger Glover was enlisted as producer, while first recordings would be released on his manager's Sunburst label.

And no time was lost. Writing and recording sessions for *David Coverdale's Whitesnake* began during August 1976, five months after Purple's final bow. These took place in the familiar surroundings of Kingsway Studios, with vocals laid down in Munich. Though recorded using a series of session musicians, the album was largely co-written with former Juicy Lucy guitarist Micky Moody, marking the start of a long association. Other contributors were Tim Hinkley on keyboards, bassist DeLisle Harper, saxist Ron Aspery and ace session drummer Simon Phillips, with producer Glover weighing in on synthesiser, bass, melodica, percussion and vocals.

The album proved an eclectic mix, featuring what in hindsight was some of Coverdale's best and most creative solo work. By the time the album appeared the follow-up, *Northwinds*, was already well under way. This was recorded in Air Studios, London and at Munich's Musicland through April 1977 and featured Alan Spenner on bass, Tony Newman on drums, Tim Hinkley on organ and a guest appearance by Dr Feelgood's Lee Brilleaux on harmonica. The album was released in the UK in March 1978 but, like its predecessor, failed to chart.

The Coverdale/Moody writing partnership was soon expanded to form what would be the first of many Whitesnake performing line-ups by ex-Hammer/Babe Ruth/PAL guitarist Bernie Marsden, former Colosseum/National Health bassist Neil Murray and drummer David Dowle, once of Streetwalkers. Initially Trapeze guitarist Mel Galley was approached but turned the gig down. First choice for bassist was Chris Stewart of Frankie Miller's band, but Marsden suggested Murray, with whom he had played in Cozy

Powell's Hammer a few years before. Although Jon Lord had been asked to join, the job of keyboards went to Brian Johnston (also ex-Streetwalkers) as rehearsals began in February 1978.

Unsure of the depth of potential support, Coverdale launched Whitesnake with a tentative low-key UK club and university tour, the band debuting at the Lincoln Technical College in March 1978. 'It was the height of the punk era,' he recalled, 'and I was told nobody was interested in hard rock. So I booked a tour of six little clubs in England, and found there were thousands of people waiting to get in. I thought, "Somebody is definitely wrong."' Indeed, given Coverdale's previous Deep Purple work, Whitesnake quickly benefited from the recent renewed interest in the hard rock genre and from the burgeoning New Wave of British Heavy Metal movement as the decade drew to a close.

More tracks were worked up during April, with Pete Solley now on keyboards. The *Snakebite* EP, released in June 1978, helped maintain the band's profile after the earlier tour while a new album was worked up. By August, Jon Lord had finally been persuaded to join the band though he'd been initially reluctant to get involved, preferring to concentrate on a writing career. Several days were spent dubbing Lord's keyboards onto the new album tracks before *Trouble* saw the light of day in October ready for the imminent round of live dates commencing in the UK. A Hammersmith Odeon gig was recorded for a planned live album.

But Dowle's jazz-slanted style was deemed unsuited to the current direction and, after Rainbow's Cozy Powell was asked to join but declined, Ian Paice agreed to link up with the band after he caught one of the early shows and enjoyed a subsequent alcohol-fuelled reunion. The announcement in July of Paice's arrival brought many music press headlines of the 'Deep Snake' variety. Yet despite the inevitable sniping about striving to rehash their illustrious past, in reality the Whitesnake sound proved far more earthy than Purple ever were.

The *Love Hunter* LP previewed a far tougher, more abrasive sound, its sleeve (a naked girl enveloped within the coils of a large snake) drawing criticism from feminist quarters. The Bilzen Festival in Belgium and the UK's Reading Festival showcased the band in blistering form, September bringing the band's first US foray via a date in Los Angeles before yet another UK tour in October.

By the end of 1979 new tracks were already being recorded at Ridge Farm studios and London's Denmark Street. One track by Coverdale, Moody and Marsden had originally been intended for BB King; however 'Fool For Your Lovin'' sounded so good the band recorded it themselves and the track was destined to be a Number 13 hit single in the UK.

In February 1980 the friendly rivalry that had developed between Blackmore's Rainbow and Coverdale's Whitesnake came to a head, both sets of musicians vying as to who could enter the singles charts higher, sell out gigs quicker, etc. Unfortunately the band leaders failed to catch the spirit of fun; Coverdale's open criticism of Blackmore and Rainbow in the press didn't go down well, and Coverdale's appearance at a Rainbow gig in Munich as a guest of the promoter culminated in a much-publicised brawl between the pair in front of (and at the feet of) several bemused guests at the after-gig party.

A first foray to Japan, where Coverdale's association with Deep Purple meant the band's profile was already high, heralded *Ready An' Willing*, arguably the best Whitesnake album of the era and a Number 6 UK smash. An associated UK tour during June was also their best yet, the two nights at the Hammersmith Odeon being recorded for a Number 5 album, *Live In The Heart Of The City*.

It was the success of bands like Whitesnake that alerted the music business to the fact that, with little outlay apart from promotion, the emerging hard rock and metal music market was a veritable goldmine. The likes of Van Halen, Def Leppard, Heart and Bon Jovi would go on to rival their 1970s predecessors, both artistically and in terms of commercial sales, and Whitesnake undoubtedly opened doors.

A headlining appearance at the Reading Festival with the likes of UFO, Def Leppard, Iron Maiden and Wishbone Ash preceded a first serious foray into the American continent in October 1980, with thirty-odd dates supporting Jethro Tull. And while the next attempt at the American market, a proposed package with Judas Priest and Iron Maiden, collapsed due to record company problems, the fact that April 1981's Number 2 *Come An' Get It* was Whitesnake's best seller so far, boosted by four straight shows at Hammersmith, suggested a bright future. Whitesnake appeared at the 1981 Donington Monsters of Rock festival – the first of three appearances at what would become the UK's premier metal event – as second on the bill to AC/DC.

But backing tracks for the next album were re-recorded after Coverdale voiced misgivings with band members who, he felt, were not pulling their weight. The singer's patience ran out in early 1982 and he convened a meeting to clear the air. Micky Moody quit and, as Neil Murray moved on to Gary Moore's band, Cozy Powell approached David to join him in the Michael Schenker Group, currently singer-less after Gary Barden's departure. Whether the band would remain MSG or mutate into the next line-up of Whitesnake was in the end a moot point as, although David did apparently try out with Schenker, little of note came from their rehearsals. Linking up with a guitarist with creative views even more entrenched than Ritchie Blackmore's seemed to promise little apart from short-term expediency.

Meantime Jon Lord, who had been working on a solo album, unveiled *Before I Forget* in February 1982. The album lacked a little cohesion, sounding more like a collection of themes and ideas gathered over a period of time. Lord then appeared in the Rock and Blues Circus tour in Germany with former Back Door bassist Colin 'Bomber' Hodgkinson. He remained with the Whitesnake organisation despite further changes, John Coletta resigning as manager and Bernie Marsden being fired. Ian Paice immediately rejoined Neil Murray by linking up with former Thin Lizzy guitarist Gary Moore for *Corridors Of Power* in mid 1982.

Coverdale finally recruited Cozy Powell, the drummer agreeing to join Whitesnake after a shared camping trip on Dartmoor.

Guitarist Mel Galley, a former Trapeze bandmate of Glenn Hughes, also joined around this time, while Micky Moody returned to the fold and Colin Hodgkinson was appointed the new bassist at the recommendation of Lord and Powell. With so many changes, *Saints An' Sinners*, which came out in late 1982 and reached Number 9, did not reflect the current line-up and gave the whole enterprise a rather curious perspective.

Late 1982 also saw a change that would have profound and far-reaching effects on the Whitesnake story when a record deal for America was signed with Geffen Records. Run by David Geffen and John Kalodner, the label had an uncanny knack of resurrecting flagging careers (witness Cher, Michael Bolton and Aerosmith) and had spotted the obvious potential of Whitesnake – the frontman in particular. A UK tour was slotted in at the end of the year and over into 1983.

The relationship with Geffen didn't get off to a good start; out went long-time producer Martin Birch, with the label suggesting former Hendrix desk-man Eddie Kramer for the forthcoming album. However, clashes with Coverdale over editing and remixing meant Birch was soon back behind the desk at Musicland in the spring of 1983.

Whitesnake headlined that year's Donington Festival and a few more European dates were slotted in soon afterwards, after which Moody announced his departure, recommending ex-Thin Lizzy guitarist John Sykes as his replacement. He was too late to feature on *Slide It In*, which nevertheless was an upbeat effort full of Galley's high-tempo rockers, succinctly underpinned by the thunderous drumming of Powell. The ribald title caused comment, and Coverdale's press interviews didn't help the situation. The album came too early in the Geffen relationship for the album to break the band in the States, though Keith Olsen's re-mix was a sign of where the band's future lay.

But not with Jon Lord, whose last show with the band took place in April in Stockholm, clearing the way for a Deep Purple Mark II reformation. The Whitesnake success story, of course, continued...

8. Back with a Bang

A number 1 album is the ultimate validation for any serious rock band. Yet when Deep Purple celebrated their third, after 1971's *Fireball* and 1972's *Machine Head*, they weren't even a functioning proposition. Nevertheless, the success of the TV-advertised *Deepest Purple*, which deposed Queen's *The Game* from the top spot in the UK in August 1980, underlined the respect in which the band were still held, and, despite the success of their spin-off bands, just how much they were missed.

'Purple to reform' headlines were an understandable fallback of the music press on quiet news weeks, the obligatory question mark sometimes omitted for the sake of a sale. The assumption was always that it would be Deep Purple Mark II that rematerialised like Doctor Who's TARDIS. Yet with Gillan and Blackmore enjoying acclaim of their own, both registering more than one Top 3 album around the turn of the decade, the incentive clearly had to be considerable for them to turn their back on solo success let alone confront their problematic personal relationship.

Even so, a Mark II reformation was said to have been simmering for some time before the inevitable happened. Roger Glover reportedly let slip to fans that, in preparation, the 'classic' line-up had got together for a jam prior to the Rainbow tour in the spring of 1981. (Ian Paice later commented it was simply a chat at Roger's house, and Ritchie was not present). There had also been approaches to both Glover and Blackmore by ex-manager John Coletta.

The initial deal was for the vocalist to be David Coverdale, who turned it down – wisely as it turned out, given the phenomenal success of the next few Whitesnake albums. This time, though, Ian Gillan was agreeable, having put his solo career on hold while he recuperated from vocal chord surgery. Shows were even pencilled in for the vast untapped markets of Eastern Europe, which were just opening up to western culture and proving to be particularly avid consumers of Purple's brand of heavy rock.

Yet again plans fell apart, one source alleging that this time it was Ritchie who had pulled out in favour of one last concerted effort to conquer America with Rainbow. It was also said he assumed the deal would be no more than a short-term get-together, whereas the others wanted a more permanent arrangement. (Blackmore: 'Ian said hurry up and make up your mind or I'm off to join Black Sabbath!'). Another version of events cited a blazing row between Gillan and Blackmore over the division of publishing royalties, culminating with the inebriated Gillan throwing a beer over Ritchie and walking out.

Whatever the reason, the redundant Rainbow musicians were all swiftly reinstated early in 1983. Drummer Bobby Rondinelli was not to remain for very much longer however, ultimately dropped because of (according to manager Bruce Payne) 'inconsistency'. This accusation was allegedly instigated by not Blackmore but Joe Lynn Turner – a sign of Joe's increasing status within the group. Rainbow played their final live show in Japan in March 1984, and two months later came the official announcement: rumour had it that each Mark II member had been offered $2 million to participate.

With the band working on what was, in effect, the follow-up to 1973's ill-fated *Who Do We Think We Are*, they chose another relatively rural location – this time, however, the other side of the Atlantic in picturesque Stowe, Vermont. Rehearsals started on 1 May at the Bass Lodge, an old house owned by the Von Trapp family of *Sound of Music* fame. The influence must have rubbed off as, after a month of rehearsals, the songs had been knocked into shape.

In keeping with the tradition of recording in less than conventional studio surroundings, the band also wanted to record the album at the Lodge, but the state authorities refused so they settled on a mansion called Horizons and started recording the album on 10 July. The band completed the mixing process in

Germany in September and, before it was released, flew to England to start rehearsing for the upcoming world tour.

With the reunion being big news in the music press, the band chose a suitable location where they would not be easily found by the press. Stuart Smith, who was working for Blackmore, suggested the area he had lived in before moving to America, the shire town of Bedford in the Home Counties. Blackmore and Smith had flown over from Hamburg a couple of weeks earlier and settled on a building called St Peter's Hall. The band moved into the hall in early October for two weeks' rehearsal, and it was here that they started to play some of the older tunes for the first time.

During their stay in Bedford a film crew spent some time with the group for a proposed documentary, although nothing actually came of it. A few brief moments of the band in rehearsal were used for the promo video to the title track, to which, Blackmore commented, 'I heard there was a part where you actually see me smiling... I tried to get that cut out right away!' Towards the end of their time in Bedford the press finally found out where they were and some of the more respected music journalists were invited along to do interviews – including Tommy Vance, who presented a full two-hour special on his Radio 1 *Friday Rock Show* the following week.

Jon Lord untypically cast modesty aside when he professed *Perfect Strangers* 'a perfect album. It said everything about the band that needed to be said. We weren't trying to be a super new 1980s band, and at the same time we weren't just a nostalgia band.' Ian Gillan later recalled 'a tremendous amount of debate before we actually decided to do it. The overriding thing was not whether we could do it but if we were going to do it [it had] better be good.'

Disappointingly, the broadcast media gave single 'Knocking On Your Door' only brief exposure. 'It was featured on radio, 'cos they had to get a handle on our album,' said Gillan, 'but even that stopped. When radio stations want to play Deep Purple and Led Zeppelin they play the same songs, they won't touch new product.

We never get played on contemporary radio because we're not regarded as contemporary.'

As *Perfect Strangers* hit Number 5 in Britain (on Polydor) and Number 17 in the States (on Mercury), the band embarked on their first world tour for over a decade. Dubbed the *Follow The Sun* tour, it kicked off in Australasia at the end of November, the band playing to large audiences at a mixture of indoor and outdoor venues. These first few shows threw up their fair share of newsworthy stories, not least events prior to the very first gig at the Perth Entertainment Centre in Western Australia.

Ritchie Blackmore and assistant Stuart Smith had flown to Perth in advance of the gig from New York via Honolulu and Sydney on a twenty-hour flight and checked into the Sheraton Hotel. Due to renovation work on the twelfth floor, the jetlagged guitarist hadn't managed to get a decent night's sleep since his arrival and, after complaining more than twenty times, sought to get his revenge. A function room at the hotel was booked in the name of J Sessions and amplification equipment from a local store was hired and smuggled in, after which Blackmore and Smith had a very loud jam session at 1.00am.

Unbeknown to the pair, Eric Clapton's entourage was also in town for a gig at the same venue and Blackmore's jam session was cut short by Clapton's bodyguard, Alfie, who stormed into the room saying, 'If I wanted to hear a rock band I would have bought a ticket to a concert. Pull the plugs out now because if I hear this again there will be some "stoush".' Although the threat was enough for Blackmore to quit playing, they had already managed to wake half the hotel's guests, resulting in a jammed switchboard and the appearance of security guards.

A sure sign that the reformed Deep Purple remained an accountant's dream was evident with the demand for tickets. In pre-Internet days, one of the New Zealand shows reputedly sold all 50,000 tickets in a day.

With all the hullabaloo the reunion caused in the press, it was as if Purple had never been away. Residents in the vicinity of

Auckland's Western Springs Stadium voiced their concerns that the band with the reputation of being the loudest in the world would be playing on their doorsteps. One woman was quoted in the local paper as saying, 'I don't mind too much the normal type of group. But these *deafening* ones...' The city council imposed a limit of ninety decibels for the gig but, according to press reports, Purple's road crew ignored the restriction and the sound reached one hundred decibels. A local acoustics expert, Nevil Hegley, helpfully pointed out that an increase of ten decibels represents a doubling of apparent loudness.

Despite the concerns with the volume the gig also made headlines for completely different reasons. 'Rock Fans Riot' was the heading in the *Courier Mail* as, when an estimated 2,000 people without tickets were turned away, some of the mob started to throw bottles and tried to overrun the security guards. Police with riot helmets and batons moved in to clear the crowd and seventy-eight arrests were made. Make no mistake; Deep Purple were back with a bang, as popular as they had ever been.

This leg of the tour will best be remembered for the appearance of George Harrison at the show at Sydney's Entertainment Centre on 13 December. Ian Gillan introduced Harrison as 'Arnold from Liverpool' who joined the band on stage for an encore of the Little Richard number 'Lucille'. Harrison, a close friend of Jon Lord, was in Australia for a book launch and it was his first appearance on stage Down Under since the Beatles had toured there in 1964.

Lord had first met Harrison in 1974 when he came into Apple Studios in Saville Row 'to check out what all the noise was about' during the recording of *First Of The Big Bands*. The pair became reacquainted in 1977 and, having become neighbours in the picturesque town of Henley on Thames, would spend many happy hours in each others' company until the ex-Beatle's death. 'He taught me a great deal about many things and I miss his wise words and his marvellous – and occasionally scurrilous – humour,' said Lord when he paid musical tribute to him in 2004 on the solo album *Beyond The Notes*.

Because of Harrison's relatively reclusive lifestyle, the Australian press had a field day. The guitarist, clearly disillusioned with the music business quipped: 'I think you have to be a homosexual nowadays to succeed. I think record companies are only catering for the fourteen to twenty year old market and forget that older people like listening to music too.'

Harrison's comments were partly accurate, but Deep Purple, lthough unlikely to have hit singles, had clearly retained a place in the hearts of album-orientated, gig-going rock fans. What was even more encouraging was the fact that most of the people attending the shows were from a younger generation of rock fans who had not been fortunate enough to see Purple first time around. Having successfully and comfortably slotted back into the rock scene with these first gigs, the huge forty-eight-date North American leg of the tour kicked off on 18 January at the Odessa Ector County Coliseum in Texas, concluding on 9 April at Tacoma Seattle Dome, Wichita. The set list as with the Australasian dates, was pretty much a fifty-fifty split between the old and the new. Five of the nine songs from the *Perfect Strangers* album were performed: 'Knocking At Your Back Door', 'Nobody's Home', 'A Gypsy's Kiss', 'Under The Gun' and the title track. They sat comfortably alongside classics of old like 'Highway Star', 'Strange Kind Of Woman', 'Child In Time', 'Lazy' and 'Space Truckin''.

The only concession to the years spent apart was the inclusion of 'Difficult To Cure', Rainbow's title for its adaptation of Beethoven's Ode To Joy from his Fifth Symphony, that was used as the platform for Jon Lord's solo spot. The encore numbers were 'Smoke On The Water', 'Speed King' and 'Black Night', though not all were played every night. The American gigs were second only to Bruce Springsteen as the biggest-grossing US tour of the year.

As the band moved on to Europe, 'Child In Time' was dropped from the set. The toil of 200-plus shows year on year and the throat problems a couple of years earlier that had affected Ian

Gillan's voice, had made it difficult for him to hit the high notes of 'Child In Time' every night with one hundred per cent accuracy. This perfectionism explains why it was rested for a while.

Nevertheless, the tour rolled on just as successfully, even though corporate decisions meant UK fans only had one show to attend. The supposed plan of following the sun hadn't allowed for the typical English weather, and the all-day Knebworth Festival on 22 June was to be one of the all-time wettest June days in recorded history. Yet despite the weather, and the fact that latest rock hot properties U2 were gigging the same day just a few miles away at Milton Keynes Bowl, Purple drew a crowd of around 70,000 on a bill that included Mountain, Meat Loaf and Scorpions. The BBC recorded the show and later broadcast it, Purple's former manager Tony Edwards subsequently releasing the recording on his new Connoisseur Collection record label.

The band undertook a few similar outdoor events in Germany but, elsewhere in Europe, had to make do with arena shows: in Paris, two nights were played at the huge indoor Palais Omnisport De Bercy, the second of which was filmed by German TV station WDR and broadcast throughout Europe. Despite Ian Gillan struggling with a cold the band was in fine form and Ritchie Blackmore even led an improvisation of the old Shadows dance routine during 'Black Night', ably joined by Messrs Gillan and Glover, that was captured on camera.

Having regained triple-platinum status with *Perfect Strangers* (which had registered the highest chart positions for a new Purple album since *Burn* a decade earlier) and followed it with a successful, lucrative and relatively uneventful world tour, Purple must have realised they still had the hardest hurdle to jump. A follow-up album was always going to be the acid test, the newness of the reunion now tarnished and the challenge there to match the best of the early years but give the music a contemporary edge.

Original vocalist Rod Evans and bassist Nick Simper, mainstays of the first three albums.

Purple Mark II make their *Top Of The Pops* debut, 1970.

Ritchie Blackmore displays his Stratocaster collection.

Ian Gillan and Roger Glover, whose importation from Episode Six in 1969 lit the touch paper.

Jon Lord in 1974, the year *Burn* launched a third Purple line-up.

Ian Paice, ever-present from 1968, hammers the skins in typical fashion.

The only deep Purple line-up to enjoy two incarnations featured (L-R) Glover, Gillan, Paice, Lord and Blackmore.

Deep Purple in transit, with new recruits Glenn Hughes and David Coverdale.

Hughes and Coverdale on stage.

David Coverdale and Tommy Bolin, singer and guitarist with Purple Mark IV.

Deep Purple Mark IV. Although promising in the studio, live performances were unpredictable.

Gillan salutes the audience as the reunited Mark II line-up

Joe Lynn Turner's Purple tenure lasted just a single album.

Glover, Gillan and current guitarist Steve Morse.

The perennial partnership of Glover and Gillan, Warsaw, June 2004.

Purple face the future with keyboardist Don Airey (second from right) now a fixture in the ranks.

9.Mixed Signals

The personality conflicts that had once split the classic Purple line-up would again become apparent during the 1986 sessions for the second album of the reunited band, *House Of Blue Light*. And, as ever, the Gillan/Glover axis found itself in conflict with Blackmore. 'Roger and I did a lot of preparation,' said the singer, 'only to find Ritchie wasn't interested in listening. It's hard to deal with that sort of thing and I didn't. Suggestions and half-worked ideas were strangled but, so long as Ritchie was happy with the guitar parts the lads were happy. I wasn't and said so. But let's not blame everything on Ritchie... I was a wanker too.

'*I* was appalled by some of this record,' Gillan concluded. 'I couldn't deal with Blackmore at all. Ritchie started getting cranky again, and I could see the nervousness creeping into everyone's eyes...' Ritchie, needless to say, disagreed: 'I would stick to my guns, not cause trouble for its own sake. Ian had a hang-up; if any idea about what we should do was to Ritchie's way of thinking, then it was wrong.' Whatever the rights and wrongs, the record tended to back up Gillan's assertion that 'There was no spirit in the group.'

One of the major problems had been that, whereas the likes of *Fireball* and *In Rock* had been written by the five musicians together, material for *House Of Blue Light* had been brought in separately by Gillan, Glover and Blackmore. A couple of years later, Jon Lord recalled Winston Churchill's saying that 'A camel is a horse, designed by a committee. Deep Purple seems to make a better horse by committee!' He also likened *Blue Light* to *Fireball* in setting the band up for a mega-album in the vein of *Machine Head*: 'We always do one good album, a confused one and then another good one.'

But there were few laughs on the tour to promote *House Of Blue Light* which, by all accounts, was nothing if not fraught. Blackmore's refusal to play 'Smoke On The Water' at the second Wembley Arena show, when he failed to return for an encore, was

seen by some as typical of the moody guitarist and UK fans
generally gave the thumbs-down to such antics that resulted in a
rather lacklustre-sounding performance with Jon Lord having to
carry the entire, guitar-based song on the Hammond organ.
Nevertheless, the track was present and correct with a version
recorded later in the year on the live double album *Nobody's
Perfect* which, while no *Made In Japan*, scraped into the UK
Top 40. (The double vinyl was condensed to a single CD,
so those with the plastic have extra tracks.)

But although Blackmore was often seen as the one who would
let the side down when it came to encores, a couple of weeks
earlier at the show in Paris, he had been the *only* one to return
to the stage! The rest of the band, apparently led by Ian Gillan,
decided not to encore on that particular occasion and the
motivation appeared to be connected with the BBC's *Whistle Test*
programme. Back in 1984, Gillan and Lord had appeared on the
show talking about the reunion, but interviewer Andy Kershaw
annoyed Gillan in particular by continually insisting the
motivation for reforming was purely financial.

Fast-forward to Paris in 1987 and the *Whistle Test* crew travelled
to the gig to film a feature for the TV show. Gillan and company
were not over-enamoured with their presence and, shortly before
the band took the stage, the film crew were told they could only
film from the soundboard area two-thirds of the way back and
only record the sound during the encore!

Blackmore, who tended to distance himself from the rest of the
group, always travelling separately and having his own dressing
room, was unlikely to have been aware of the feud with the
Whistle Test crew, and so, after the rest of the band decided they
didn't want to go back on stage after the closing 'Space Truckin'',
Ritchie decided otherwise. Getting one of the road crew to join
him behind the drum kit, he started cranking out the opening to
'Smoke On The Water', then stopped, held his arms out and
looked around as if to say 'Where are they?' Thanking the
crowd, he then walked off.

In an incredible turnaround, Blackmore all of a sudden became the group's spokesman and the *Whistle Test* crew were desperate to get a few words with him. Filmed in the empty arena, he was somewhat diplomatic about the whole incident, but his usual dry sense of humour was still evident. 'Rock 'n' roll is built on an edge,' he commented. 'That's why sometimes I won't do an encore and sometimes the band will. But I refuse to be a robot. I'm a very emotional kind of person and very sensitive. Sometimes I don't play an encore because I don't feel that I want to, if I don't think the audience is channelling in on something I want to think about. But tonight I wanted to do an encore and the rest of the band didn't, so it made a change!'

The *Whistle Test* team appeared to get the last laugh as they put together the programme. Having been unable to record any live performance from the band, they used a brief clip courtesy of French television, recorded at an earlier show in Cologne, with the band playing 'The Unwritten Law' from *House Of Blue Light* featuring, it has to be said, a very rough vocal performance from Ian Gillan.

Two days after the last date of the European tour, Blackmore teamed up with his old 1960s colleague Jackie Lynton for an impromptu gig at the Kings Head pub in Fulham, West London, where delighted punters saw the unadvertised guitarist play a full set of rock 'n' roll standards with Lynton's band.

The commercial fortunes of *House Of Blue Light*, in chart placings at least, represented a decline on the glorious comeback of *Perfect Strangers*. The UK peak of 10 compared with 5, while a US position of 34 showed a similarly proportionate fall from the heady heights of 17.

The House Of Blue Light tour, just two or three weeks old, ended abruptly on 30 May in Phoenix, Arizona, when Ritchie Blackmore broke his finger while attempting to catch his Fender Strat at the climax of the act. 'I woke up next morning to find no tour and a ticket home,' Lord recalled sadly. 'I didn't even get to say goodbye to the crew.'

Gillan and Glover, on the other hand, failed to feel sorry for themselves and managed to turn their unexpected spare time into something positive. They turned the tour bus towards New York and found the musicians who could help them complete a half-finished duo recording project. With the help of top jazz-rock horn man Randy Brecker, crack drummer Andy Newmark (Steve Winwood, Roxy Music) and New Orleans piano legend Dr John, they came up with *Accidentally On Purpose*, an album that was a long way from Deep Purple, but as a whole is still regarded by Ian Gillan as 'the one I play the most of all the records I have made'.

The feel of the original material ranged widely; few other albums the duo had graced since Episode Six days could beat the contrast of the adjoining 'Dislocated', with its reggae offbeat, and the retro-rock of 'Via Miami'. There were a number of covers on board. Having been referred to in the lyric of Purple's 'Speed King', Little Richard received yet another tip of the hat in a rollicking cover of 'Can't Believe You Wanna Leave' (given an authentic N'Awleans feel by Dr John). Very different was the treatment of the Doc Pomus-penned 'Lonely Avenue', a Ray Charles song, while Dr John came into play again on 'Purple People Eater', a 1958 novelty hit for Sheb Wooley.

Accidentally... was a holiday album, but it marked the end of Ian Gillan's holiday with his record label. 'This was the first album I'd delivered to Virgin since 1982, and I had a great relationship with them. But Virgin changed quite a lot and when I wanted to talk to someone no one knew who I was!' From being Virgin's highest-selling artist in his first year there – an accolade inherited by one Phil Collins – Gillan had seen his position change. The fact that he was back riding the Purple gravy train on another label and unable to cut significant solo material undoubtedly contributed. 'I thought it was the best album I'd ever done but Virgin didn't make any effort whatsoever. So I wrote to Richard Branson saying I guess we don't love each other any more...'

The 'day job' of touring with Purple had recommenced in Europe in August and September, Ritchie's finger having healed. Once over, a reappraisal of the band's objectives was next on the agenda. Gillan believed a more progressive approach without regard to chart positions was the answer: 'I was rocking the boat hard,' he later admitted, 'because I thought the band was stagnating. I wanted us to become more creative and aggressive, and I was sick of it.' Almost inevitably, however, Ritchie Blackmore was looking to pursue a more commercial direction in similar vein to Rainbow and their run of major hit singles in 1980.

Recordings from the *House Of Blue Light* tour were compiled for the double live album *Nobody's Perfect* but, in keeping with the previous live album the band had produced back in 1972, the group generally showed little interest in it. Blackmore sat in the studio for a couple of days listening to the playbacks with the rest of the band but invariably found it ended up with a situation where four of them would be happy with a particular performance only for the fifth member to be critical of his own performance – and so it would go on.

Ritchie was first to tire of the process and left it to the others to put it together. Roger Glover was really the only one to nurse it all the way through, and, even though they had recorded several shows in both the USA and Europe, invariably versions of songs would be incomplete due to the time limitations of the tapes – or, less forgivably, because they had not run two tapes to overlap. As such, Glover married up recordings from different shows, and although it was a technique that people like Frank Zappa had used for many years, some Purple fans somehow felt it was a dishonest way of doing things. During the mixing of the album in February at Hook End Manor in Oxfordshire, a couple of spontaneous recordings of 'Black Night' and 'Hush' were done, and the latter was considered good enough to include on the live album as a kind of bonus track.

The launch party for *Nobody's Perfect* took place at the wonderfully named Fort Frankenstein in Frankfurt, where everyone, from the band to the journalists, had to dress in medieval period costume. All this was instigated by Blackmore, for whom that time period had long held a fascination. Jon Lord

elected not to attend, but all the other members were there and
partook in events such as archery. The musical entertainment was
provided by a medieval group called Des Geyers Schwarzer
Haufen who, ten years later, were to have a huge influence on
Blackmore's change of musical direction.

The album, when released in July 1988 was quickly written
off as a pale imitation of the magnificent *Made In Japan*. The fact
that much of the older material was included drew the inevitable
comparisons and undoubtedly affected the album's standing
against its more powerful predecessor. Ian Gillan was particularly
critical of it ('We'd hardly changed at all... just become more
slick') and had been generally against the idea of producing a live
album anyway... but then he had felt the same way back in 1972.

Some time later Gillan claimed the band had been totally united
– apart from himself – in okaying the release. 'If there's going to
be a live album there has to be a valid reason for doing it.' He
pinned much of the blame on manager Bruce Payne who, he said,
'had lost all direction'. The re-recording of 'Hush' was issued as a
single but if this was aimed at a Top 10 populated by the likes of
Kylie, Belinda Carlisle and Debbie Gibson, then a Number 62
chart position in mid 1988 suggested it had failed. (Ironically,
Kula Shaker's cover would do considerably better nine years
later, reaching the heady heights of Number 2.)

To coincide with the release of *Nobody's Perfect*, a large
North American tour was planned for the summer, commencing
in Saratoga at the end of July and continuing through August
and September. Some of these dates were cancelled, apparently
because of poor sales of the new album which subsequently had a
knock-on effect on ticket sales. It's fair to say, though, that Purple
wasn't the only band that summer to suffer from the problem.

After a warm-up gig in a club called Hammerjacks in Baltimore
on 11 August, what should have been a tour of twenty-plus dates
ended up as just one gig in New Jersey – though this was at the
Giants Stadium with fellow classic rockers Aerosmith and up and
coming Guns 'N' Roses. Jon Lord disguised the disappointment of

the cancellation of the rest of the tour when he said, 'There were 80,000 people there, it was lovely,' adding hopefully, 'I'm glad to say our drawing power hasn't diminished and that we can still be counted among the top five rock bands.'

With the potentially more lucrative US gigs having fallen by the wayside, attention switched to Europe, where sales of the album had been generally healthier, for a rather hastily arranged set of dates billed as the *Nobody's Perfect* tour. It was rather unusual to put together a tour to promote a live album but then Deep Purple has never operated like a normal band. Even some of these European dates got cancelled and all that was left were a few Italian shows and four German dates with Copenhagen sandwiched in the middle of them.

The set that had been rehearsed for the US gigs was played at these concerts, stripped back to a concise ninety minutes with shorter solos and tracks such as 'Space Truckin'' cut down to a maximum of five minutes,. Despite the indifferent reception the live record had received, those who witnessed this short tour generally agreed the band was firing on all cylinders with stronger shows than had been witnessed on the later dates of the *House Of Blue Light* tour. The band also performed 'Hush' during the encores, which was an unexpected highlight.

The indifference that initially greeted *Nobody's Perfect* was disappointing in itself – but the release was put into perspective when, in November, a stunning live recording of the band from Stockholm 1970 appeared on Tony Edwards' Connoisseur label. All five members had agreed to the release on the understanding it was held back a few months so as not to clash with their new live effort. The delay didn't make a blind bit of difference and, as far as most fans were concerned, there was little comparison in the quality of performance between the two recordings. This, needless to say, only served to further the frustrations of the fans that had hoped for an equally raw recording from the reformed group.

Rumours of a split were denied by management, and Jon Lord ventured into print with *Metal Hammer*'s Chris Welch, insisting that 'there are six semi-completed [songs] and a further half-dozen in a rough state' ready to be worked up into an album. After 'a few one-off gigs in the summer', he was convinced it would 'be out in November, in time for your Christmas stocking'. As such, Deep Purple went back to Stowe in Vermont after the brief tour to work on the new material.

This would be for a new record company, the band having decided to switch from Polydor to the BMG label for their next release, feeling that a change was as good as a rest. In Jon Lord's words, 'They [Polydor] didn't give us the feeling that they still thought Deep Purple was a current band.' Certainly, the live album had contained precious few post-reformation songs. Also, many of the personnel that had signed Purple to Polydor had now, thanks to the music-business merry-go-round, ended up at RCA – 'another of those huge German conglomerates', as Lord called it. And since Germany was undoubtedly one of Purple's main markets that was not necessarily a bad thing.

Whatever rifts may have been developing in the Purple camp were nothing compared to the horrendous Armenian earthquake disaster on 10 December 1988 that resulted in over 45,000 deaths and left half a million people homeless. It prompted several people in the music business into putting together a charity concert to be performed in Moscow. A huge festival billed Deep Purple alongside such disparate acts as UB40, Bonnie Tyler and Joe Cocker. Originally planned for February, then put back to March, then back further to May with talk of satellite link-ups around the world, the event never actually got off the ground – and, given the growing disharmony within the ranks, it's unlikely Deep Purple would have committed to such an event anyway.

By the beginning of that year the relationship between singer and guitarist had once again deteriorated. Both parties maintained very set opinions on the direction of the band and its future material. Ian Gillan's demands for a more instinctive progressive approach *à la Fireball* conflicted with Blackmore's ideas (earlier attempted with Rainbow) for a more commercial and immediate melodic stance that was proving popular in the USA at the time.

Gillan's upbeat work ethic was also at loggerheads with the rest of the band's more studied and leisurely approach to things this time around; their reticence was understandable given that work-related stress in 1972 had been central to earlier tensions within the quintet.

Irrespective of who was right or wrong, this polarisation of Purple's collective creative effort became ever more acute. Demos for the next album were worked up early in 1989 and forwarded to Gillan. Despite a valiant effort to make something of them, Ian rejected the backing tracks (these became 'Slow Down Sister', 'King Of Dreams' and 'Wicked Ways'). With this seeming impasse on a creative front, Ritchie started having thoughts of reactivating Rainbow as an outlet to vent his creative frustrations.

Meanwhile, tired of the band's current inactivity and ever the workaholic live performer, Gillan embarked on a tour of the UK as his *alter ego* Garth Rockett and the Moonshiners. Reprising standards along with his Gillan material and choices from *Accidentally On Purpose*, the set proved entertaining if often undersubscribed.

Although the official line was that this was a little extracurricular fun, things did not go down well with the management (and band), who thought the singer should be concentrating his efforts working up material for the forthcoming album. This was all rather ironic, given that Jon Lord had spent some time in Germany the previous year with long-time friend Pete York recording a TV project called *Superdrumming* that was launched on German TV in May, with Lord as part of the resident house band.

This, coupled with Blackmore's recent request that Gillan be absent from band rehearsals (which the band agreed to) meant that things were – as in 1972 – coming to a head. April 1989 saw a planning meeting in America where Ian demanded a proper New York studio environment this time around. Given Blackmore's hatred of recording studio sterility this was argued against, with Jon Lord also nixing the idea ('The idea of recording in New York fills me with dread'). After a full-blown row Ian stormed out and flew back to the UK, where his dismissal was confirmed to his personal manager a few days later.

The final straw had been an evening at snowbound Stowe, recounted with mournful humour in Gillan's autobiography, where he'd indulged in a drinking session at a nearby watering hole and returned to the communal house 'wearing nothing except two bin-liners tied below my knees to keep my feet dry.' Having kicked the door open, he swayed unsteadily across the room to end up somersaulted behind the sofa, having brought down a pair of heavily laden shelves with his feet. 'Still naked, except for my improvised wellies, I drifted off to sleep. Back in England, a short while later, I got the call telling me I was fired.'

The first firm confirmation of the singer's departure from Purple was Ian's signing of a fan's cutting from *Kerrang!* on the split rumours with a succinct 'Bye Bye...' The UK music press as usual caught up with the story late, perfunctory articles in July relating to the parting of the ways.

No sooner had Gillan's sacking been announced than, bizarrely, he was back working on a project with the very person who was instrumental in his departure. With the proposed Moscow Armenian Earthquake benefit concert having fallen through, a charity record was produced instead. The track chosen for an all-star recording was Purple's own 'Smoke On The Water' and such luminaries as Paul Rodgers, Dave Gilmour, Brian May, Roger Taylor, Alex Lifeson, Chris Squire and Bruce Dickinson got together in the Metropolis Studios in Chiswick, West London on 8 July. Both Jon Lord and Ritchie Blackmore were also mentioned, but in the end only the latter ended up playing on it.

Despite knowing that Blackmore would be present, Ian Gillan invited himself to perform on the track as, after all, it was his song. Any concerns that he and Blackmore might bump into one another in the studio were erased when Ritchie insisted on doing his parts last, once everyone else had left the studio. The song made Number 39 in the UK, all profits from the record going to the earthquake victims.

10. Purple Rainbow

Although Deep Purple had started 1988 having signed a lucrative new deal with BMG, with the singer now departed it looked to most outsiders as if the band was about to fold. Especially when Jon Lord once again teamed up with Pete York plus, Tony Ashton, Colin Hodgkinson, Miller Anderson, Zoot Money and Chris Farlowe for a lengthy Austrian and German tour in October and November, billed as the Olympic Rock and Blues Circus. Although there must have been pressure from the new record company for Deep Purple to continue, Blackmore's apparent interest in putting Rainbow back together seemed less important now Ian Gillan was no longer in the band. In fact if the right vocalist could be found, Blackmore could, to all intents and purposes, produce Rainbow-style music under Deep Purple's more commercially viable name.

Just a few months after getting the sack, Ian Gillan put forward his side of the story to members of the DPAS, admitting that he had got over the shock but not the disappointment of how Lord and Paice had basically gone along with Blackmore's decision. Roger Glover, who was definitely the closest to Gillan, was apparently in tears when he eventually phoned the singer after his sacking and they remained in constant touch thereafter.

Gillan also claimed that Jon Lord, in particular, had been excluded from writing and that, in his eyes, Purple had become nothing more than Ritchie's backing band. He was also critical of manager Bruce Payne and referred to a situation prior to the *House Of Blue Light* album. 'He said we've had a band meeting and decided it might be a good idea not to use Roger as the producer. I said "Have you spoken to Roger about this?" and he said no. I said, "Well you've not spoken to me about it either, so how can it be a band meeting?"'

With large 'Vocalist wanted' adverts placed in the rock press optimistically hoping for another find of the David Coverdale type,

Blackmore and the band now drew up a list of candidates. Doug Pinnick of Kings X (whose management shielded all approaches) and Ronnie James Dio were mooted, but those rumoured to have actually auditioned included Aussies John Farnham (Little River Band) and former Cold Chisel singer Jimmy Barnes, Brits Kal Swann (a Coverdale soundalike, ex-of Lion and Tytan) and Bad Company's Brian Howe. Paul Rodgers, the man Howe had replaced, was also mooted but sources claimed he was 'found wanting' – unlikely given Ritchie's love of the Free vocalist's style.

The duo that came closest were unknown American Terry Brock (of Scottish band Strangeways, who only lasted three days!) and ex-Survivor/Cobra frontman Jimi Jamison. Jamison, a 'name' in AOR circles, was an undoubtedly powerful singer and seemed to satisfy all the criteria. Despite recording a couple of vocal tracks over the album backings in September 1989 he finally turned the offer down on management advice in favour of a solo career (singing the *Baywatch* theme!) Purple had underestimated the uniqueness and identity Gillan had given them – few singers gave them the same sound and flavour.

According to Marc Brans of the longest-running Deep Purple fan club in the world (in Belgium), Roger Glover confirmed to him that they had even discussed the possibility of a female. How serious Glover was about that is open to debate. What's certain, though, is that by the end of December 1989 all possible options seemed exhausted and the name of former Rainbow frontman Joe Lynn Turner was raised by Ritchie. An audition was arranged.

From Hackensack, New Jersey, Joe had started out in the early 1970s with a Hendrix and Deep Purple covers band called Ezra. After leaving college with a degree, he went fully professional with Fandango in 1976. 'We were good writers, but we didn't know whether to be the Eagles, Kool and the Gang or Bad Company,' Joe remembered. 'A lot of potential, a lot of talent, but no direction.'

Nonetheless the group built up a healthy following on the East

Coast circuit, supporting the likes of the Allman Brothers and the Marshall Tucker Band. Between 1977 and 1980 they released four albums of competent soft rock on RCA: *Fandango, One Night Stand, Last Kiss* and *Cadillac*. The latter's most familiar track, 'Blame It On The Night', has since been covered by the likes of Ted Nugent and Rage).

Turner's post-Rainbow CV had been interesting, if ultimately unrealised. He had embarked on a solo career as planned, although things didn't start off too well: 'Bruce Payne was supposed to be handling my solo stuff. The longer things went on the more obvious it became that he was too busy with Purple to really give a shit about me – I can understand that though as Ritchie's his gaffer and he doesn't want to screw that up! So I was living off royalties for a year, writing and waiting.'

Tommy Aldridge and Rudy Sarzo requested Joe front their band project Driver, and with such high-profile outfits like Survivor and Toto also said to interested in recruiting him the singer had plenty of career options. Joe also worked on advertising and commercial soundtracks – initially rather reluctantly. 'Michael Bolton got me into it. This was before his rise to fame and fortune. He said "Man, you gotta do this." So I did a Budweiser commercial. Then I saw the cheque in the mail the next month and I said "This will work!"'

Parallel to this, solo work continued through mid 1984 with former Foreigner and Spys keyboardist Al Greenwood. These ultimately led to a record deal with Elektra Records in April 1985 and a moderately successful solo album, *Rescue You*, was released that October. Largely co-written with Greenwood, the album was packed with ballads and lush keyboard-orientated melody, veering to the softer end of AOR.

The album retained Chuck Burgi on drums and included Bobby Messano (ex-Starz) on bass and guitars. The recording personnel formed the Turner touring band and, with Pat Travers' bassist Barry Dunaway, supported Pat Benatar through the US in the spring of 1986. Offers from other groups continued to come in; Joe turned down both Foreigner and drummer Jason (son of John) Bonham's group project.

Further solo plans were put on hold after an agreement in June 1987 to link up with Blackmore clone Yngwie Malmsteen. Turner's recruitment was at the behest of Polygram, who desperately wanted someone who could help the Swede commercially and add a more contemporary sheen to Malmsteen's impressive but often overwrought guitar work. Joe joined for an album and a world tour with a long-term solo deal promised. The result was the excellent *Odyssey* which nodded towards the best of the JLT-era Rainbow sound with fluidly frenetic neo-classical guitar tempered within the framework of genuinely melodic songs. The LP, which eventually sold over a million, debuted at 40 in the US *Billboard* charts.

A tour of the then Soviet Union duly followed, playing 20 shows to huge enthusiastic crowds totalling over a quarter of a million people. The patchy *Trial by Fire – Live in Leningrad* CD and concert video of October 1989 marked the commercial high point of Malmsteen's career. Given the Swede's volatile persona the band was always going to be on borrowed time and, once the album had opened up the US market enough to Malmsteen's satisfaction, the inevitable split with the vocalist occurred in 1989. ('Malmsteen and I broke up over religious reasons… he thought he was God, and I didn't agree,' joked JLT. 'The cheques just stopped coming so I guess I'm out of the band!')

Numerous sessions writing and recording for other people followed, with two tracks earmarked for Paul Rodgers and the Who's drummer Kenney Jones' studio project the Law. (One of these – 'Too Much Is Not Enough' – eventually somehow found its way onto Deep Purple's *Slaves And Masters*.) Some writing also took place with Glenn Hughes in the autumn of 1989. For a while Joe became in effect an in-house writer and backing singer for Geffen Records, his compositions and performances appearing on a number of that label's releases. Attempts to once again kick-start his solo career resulted in the formation of a new backing band provisionally called Jolt. However plans soon fell apart as, in the winter of 1989, the call from Deep Purple came.

The fruitless auditions for Gillan's replacement had proved to the Deep Purple organisation the difficulty of replacing a singer who gave the band its unique sound and signature. While the likes of AC/DC had managed to sustain viability after losing the face and voice of the perceived 'classic' line-up, others (like Black Sabbath and Bad Company) quickly found the new-singer novelty wore off and commercial popularity waned after one album.

Because of the Rainbow connection and the associations it entailed, the band had initially and understandably dismissed the idea of Joe Lynn Turner. However, with BMG now pressing for the new album, he was finally tried out and did well enough to initially at least dispel most reservations. 'I got a call to go up to Vermont to wing it with the guys for a day or so,' Turner reminisced about his audition. 'I arrived at this deserted golf club-house and, without even being formally introduced to Ian Paice and Jon Lord, was invited by Ritchie to start singing.

'He just started playing "Hey Joe" by Hendrix. I immediately picked up the mike without even saying hello... We started getting into this really long jam. We ended that, started slapping five and everything, and made our introductions.' (A version of 'Hey Joe' – a track Mark I Purple had recorded some two decades earlier, remember – is also said to exist among Roger Glover's session tapes.)

'Ritchie then started this riff that became "The Cut Runs Deep" and... asked me if I'd got anything in my "magic bag", a reference to my ability to come up with melodies and lyrics on the spot, and I think what I came up with probably convinced the rest of them. They were all up for it.' An attractive financial deal resolved any of Joe's hesitancy over joining (he had recently become a father) and terms were agreed late in 1989.

The new boy soon set to work on the few backings already started. The methodology seemed to be to jam around collectively, developing each new song in turn before starting the next one,

which lengthened the sessions well into the following year.
Fourteen backings were said to be have been finished by mid June
including the 'Hey Joe' version. The album became *Slaves And
Masters*, the title inspired by the names of the tape machines used
during recording, and was released in October 1990.

The choice of Turner was a decision which had surprised many,
but in retrospect can be seen as fitting Blackmore's idea of the
more melodic AOR direction followed by latter-day Rainbow.
Ironically, 1990 also saw Ian Gillan hit the road to promote *Naked
Thunder*, his twelfth solo album, which hit the shops three months
before Deep Purple's new offering.

The new Purple opus drew comparisons, commendations and
criticism in equal measure. For fans of the Turner era, and of AOR
in general, *Slaves And Masters* was the definitive Rainbow album.
For the vast majority, things were just not Deep Purple. Joe
understandably supported the release: 'This album is not as forced
as the Rainbow albums, as we wrote songs, not jammed them, and
this album is dirtier and nastier. Everyone was anxious to be Deep
Purple but also be a bit up to date. Some may say it's not as
aggressive but I think the album has drama, and lots of
different grooves.'

Certainly 'The Cut Runs Deep', 'Wicked Ways' and 'Fire In The
Basement' showed promise, though the likes of 'Love Conquers
All' and 'Too Much Is Not Enough' were middle-of-the-road rock
at its most insipid. The record-buying public were curious but
cautious; the album barely made the UK Top 50, while elsewhere
its popularity proved fleeting.

As with his original tenure with Rainbow in 1980, Turner a
gain found himself following in the footsteps of an individualistic
singer who enjoyed a particularly strong relationship with fans.
But whereas Joe took things in his stride in 1980, Deep Purple
history was a wholly different proposition to Rainbow.
Increasingly frustrated with the ongoing and understandable
critical comparison with past so-called 'classic' line-ups, he dealt
with the situation in his typical (in other words, brutally honest)

way with an increasingly aggressive stance against what he saw as an often unfair and blind devotion to his predecessor.

For many fans, any Purple was better than none at all. But Joe's public dismissal of the group's recent efforts risked alienating even those who were prepared to concede to events and allow the new line-up a fair chance.

With the valuable commodity that is hindsight, any singer's recruitment (apart from maybe Coverdale's) was asking for trouble and the band's credibility nosedived with the hard-core fan following and simply caused confusion in the more general rock fan-base who identified the band with *Machine Head* or *Made In Japan*. With three-fifths of the band now formerly Rainbow, the elements of the sound developed circa 1983 bubbled to the surface once again. Although the two reunion albums thus far had indeed borrowed from the 1980s Rainbow sound honed by Blackmore with Glover's help, the finished product had been suitably 'Purple-ised' by Paice, Lord and – most importantly – Gillan. But with Joe fronting the band the creative forces at work were biased again towards a more soulfully melodic direction.

With the album ready for release on the band's new German-based label the launch party, complete with topless female wrestling, was held in Hamburg in October. During the initial month of promotion, back over in America, Glover and Turner did a Rockline Radio phone-in show on 19 November and performed an excellent acoustic version of 'King Of Dreams' live on air.

Undeterred by *Slaves And Masters*' decidedly lukewarm reception – it reached Number 45 in Britain, seven places below its predecessor, *Nobody's Perfect*, improving slightly in the States at Number 87 – the band sequestered themselves in Florida before Christmas to bring their live act up to scratch. The new year of 1991 saw them regroup in Thamesmead, South East London to rehearse for a tour that kicked off in February in Ostrava, Czechoslovakia – this very first show being filmed and broadcast by Czech TV – progressing through Europe and Scandinavia before a seven-date UK leg in March.

The tour had been due to start with four dates in Italy but these were cancelled, once again due to poor ticket sales. The band then took in the USA for a few dates, then Japan, Thailand, Singapore and South America before a return to Eastern Europe and Israel. This was no time to be touring with the first Gulf War still raging, and the troubled nature of the times was underlined when Iraq fired Scud missiles at Tel Aviv the night Purple had been due to play there.

Even so, several parts of the world had been played for the first time by the tour's end in September 1991. Any reservations more established markets had for this incarnation of the Deep Purple were not reflected by these newer areas where audiences, starved of seeing western rock music in the flesh for so long, embraced the Purple shows unreservedly.

The band had allowed Joe to review the band's back catalogue and choose the songs he wanted to do – 'Pictures Of Home' was one the singer stated he was keen to try. Ritchie however (and alas) had a veto on the set list, so the track unfortunately never got tried out. 'Fireball' and the new album's 'Too Much is Not Enough' were rehearsed for the tour but never performed. Ironically, the set was significantly revamped from the *Made In Japan* biased shows – something fans had wanted since the end of the *Perfect Strangers* tour. 'Burn' opened up the set and up to six *Slaves And Masters* songs were featured over the tour. Ever the improvisers, this time around snatches of standards like 'Hey Joe', 'Stand By Me', 'A Whiter Shade Of Pale', 'Tutti Frutti' and 'Yesterday' were included, often at Joe's initiation.

The optimistically titled 'Love Conquers All' entered the British singles charts in March, but would fail to improve on an initial Number 57 placing. As was to be expected, though, it was the States the Turner-fronted band had squarely in its sights, and 10 April saw them kick off the North American leg of the tour at Burlington, Vermont's Memorial Auditorium. But it was soon clear that not all was well within the camp, and just twelve days later the tour was aborted at Pittsburgh with fourteen US concerts remaining. Though many other rock acts had suffered poor ticket sales thanks to recession in the US markets, many thought it was a rejection of the band's current efforts.

The ongoing debate was never far below the surface, with the tour adding further fuel to the fires with critics zeroing in on Joe's struggle with some of the obligatory Purple standards such as 'Highway Star' – conveniently ignoring the fact that a lot of the newer material aired (even the mawkish 'Love Conquers All') did come over far better than many dared to hope for – and didn't Coverdale and Hughes struggle with 'Highway Star' too? As with the Bolin era the line-up had potential; the question was, would it ever realise it?

The reservations over album and concerts notwithstanding, other forces were at work to curse the future viability of the band. The growing Seattle grunge movement in the early 1990s spelled banishment to a commercial desert for many an AOR or 'big-hair' band. Thankfully Deep Purple's iconic status did mean they could carry on in some shape or form until musical tastes again found favour with their sound. But how long could they sustain things with a 'compromised' line-up?

11. The Prodigal's Return

The drop in sales and interest within the rock fraternity manifested an unease with the situation at BMG. Internally, the band's growing dissatisfaction over the lack of identity Joe Lynn Turner's efforts gave the group suggested his tenure with the band might be on borrowed time. Work started in November at Greg Rike studios in Florida on ideas for a new album. Things were a struggle, with an absence of cohesion during the early round of writing sessions. Turner complained: 'We'd come out with some great tracks and they'd all turn round and say "It's awful" ... Singing with those guys was a dream come true and a nightmare waiting to happen.'

While some material was recorded through January 1992, professional pride was swallowed and outside help proposed in the shape of Survivor's prolific songwriter Jim Peterik. This did not go down well with the rest of the band, particularly Glover, who saw his role in the creative process undermined.

Joe: 'We brought in Jim Peterik, and he was writing with us, and we had some really cool stuff! We had this one called "Lost In The Machine" – which was fuckin' heavy. We had another called "The Stroke Of Midnight", another called "Little Miss Promiscuous". We were just ripping it up with social statements, and all that kind of stuff. And we were sort of becoming like an angst band, but with a commercial attitude, and a lot of great music! But the other guys were just... "Oh – the twenty-fifth [anniversary] reunion, we can't survive without Ian Gillan." Roger felt pushed out, and sided with Jon and Ian.'

Roger recalled the songs in their rough form at this stage; 'I recall the titles "Just Don't Call It Love" and "Put Your Money Where Your Mouth Is" ... "Vicious Circle Of Friends" was a great idea never brought to fruition, I have a demo somewhere.' ('Little Miss Promiscuous' may have turned into 'Lick It Up', 'Stroke Of Midnight' may have became 'One Man's Meat', while 'Lost In

The Machine' became 'The Battle Rages On'.)

With the inevitable exception of Blackmore, the rest of the band were now of the unanimous opinion that Joe's style wasn't what they wanted. As Ian Paice later commented: 'He comes from an American pop background, and we've come from a European rock 'n' roll background.' Ritchie wanted yet another new singer in the band but for once was in the minority with the other members prepared to stand up for a Mark II re-reunion. Feelers were put out to Gillan's management early in the decade regarding a return.

Not that his return was exactly a foregone conclusion. After accepting the other three members' desire to sack Turner, Blackmore had set his heart on Riot singer Mike DiMeo, who would later reveal he was recruited to work on the album before Gillan's return. DiMeo: 'Ritchie Blackmore asked me to join Deep Purple! That's the stuff that I like to sing, you know. I was supposed to sing on *The Battle Rages On*. I had started to work on that record with Roger Glover. I only worked with them for about three months before BMG pulled the plug. They decided they wanted Ian Gillan to do the twenty-fifth anniversary. I have those same songs on a CD with me singing on them.'

Ten years later Roger Glover recalled the situation. 'Some time before 1993 Ritchie did want to try out a singer and he and I went into a studio in Norwalk, Connecticut to see what he sounded like. I wrote a few lyrics and he sang over the backing track to what would later be called "One Man's Meat". It was called "24 Hours" and, although it was okay, it wasn't too great. At least I wasn't convinced enough to pursue it any further. Ritchie really liked him, however. I don't know what was said between them. I never heard about him again, until now. I still have the tape somewhere, so there's no danger of it ever being released.'

Normally the likes of Jon Lord, by his own admission, had 'gone with the flow' but this time things were different and Blackmore received an ultimatum to accept Gillan back on board. After a great deal of persuasion (and a rumoured financial incentive) from the management, Blackmore decided to accept what was on offer.

As Joe explained: 'They wanted Ian Gillan back but there was no way Ritchie would agree to it… BMG eventually sat Ritchie down and persuaded him that bringing back Gillan would be a good idea… There was all this stuff by them at the time that I couldn't sing any more. Hey, call me an asshole, but don't say I can't sing…'

Blackmore recalled the situation somewhat more dispassionately: 'The rest of the band wanted Ian back in. I wanted to bring someone else in, but I was outvoted, so I said "I'll go along with that…" They needed a scapegoat and Joe was it.' Turner was told of his dismissal by Bruce Payne in August 1992 midway through the aforementioned sessions.

Roger Glover had been the one to broach the subject of recruiting Gillan and, a phone call later, the deal was under consideration. Given a few days and the inevitability of things Purple, Ian once again opened himself up to conflict and disharmony by rejoining.

The public reaction was one of both relief and cynicism. 1993 was the twenty-fifth anniversary of the band and it wasn't hard to see a lucrative tour and album would generate more interest, especially the bona fide Mark II line-up. Questions remained: how would Purple carry things off without imploding yet again; would Blackmore simply go through the motions; would the studio material improve given the tensions within?

Gillan put past protestations – 'I look at Purple as an ex-wife I made my mind up never to marry again' – to one side and prepared to rejoin the fray. But what he had been doing in those three years that constituted his 'lost weekend' away from the Purple pack was a salutary lesson that the outside world was no longer as welcoming to a singer nearing his fifties. The *Naked Thunder* album, whose release had attempted to steal Purple's thunder back in July 1990 was, in hindsight, a poor effort and – ironically given his demand for more progressive directions in his former outfit – a very AOR affair. Ian was no longer interested in the uneasy

democracy of a band. He was no longer one of the boys...
'I always enjoyed being in a band but the mechanics of running it weren't give and take, it was all take and it got to where frustration set in. I've had enough of all that band business after twenty-eight years.'

So Gillan called the shots on *Naked Thunder*, although delegating some authority to producer Leif Mases who'd just got a Grammy award for Jeff Beck's *Guitar Shop*, which he co-produced. Five of Ian's eleven non-Purple albums prior to this one had charted, so he had high hopes when he signed to the German Teldec record company. The album was released in Britain on EastWest, where his label-mates included Simply Red! Thankfully, the music had little in common with Mick Hucknall and his Mancunian soulsters.

Instead, Gillan had looked 30 miles down the East Lancs Road for his musical inspiration – and it came in the shape of guitarist Steve Morris, 'born and bred in Liverpool, a typical Scouser'. Having told his new boss he wrote songs and been invited to submit a demo tape, his effort was consigned to the bin when Ian gave up trying to open the securely taped envelope it arrived in! Road manager Graham Underwood rescued it from the garbage, and three of the four backing tracks it contained ended up on the new release with Gillan lyrics.

Morris was to claim a place in the touring band along with veteran keyboardist Tommy Eyre, who'd made his reputation in the Grease Band behind another great British rock voice, Joe Cocker. Peter Robinson (ex-Brand X) and Simon Phillips had added keyboards and drums respectively to the album, while guest appearances were made by Roger Glover and John Gustafson. What Glover thought of the picture sleeve of the single 'No Good Luck' is unknown, since it featured a parody of Purple's *Fireball* and *In Rock* cover designs. Gillan was picked out in gold, while his former colleagues looked rather the worse for wear...

As might be guessed from that display, Gillan would later confess he was still recovering from his ejection from Purple.

'I should have come out with all fists flying,' he admitted in his autobiography *Child In Time*, 'but I didn't want to be undignified nor appear to be in a corner. The first divorce [from Purple] had been bad enough, but at least I'd walked out... this time I'd been *thrown* out.' The single failed to chart.

It had been a difficult experience all round, playing demo tapes to a generation of record-company A&R men who might not even have been born when Ian's career had begun. *Naked Thunder* peaked at a modest Number 63. When it came down to it, Ian might be older, wiser, soulfully seasoned as a performer and more interesting as a songwriter, but so what? Fans, it seemed, would be happier to hear the kind of music he'd found fame with two decades ago. 'Yeah, *right!*' was his reaction. 'I'm gonna scream from the start to the finish of every song!'

The follow-up, however, proved one of Gillan's most enduring solo creations. No less a rock journalist than Chris Welch, the man who 'discovered' Cream, said of it that 'If *Toolbox* isn't a great success then maybe rock 'n' roll is really dead.' Retaining only Steve Morris from the previous album, Gillan recruited a rock-solid rhythm section of Californians Brett Bloomfield and Leonard Haze. The latter had achieved minor legend status drumming for Y&T, a US band *Kerrang!* magazine reckoned 'never achieved the success they deserved, but whose records remain very influential'. The producer was Chris Tsangarides ('Tangled hairdo', as Gillan inevitably dubbed him), whose track record included the likes of Gary Moore, Thin Lizzy and Tygers of Pan Tang.

Toolbox was intended to put Gillan back on track as a hard rocker and was launched at the Marquee Club in London where the man and his band played a showcase gig to launch the album in front of an audience including one-time Gillan guitarist Janick Gers (who had joined Iron Maiden the previous year). The tour that followed this album flew against the trend of a worldwide recession, visiting 27 countries from Australia and Japan through Lithuania to Brazil and Venezuela. It was, Gillan later reflected, one of the most enjoyable professional experiences in his three decades in the rock business. With just four musicians and as many crew, it was a far cry from the Deep Purple entourage of old – and, having produced an atypical if entertaining solo 'debut' in *Naked Thunder*, Ian had now rediscovered his hard-rocking stride.

Sales, though, were far from Purple proportions and discussions ensued as to what could be done about this. With a band he'd stake his life upon, Ian was about to renounce his hard-won solo act status and re-brand his group Repo Depo – a term coined by drummer Haze on surveying the devastated state of their rehearsal space. Even parting company with their European record label (*Toolbox* would not appear in North America until 1997) failed to dent enthusiasm. 'We were evolving into something a bit special,' Ian noted. 'We had total belief in ourselves, so we thought "Let's go for it".'

In terms of songwriting the man was on a roll – but four new tracks cut with a mobile studio in Gillan's backyard by the road-toughened outfit (with Dean Howard, late of 'China In Your Hand' chart-toppers T'Pau, now replacing Steve Morris) failed to excite the music-business ears to which they were aired. And though Gillan had once memorably stated 'I'd rather slit my throat than sing with that band again' the lure of Purple was ultimately too strong to resist.

As could have been predicted, Gillan's reinstatement during the summer of 1992 did little to restore the relationship between singer and the guitarist who'd proved his *bête noire* over so many years. Matters both musical and creative were at best strained, at worst downright hostile. Most of the backing tracks for *The Battle Rages On*, the first album from the reunion, had been done at Bearsville Studios in Woodstock, New York, while the final work was cut at Peter Maffay's studio in Germany and emerged in the following July. Gillan was required to write new lyrics and record the vocals over existing tracks in a relatively short space of time. From the outset, Blackmore was quick to comment that the original recordings done with Joe Lynn Turner were, in his opinion, superior. It was clear that he had lost all interest in Gillan's vocal style and, no matter what the public felt, was stuck in a situation he was not happy with.

A few years later Blackmore commented about the album: 'That was shaping up to being a good LP without the vocals – if you heard just the backing tracks they sounded really good. Then when the vocals got put on... we did two tracks with Joe, "Stroke Of Midnight" – you should hear that – and "Lonely For You", an excellent song. It would have been a Number 1 had it been released; so catchy, Joe sang it, it was brilliant. I thought: "We've got to do this; if we take on Gillan we've got to do this song." Do it exactly the same.

'But I spoke to management: "Does Gillan realise that he has to sing that one song exactly like this?" Because I knew he was going to be a headache. "Oh yes, he knows all about it." I said: "Great, okay, that's one of the conditions of him joining Purple again." He didn't know anything about it when I spoke to him. I saw him in the studio: "Ian, do you know about doing this 'Lonely For You' song?" "No." "Bruce Payne didn't tell you that I wanted you to do that song with exactly the same melody?" He didn't know anything about it. That didn't help matters. That wasn't Gillan's fault, it was the management.'

The two songs in question ended up on the album as 'Time To Kill' and 'One Man's Meat'. With the backing tracks already laid down, there was little reason for Gillan and Blackmore to come into contact on a regular basis in the studio. Blackmore, his work done, was off and Gillan was left alongside Glover to work on the vocals and lyrics.

When the resulting album, aptly named *The Battle Rages On*, was released in July 1993, it was widely acclaimed as Deep Purple recapturing the sound of the early 1970s, brought up to date with a modern production. Despite the obvious frictions it was evident that here was a band still able to produce great music. The question would be, when the band hit the road, could it work live?

On tour, the increasingly angry Blackmore seemed determined to blow the rest of the band off stage – and succeeded on several occasions. The venture, celebrating twenty-five years of Deep Purple, was always going to be marred by in-fighting. Even before the tour had started, both Gillan and Blackmore had agreed to be interviewed (separately) by Swedish journalist Anders Tegner for his TV show *Metall Magasinet*. Both played up to the general belief that no love was lost between them and made it clear how they felt about one another. As is so often the case with Blackmore, his comments were tongue-in-cheek when he told Tegner that he wanted to beat Ian Gillan up. 'He's bigger than me so maybe I'll get some friends, maybe Swedish and we will beat him up. But he won't know it's me!'

Gillan's comments seemed more spiteful. 'He's an intellectual dwarf. I didn't say that,' Gillan repeated three times before saying, 'Yes I did.' Blackmore hinted at why he thought Gillan was back in the band when he said, 'I think it's money. I think Ian needed some money so we said okay let's do it.' The lure of extra cash in the guitarist's bank account, of course, appeared to have influenced the decision as well.

Blackmore was certainly aware of the musical chemistry the band was capable of when he spoke to *Rock World* magazine in 1993: 'Although none of us will ever be the best of friends off stage, it's an explosive gelling of individuals which hits the button on stage and record.'

The world tour got off to a rocky start with the cancellation of the proposed US leg. At this point in time, the American audience for rock music, not just for Purple but for pre-grunge bands in general, appeared to be dwindling and poor ticket sales forced the curtailment of the tour, leaving Europe and Japan the only dates. Even the proposed start of the European leg had a setback with the first date in Turkey being cancelled due to the political situation, which in turn meant Greek shows were abandoned.

On 21 September, Blackmore, Gillan, Glover, Lord and Paice convened in Bregenz, Austria for rehearsals, and MTV was there to film it. Prior to this the band had maintained a defiantly low profile, refusing to do a video and even denying photographers a group session. All the press got was a jigsaw with cartoon drawings of the group! UK tabloid the *News Of The World* responded by blowing the friction out of all proportion with an article headlined 'Deep Hatred'. In Bregenz, Roger Glover, the eternal optimist, had suggested to MTV the tour 'would go a long way to cementing the good feeling within the band again'. How wrong he would turn out to be.

All in all there were to be only thirty-seven shows. After a full run-through the day before at the Palaghiaccio in Rome, the Twenty Fifth Anniversary Tour finally got under way. It didn't take long for news to filter back to fans around the world that the friction between Gillan and Blackmore was making itself known on stage. On previous tours the guitar/vocal duet section of 'Strange Kind Of Woman', the Italian encore number, had often turned into an impromptu performance of 'Jesus Christ Superstar', as sung by Gillan on the original movie soundtrack. Now, every time Gillan started to sing it, Blackmore completely ignored him and refused to play the tune. Not surprisingly it was dropped from the show as the band moved through the rest of Europe.

Elsewhere though, friction boosted the level of performance, with Blackmore as ever the catalyst. His natural gift for improvisation and the unpredictable took the shows to heights not seen or heard since the halcyon days of the early 1970s, giving the lie to those critics who'd suggested the band had rested on their laurels after the initial bout of reunion touring, and were going through the motions.

The whole band seemed to be feeding off the improvisation and passion Blackmore was showing. Jon Lord in particular was playing with more commitment and desire than on previous tours. As he said shortly afterwards, 'The shows were done at an energy level and ability level I've rarely seen attained before. I think we played as well as we've ever played.'

Although the set list didn't deviate, except for occasional changes in the encores, Blackmore would often throw in brief renditions of various pieces from Purple's past along with classical themes. At some shows, riffs from 'Rat Bat Blue', 'The Mule' or 'Wring That Neck' would be thrown in; at other times Blackmore would start to play an old classical favourite, Grieg's 'In The Hall Of The Mountain King'. On a couple of occasions the whole band joined in for a couple of minutes before getting back on track.

Yet insiders felt the likelihood of the scheduled sixty-nine dates of the tour ending as planned in Osaka – with its *Made In Japan* associations – in early December was debatable. A fortnight of shows in Germany prior to the UK dates saw the tension between Blackmore and Gillan escalate when the guitarist instructed his assistant Rob Fodder to attach the lyrics to a particular song to Gillan's mic stand. Ritchie was allegedly fed up with Gillan forgetting the lyrics, as Fodder recalled. 'In the dressing room before the Cologne show, Ritchie asked me if I knew the words to "The Battle Rages On", which I did, and told me to write them out on sheets of A4 [paper] which we taped together. My instructions were to tape them to Gillan's mic stand just as the lights went down and the intro tape started. Gillan walked out, noticed the lyrics, tore them from the stand and threw them away. He didn't look too impressed!

'During this show I noticed that Gillan would stand in front of Ritchie and jump up and down as he was soloing. However, Gillan hadn't noticed that Ritchie had switched his guitar in "Smoke On The Water" and proceeded to trash it within inches of Gillan's feet, causing Ian to jump out of the way…'

The best shows were Munich and Stuttgart, both recorded for a proposed live album. At Munich the whole band was really on top form, and after the show Roger Glover said; 'We always know if it's going to be a good show, when Paicey starts the intro to "Highway Star" and Ritchie starts doodling over the top of it.' As ever, Blackmore the catalyst was pushing the band on. At the last German show in Stuttgart his improvised solo in 'Anya' defied description and, as the song finally concluded nearly quarter of an hour later, the whole band stood applauding, something never seen before or since.

As the tour continued around Europe the performances continued to get the thumbs-up from fans and press alike. But Blackmore's dissatisfaction at Gillan forgetting the lyrics and the quality of his voice was becoming increasingly difficult for him to conceal. By the time the band arrived in Prague he had decided enough was enough and, after the gig, he told his assistant he was leaving the band.

Tour manager Colin Hart had the job of telling the news to the others, who had convened in the bar area. As Hart relayed Blackmore's decision to quit at the end of the European tour, there was a stony silence. Roger Glover's belief that the tour would go a long way to patch up differences had clearly been misplaced. It was testimony to the professionalism of the musicians involved that the next show in Poland was at the same high level that the tour had already produced.

Deep Purple then moved on to Holland before the long-awaited return to their homeland. During the final number of the Rotterdam show, the inevitable 'Smoke On The Water', Gillan continued singing during the guitar solo. When it came to the sing-along towards the end, with Gillan encouraging the audience to join in, Blackmore went to the front of the stage and proceeded to play his bass pedals loudly and discordantly. At this point Gillan took hold of his mic stand and gestured as if to throw it at Blackmore.

This particular act of petulance from both parties can probably be attributed to an incident earlier that day, when Ritchie had found out that the Japanese promoter had not been informed that the guitarist would not be performing and that the management seemed prepared to still sell tickets on the pretence that Blackmore was going. He tore out the Japanese work permit from his passport to show there was no going back, then phoned the promoter personally, apologised that he wouldn't be going and told him the news.

By the time of the first UK show, although no-one was publicly aware that Blackmore would be finishing with the band at the end of the European tour, news of the conflict between guitarist and singer left many UK fans wondering if they could really cut it on stage. The second of two Brixton shows saw Ritchie severely damage his ankle after slipping on stage during 'Highway Star'. A doctor was called before the following gig and advised that they should cancel, but the final UK show at the NEC in Birmingham went ahead as planned – just as well, as it was to be filmed for possible video release. Blackmore, however, had been in favour of filming one of the earlier shows in Germany where, in his view, Gillan's voice would have been in better shape.

The film company insisted that Birmingham was their favoured venue and Blackmore consented on the understanding that no cameras would be allowed on stage. After the house lights dimmed, Ian Paice's familiar drumbeat heralded the beginning of 'Highway Star'. Something seemed afoot as the intro continued for longer than normal, then after a while it was apparent Blackmore was not to be seen. Eventually the other four decided to launch into the number. Blackmore eventually appeared on stage but, during his solo, picked up a glass of water from atop the keyboards and hurled it at a camera stage right. As Gillan was just in front of the camera, merrily banging away at his congas, it appeared to be aimed at him but Blackmore's accuracy ensured the cameraman got a soaking. He continued to wander on and off stage during the opening two numbers and subsequently appeared less than interested.

To this day, Blackmore insists 'The incident was in no way directed towards any member of the band; certainly not towards the audience. I had already made my mind up to leave Deep Purple for reasons of my own; I was told by my management at the time that [record company] BMG wanted to film the show at the NEC. I agreed to this providing there would be no cameramen on the side of the stage… As the intro to "Highway Star" started I walked out only to trip over one right in my way. I pushed him off the stage he should never have been on in the first place… It is a very nerve-wracking experience to play a show like this; I feel I have earned the right to have a set-up which will enable me to give my best to everybody.'

Stories abound that the rest of the band believed Blackmore manufactured the situation as he had just been handed a solo contract. Whatever the truth, it was after this show that the news was leaked of Blackmore's imminent departure, though Gillan had allegedly relayed the story to someone else by saying the guitarist had been sacked.

The tour concluded with four shows in Scandinavia, all continuing the previous high standard. A particularly aggressive performance was witnessed at the penultimate gig in Oslo and, at the end of 'Smoke On The Water', Blackmore trashed his guitar for the last time and left it to reverberate as the band left the stage. After the final show in Helsinki he stayed on stage for a little while longer than normal to shake hands with the first row and then it was back to the hotel. They all knew the end of an era had come but only Ian Paice, forever the diplomat, went up to Ritchie to say goodbye, saying something along the lines of 'I think you are making a mistake but I wish you all the best anyway.'

While neither Gillan nor Blackmore look back upon their last stage stand with any great fondness, many fans look back on this tour as one of the greatest the band ever did. Ritchie Blackmore bowed out of Deep Purple in some style, leaving them in greater shape than for many years. Since his departure the battle still rages on, with fans divided between those who feel the band continued firing on all cylinders and those who believe Blackmore's departure took away the very spirit of Deep Purple.

With Ritchie's volatile performances pushing the others on, fans had witnessed some of the best concerts Blackmore and Purple had been involved with since the original reunion. Indeed, there is an argument that those thirty-seven shows were a pinnacle of Deep Purple and Ritchie Blackmore's career.

'The spirit was barely fluttering and we knew there was no future with him, so he did us all a favour by leaving,' commented Gillan, who was understandably pleased by subsequent events. 'There were all these power games going on... we were spending all our energy resisting someone who was becoming a megalomaniac. You try to conceal it like some family row for the sake of the kids, but at the end of the day it's like realising you're no longer in love with someone you married years ago. Also the style he wanted to take us in was so limiting. We were going down the tubes.'

Since the whole band except Gillan had signed to the BMG label as individual artists in the late 1980s, Blackmore was able to take up his option to pursue a solo project – though the label insisted this be named Rainbow, against Ritchie's wishes: 'I wanted to call it Moon, after my grandfather's surname, but the record company said it has to be called Rainbow for sales... you know what record companies are like.'

Having tentatively contacted Joe Lynn Turner to serve again as frontman for the band – 'I didn't really think he was serious and said yes. We had such big problems before that I didn't mean it' – he took on unknown Scotsman Dougie White, but this Rainbow line-up would produce only *Stranger In Us All* before the guitarist underwent a dramatic change of musical tack and went 'unplugged', teaming up with his girlfriend, Candice Night, for the Renaissance inspired Blackmore's Night. But what of the band he left behind?

Financially, cancelling the Japanese tour wasn't really an option, and initially Purple approached former UFO guitarist Michael Schenker. 'After Blackmore left Deep Purple, I was asked to join. I turned the offer down, because I didn't want to play other people's solos.' If playing lead guitar with Deep Purple represented a dream job for thousands of would-be superstar axemen, the task of filling the shoes of the Man in Black was certainly not. After all, the only man to have done it on a full-time basis was no longer around...

Yet this didn't stop Purple from going for a third American (if you count Randy California) in the shape of Joe Satriani. Not that this was ever considered more than a stop-gap measure: the fleet-fingered Satch was clearly on a steep upward career curve, and his spell in Purple, which began in November 1993, could only be a diversion.

'He helped us to finish off the tour when Blackmore quit,' said Gillan, 'and was with us a year. He was note-perfect after a day's rehearsal – a thorough professional and a great guitar player. I remember him saying to me, "Gee, I'm gonna play 'Smoke On The Water' with Deep Purple." I didn't realise how much it meant to him.' Roger Glover was equally happy: 'We needed someone who could learn our stuff fast and who was also acceptable to our Japanese promoters and the audience. Satriani was the right man in the right place.' He also added, willingly, 'It was a delight to perform without a black cloud on stage.' Glover's comment was slightly disingenuous; in truth, Japanese promoter Mr Udo insisted on a heavyweight name to ensure the tour wasn't a financial disaster and it was he, along with Bruce Payne, who suggested Satriani was drafted in.

New Yorker Satriani was born in 1956, and was strongly influenced in his formative guitar-playing years by the late-1960s British blues rock of Clapton, Beck and Page. In 1974 he took tuition from jazz guitarist Billy Baurer and keyboardist Lenny Tristano, and four years later was teaching guitar in California: students included Steve Vai, Metallica's Kirk Hammett and Counting Crows' Dave Bryson.

After spells with pop bands the Squared and the Greg Kihn Band, he came of age in 1986 with his first full-length album, *Surfing*, on the US Relativity label. Mick Jagger, no less, invited him to tour with him in 1988, while that year's Grammy-nominated *Dreaming No 11* EP and 1989's *Flying In A Blue Dream* kept him in an ever-increasing spotlight. Guesting with Alice Cooper and Spinal Tap, he continued his career with *The Extremist*, a US Top 30/UK Top 20 entry in late 1992, while a double 'odds and ends' compilation, *Time Machine*, would do almost as well a year later. This was a man going places.

Nevertheless, he was enough of a Purple fan to fly out to Tokyo at less than a week's notice for a single afternoon of rehearsal. 'They were so great to play with. So easy to play with and so much fun to be around that I really wanted to do it some more but

I really couldn't be in the band. At the time I was in the middle of promoting the *Time Machine* album, so eventually what happened was that I went on my own tour again for a couple of months and met with them in Europe. We toured in Europe for two months in the early summer of, I guess that was '94.'

With Blackmore having left the band at such short notice, the Japanese promoters had no option but to place adverts in the press explaining the situation with the current band members listed, a photo of Satriani and the comment, 'due to Ritchie Blackmore's resignation from Deep Purple, the show will be performed by the above line-up.' It also explained that those who had already purchased tickets were entitled to a refund if they so wished and, in a land where Blackmore has Clapton-like status, approximately 2,500 did.

The one person, predictably, most happy with the outcome was Purple's vocalist. 'When we finally parted from Ritchie, it was like a divorce,' Gillan commented in 1995. 'Things had been going very badly. We were in a deep trough. With a divorce you feel a wrench, a sense of relief and then you don't know what to do. So Ritchie went and everyone felt very low. These guys are fantastic musicians, but they were playing like journeymen at the time. Then it all started picking up.'

12. Morse Dancer

If some were disappointed that the Mark II line-up would not be performing, Japananese Purple connoisseurs were beside themselves: the set list on the tour was the most imaginative the band had performed since the reunion. It was also galling for the European fans to discover it was the set they would have played in Europe had Blackmore not refused to play some of the tracks. The full set list was: 'Highway Star', 'Ramshackle Man', 'Black Night', 'Maybe I'm A Leo', 'Twist In The Tale', 'Perfect Strangers', 'Pictures Of Home', 'Knocking At Your Back Door', 'Anyone's Daughter', 'Child In Time', 'Anya', 'The Battle Rages On', 'When A Blind Man Cries', 'Lazy' and 'Space Truckin'', with encores of 'Hush', 'Speed King' and 'Smoke On The Water'. Perhaps mindful of the fact that the tour with Satriani would be a short-lived affair, BMG made the decision to record the show at Tokyo's Budokan, but this has not seen the light of day and may never be released.

The American guitar virtuoso was at pains to mention to journalists who asked the endless question that he was celebrating the legacy of Deep Purple with the audience while up on stage rather than 'stealing Ritchie Blackmore's gig... I had no intention of staying but these guys needed a guitar player now and they are in the process of weaning themselves off of Ritchie Blackmore and finding a new permanent member.

'We mutually benefited from the association and I really enjoyed playing. Half of the songs I really stuck to Ritchie's blueprint but there were other songs where he clearly, from the tapes that I had, turned his back on the recorded performances and was trying to do different things every night. I took the cue from that and from what the band liked – maybe two-thirds of the material [was] reinvented.' Certain other songs, like the inevitable 'Smoke', remained faithful to the recorded versions.

The Japanese tour had been so enjoyable for the band that all concerned decided to carry on, with a full-length European tour scheduled for the following year, kicking off in Holland on 27 May. Just prior to the tour, Satriani spoke to German magazine *Metal Star* and recalled the moment he was called up for the job: 'Bruce Payne and Mr Udo came up with the idea and rang up my management. I asked for a few days to think it over. I thought it was quite a dramatic thing for Purple fans. But after an hour I called back and accepted. I was worried they might have changed their minds!'

When asked how long he intended to stay in the band he replied, 'I'd like to stay forever! But we have a strange situation with contracts and record deals. It's very complicated. But if what Roger says is true then the band wants me to stay. It's my greatest wish. We would all like to forget the past and discover something new.'

The European tour stuck with the same set that had been employed in Japan, with the added bonus of 'Fireball', not played since 1972. Despite a couple of the German dates being cancelled due to their close proximity to other gigs that adversely affected sales, the tour was successful enough for the band to realise Deep Purple still had a future – even though some fans had clearly decided that a band without Blackmore wasn't to their liking. Spain, a country where Satriani's status was extremely high, received the 'new' line-up very well.

The parting of the ways came with two dates in New Zealand which had been booked for October. Although Joe Satriani had helped the band get out of a sticky situation, his commitment to his own career affected future plans. He was required to record a solo album around the time of the New Zealand gigs, and furthermore it was reported that his contract restricted him from playing with Purple in America. The band had no option but to seek a permanent replacement.

(Though that was the end of the association, a brief reunion took place on 30 July 2002 when Joe rejoined Purple on stage at the Hilton Amphitheatre in Reno, Nevada. They performed 'Smoke

On The Water', 'Hush', 'Highway Star' and a lengthy guitar jam.)

When the time came to replace Satriani, the remaining four members of 'classic Purple' at least had the luxury of time. They decided to write their own personal Top 10 guitarists as a 'wish list' from which to select. In the end, the man they came up with selected himself by being the only individual to appear on all four lists. Step forward Steve Morse... another American.

This was a name that would mean something to only a proportion of Purple's following – unless that was they were guitarists themselves. *Guitar Player* magazine's readers had voted him their top pick for five years running between 1982 and 1986 before the inevitable request came to 'retire' and give the also-rans a sporting chance. This path had been followed before by Yes's Steve Howe and then Eric Johnson, so Morse could claim to be in good company.

Born in Hamilton, Ohio on 28 June 1954, Steve Morse had studied classical and jazz guitar at Miami University before forming his own band, Dixie Dregs, in 1975, with bass-player Andy West (the pair had studied together and played in an earlier band, Dixie Grits). Neither they nor Kansas, with whom Steve spent a late-1980s spell, could really be classed as Premier League outfits, but the Dregs in particular had a higher than average proportion of musos in their fan following thanks to their eclectic mixture of jazz, rock, classical and even bluegrass.

They also contained another higher-profile player in their midst in the shape of future Winger drummer Rod Morganstein, while anyone who'd tuned in to Radio 1's *Friday Rock Show* under the aegis of Purple pal Tommy Vance would have recognised the theme tune 'Take It Off The Top', even if they'd be hard-pressed to identify who played it.

In 1983 he formed the Steve Morse Band before his Kansas stretch, which resulted in appearances on two albums, *Power* (1986) and *In The Spirit Of Things* (1988), but by this time the band were definitely on a decline from the commercial heights scaled by the likes of hit single 'Carry On Wayward Son' and US

Top 5 album *Leftoverture* in 1976–1977.

Unusually, Morse had taken a step back from music, which had been his life since childhood, to indulge another long-held ambition – to be an airline pilot. Talking to journalist Anil Prasad in 1992, he explained he enjoyed the contrast with rock-band touring. 'Being a pilot was neat because you have regularity about your work and you have a chance of doing your job in a very finite and finished way. When you're done, you're done. But on tour you spend the day flying and get off the plane and then go to soundcheck, do an interview, a clinic, and hurry up and check in the hotel and take a shower, and go to the gig and take care of business after the gig and work out your time for the next day, get something to eat, and go back and sleep for a few hours and get woken up and go do it again!'

He'd found the flying job challenging and enjoyed being part of a team – 'You have another pilot you have to work with, so, if you miss something, he'll catch it' – but ultimately missed the creative aspect of music and having total control over his career. 'But I do fly in my music job too, so it's a nice compromise.'

Morse had never seen the band live before he received his invitation, and took his seat at a Purple/Satriani show admitting he didn't know what to expect. 'I was prepared to be a little disappointed, but the biggest shock to me was how comfortable and focused they still are. My experience,' he said with his recent stint in Kansas quite possibly in mind, 'is that once people peak they start going the other way. I'm sure the guys don't like me saying I was surprised at how good they were, but I was!'

The feeling was, needless to say, entirely mutual. 'Playing with Steve we've been tremendously relaxed and it's been much easier to express ourselves,' said Gillan, who included Dixie Dregs albums in his personal collection. He didn't see any problem in Morse's jazzy background, pointing out that 'Ian Paice comes from the Buddy Rich school of music, Jon's roots are in classical, jazz and blues, Roger's a hippy so he doesn't count and Ritchie was into the Nashville thing. And I was rock 'n' roll and blues.

Steve grew up with bluegrass in his veins.'

The same question was asked at a Moscow press conference, at which Morse ably conducted his own defence. 'Firstly, nobody told me I could only be good at one thing. And second, yes, it's true – I have played with some of the greatest living jazz musicians. But I've never played with musicians as good as Deep Purple. I have to work at my absolute peak to keep up with these guys.'

The first test for the band and their new member would have been the previously mentioned New Zealand shows, but with around 4,000 tickets having been sold for each, while one of the venues had a capacity of 13,000, the promoter apparently opted to pull the dates. Morse's initiation would be a four-night mini-tour of Mexico in November 1994: the chemistry proved immediate and it was to prove a permanent bond.

The only sticking point for Morse, a recent father, was the absences from home and his son, who was aged three when he joined the ranks. With other band members' progeny in their more independent teenage years, he was keen to ensure he had adequate quality time with his offspring. 'By the end of the first tour I was freaking out,' he candidly admitted to *Classic Rock*'s Dave Ling in 2001. 'I was so comfortable being in Deep Purple but I realised that I couldn't do it. I was missing out on a magical age. But we sat down and talked about it and, while there are still times when I'm counting the days when a tour's been going on for too long, it's been fixed.'

Gillan claimed Morse 'was the only name on our list, the only phone call we ever made. The music was always going to work, we felt good about that, but it was just a question of personal chemistry, because you don't want to commit yourself for a long period of time to somebody you don't like very much. It went beautifully, we did a few shows off the beaten track and we all seemed to get on very well. Yes, he's American, but having said that don't read the wrong thing here – he's got a great sense of humour and he's extremely intelligent.'

The key relationship was not between singer and guitarist, however, but between the newcomer and keyboardist Lord. The initial spark between Jon and Ritchie Blackmore had been a feature of 1970s Purple which, Gillan explained, had been long dormant: 'When it came to jamming Ritchie would never follow Jon so that's the difference between then and now.' Morse described his new instrumental sparring partner as 'a genuine improviser and a natural born musician with great poise. He's a pleasure to work with.' He was also impressed that Ian Paice would pick up on his riffs and answer them with drum patterns. 'He can read what I'm trying to do,' he revealed, explaining that, while many lesser musicians had to hear something over and over before they discerned a pattern, 'Ian gets it instantly.'

Morse was also happy to share the visual load with frontman Gillan, who encouraged him thus: 'Hey, I want you up the front here with me. Let's go play.' Thus the blue Music Man guitar would become as prominent as the Blackmore Strat had been in earlier years. He also had an immediate impact on the repertoire, requesting the return of 'Hush' and 'When A Blind Man Cries'.

This historical reassessment met with Ian Gillan's full approval. 'I was frustrated with the band when I joined them because I thought "Hush" was brilliant. But the rest of the band hated it because to them it represented an era they wanted to put behind them. The "bouffant hair-do" era. All those hits – "Hush", "Kentucky Woman", "River Deep Mountain High" – they wanted nothing to do with. But when Steve joined the band he said "Man, you're crazy, you've got to play 'Hush' – it's brilliant." There was resistance from four of us, including me, but it turned around and I love it.'

Did Purple now intend to reach out to new converts as well as 'old stagers'? 'Our old audience grew up and moved on,' Gillan conceded in 2001, 'but there was a turning point about ten years ago when a new crowd came through. We noticed this after Ritchie left and we got young kids in. That's probably because Steve Morse is a handsome-looking young guy. Well, he's a kid to us!

People could relate to him and also people had got fed up with techno and sampling. They wanted to hear some "live" music. Now we are getting some amazing audiences. So we're very excited about the future. The honeymoon is over now. Steve is a full member, even though he still calls himself the new boy. We care about him and listen to what he has to say.'

The challenge for Morse, as with anyone following in famous footsteps, was how to keep the balance between integration and innovation. New material might offer a blank page, but riffs like 'Smoke On The Water' were definitely not to be messed with. People wanted to hear what they knew, a fact Morse was more than aware of. 'I'm a fan, and play the songs like a fan,' he told Dave Ling. 'I mix a little bit of Ritchie's sound with my own style but I can't really cop much of his because the best thing about Ritchie is that he's unique.' The success of his softly, softly approach came the fact that he claimed, in 2001, to have suffered only two verbal assaults from the audience in seven years. And that's a total unlikely to have been added to as Purple fans took him to their hearts.

While most fans warmed to the American immediately, it took longer for Steve Morse to be represented on disc, the chance finally coming on 1996's *Purpendicular*. Its Number 58 UK chart position, achieved that February, was a considerable disappointment after the showing of the last Purple album with Blackmore, *The Battle Rages On*, which had peaked at Number 21 in August 1993. (*Purpendicular* also became the band's first LP to totally miss out on the US Top 200.)

Press reviews were, as was by now expected, poor: *Melody Maker*, once the muso's bible but now in its last throes, was particularly bilious in its condemnation. '*Purpendicular* is, hold onto a chair and prepare to be flabbergasted, fucking rubbish. It's almost impossible to give the songs on this album a fair hearing because none of them are bearable for more than about a minute. An aural, indigestion-inducing farrago of twiddling twaddle...'

Frontiers magazine, however, went in entirely the opposite direction, as would be expected for a specialist progressive rock magazine. 'If you'd told me a year ago that Ritchie Blackmore's departure could actually save the legend of Deep Purple I'd have told you to have a long lie-down. Now I suspect Messrs Gillan, Glover Lord and Paice are kicking themselves he didn't walk a damn sight earlier.' It has to be said that *Frontiers* was in a minority, and a minority of one, in its conclusion that this was 'arguably the finest album Deep Purple have ever made'.

Not surprisingly perhaps, given the mixed and often heated reaction, another two and a half years would elapse before the result of a studio session was again released. As ever, though, live material from an earlier era was to prove plentiful, and this would lead to Steve Morse making the decision during the *Purpendicular* tour not to sign bootlegs. The seeds of an idea were sown by Simon Robinson of DPAS when he suggested that the band should consider letting limited edition CDs be available of selected live gigs, and one in Paris was considered for possible wider consumption.

This reached the racks relatively rapidly in the shape of *Live At The Olympia*, a double set released in June 1997. Purple had been augmented by a brass section for two *Purpendicular* numbers, 'Cascades' and 'Purpendicular Waltz', a sign that they were relaxed enough in their new incarnation to experiment a little and deviate from the accepted formula. This was, indeed, typical of the studio album's ambience, aligning it with *Fireball* as something different.

The vehemence of the anti-*Purpendicular* feeling was probably partly explained by the fact that there were die-hards who still insisted that, without Ritchie Blackmore, this could not be the 'real' Deep Purple. They contrasted the recently reunited Robert Plant and Jimmy Page, who had made a point of not resurrecting the Led Zeppelin name. 'I think if one guy's out of the band you can get away with it,' said Gillan comparing the two outfits, 'you can probably do it – don't forget there were only four of them anyway. The absence of fifty per cent, its really in your conscience and in your heart and if your really believe you've captured the spirit of the band then I think you're probably entitled to do so. If you're trying to do something else under the umbrella of the band, with eighty per cent of the band I think you're on fairly safe ground. Mind you there's an awful lot of bands around with only one or two members in!'

The *Purpendicular* tour began on 15 February 1996 at the Plymouth Pavilions, two days after the album entered the UK listing at what would prove to be its peak position. (Their failure to penetrate the Top 50 was compensated for by a Number 1 rating on *Kerrang!* magazine's influential chart.) The UK leg climaxed with a pair of dates at Brixton's Academy on 8 and 9 March.

Purple found themselves in huge demand worldwide, not least in countries that had rarely figured on the rock 'n' roll map. Many were former Iron Curtain countries where tours would have been impossible before the fall of the Berlin Wall in 1989, while India was another rock-starved territory where Purple were received like royalty. 'It was a fabulous surprise,' admitted Roger Glover, while Jon Lord advised local bands not to try to be famous but 'try to be good… it requires an enormous amount of energy trying to be famous!'

July saw Purple fulfil an invitation to the prestigious Montreux Jazz Festival, which they first played back in 1969, while fireworks were seen at Toronto's Warehouse in November where a sell-out crowd witnessed the start of the US leg of the tour. Most exciting of all was a first visit to South America in early 1997, where the band's classic rock status saw them well received in Argentina, Bolivia, Brazil and Peru: a summer season in Europe playing the festivals preceded a US tour in the autumn that followed an increasingly popular pattern of playing a series of venues known as House of Blues.

Gillan would look back at *Purpendicular* as 'a springboard in the way *Fireball* was to *Machine Head:* it laid some foundations.' He felt it was logical that the new man would 'take some time to pick up the etiquette, the smoking rules of the office.' He rebutted accusations that Purple's past had given rise to unreasonable expectations. 'Ten years on you can judge by how many of the songs are still in the set,' he insisted. 'Basically, we look on albums as demos for the next tour.' He pointed to *Perfect Strangers* as a 'new' classic, as fans were now measuring the new material up against it. 'Only when time's passed can you judge these things.'

With *In Rock* having hit its silver anniversary in 1995, a series of remastered CDs began, overseen by Roger Glover, that would result in *Fireball*, *Machine Head* and *Burn* following it back into the racks in superior form with studio chart, outtakes and, often, contemporary mixes. Reissues and compilations had traditionally been the bane of Purple's life, their new music having to compete with the classics of the past, but at least this way they had some control over what was being reissued.

Next up for the current band would be *Abandon*, their second post-Blackmore studio effort. Its recording in the States followed the same pattern as its predecessor but this time, with Steve Morse fully integrated, the songs came much more easily. The presence of a remake of *In Rock* classic 'Bloodsucker' was no indication that the fire had burned out, more recognition of the song's reception when reintroduced to the live set. Several of the new songs had been road-tested too, another return to the practice of old – though clearly risking playing into the hands of bootleggers. (That issue was soon addressed with a twenty-four-CD set, issued in two halves, that documented the band's live evolution from 1984 to 2000, but with emphasis on the post-Blackmore era.)

On *Abandon*'s very first cut, 'Any Fule Kno That', Gillan bemoaned the fact that, 'for the last twenty years the music business has been looking up their own backside! It's all media-driven now,' he lamented. 'The writing was on the wall years ago – so we wrote a song about it and sent them the lyrics!' There were, however, signs that the band had been keeping an ear to musical trends in the distinctly modern stylings of 'Watching The Sky'.

Promoting the album after its May 1998 release put the band back on the road for the usual incessant touring. But the superficially exciting concept of teaming Purple with the reactivated Emerson Lake and Palmer to recreate the bill of 1974's legendary California Jam (albeit played by the Mark III line-up) was fated to fail. A three-week summer tour was so poorly supported that ELP had split again by the year's end, the addition of young US progressives Dream Theater seemingly doing nothing to boost ticket sales.

Not that this stopped Purple circling the globe in time-honoured fashion from June 1998 to July the following year, a Yuletide break the only scheduled respite. There had been much turbulent water under the bridge, but Gillan was singing with all his old energy and enthusiasm. The band went back to Santiago, Chile where there had been an accident the year before on the *Purpendicular* tour. A lighting rig had collapsed and they'd had to play without PA in a darkened stadium. They also went to the Lebanon, which Ian hadn't visited since 1967 when he was in Episode Six. Everywhere Purple went, they were greeted by younger audiences seeing the band for the first time.

Somehow Jon Lord, the man traditionally responsible for Purple's classical collaborations, had managed to release a rare solo album, *Pictured Within*, in 1998 and even found time to tour it in continental Europe the following year with the help of vocalist Sam Brown and others.

He found this re-ignited his appetite for that side of his musical repertoire, with the result that much of 1999 was taken up with Purple revisiting their legendary *Concerto For Group And Orchestra*, first performed thirty years earlier. The loss of the musical score had precluded any repeat performance of the piece – a venture suggested on the twentieth anniversary in 1989 – but Purple fan and budding composer Marco De Goeij had meanwhile completed the daunting task of recompiling the score from video footage and sound recordings. The young Dutchman accosted Lord in Rotterdam in February that year, blurting: 'It's about your

Concerto – I think I've managed to create it!' Though only the first movement was complete, Lord was overtaken by the enthusiasm De Goeij showed and willingly helped him complete the restoration work.

The Royal Albert Hall was booked for two repeat presentations on 25 and 26 September 1999, and these were recorded for a double CD (and later DVD) entitled, *Deep Purple In Concert With The London Symphony Orchestra*. Interestingly, these appeared not on EMI, who had released the last two albums, but Eagle. 'EMI didn't want to do the Orchestral thing,' sniffed Gillan in 2001. 'They didn't think it would sell. It turned out to be out biggest-selling [Deep Purple] album in years, platinum discs all over the world.'

Indeed, such was the success of the concerts and the subsequent multimedia releases that a complete change of plan was called for. As Purple entered the twenty-first century, they decided to put a scheduled new studio album on hold, choosing instead to take the *Concerto* to audiences around the world. And even Gillan, who had been notoriously sceptical about the project in its infancy, enjoyed the challenge of recreating this historic piece. Playing the anniversary shows on home turf in London was one thing. Taking it on the road was quite different, with a whole new set of challenges and responsibilities. Purple engaged Paul Mann as conductor, working with different local orchestras as they circled the globe on a three-month venture.

After a break, the touring continued in non-orchestral fashion from September 2000. How did Ian Gillan feel taking a 1970s supergroup into the new millennium? 'It was strange,' he conceded in 2001. 'Everybody seemed to be expecting something to happen. Back in 1969 when the band started, time seemed to stretch for eternity. Every day and every summer seemed long. Now the days flash past! Arriving in the year 2000 is not so significant. What's important is that the band is back on course. It's been a long haul with lots of ups and downs. It's like a family. Despite past squabbles we are committed to each other and there is a family spirit.'

The following year found Gillan adding a rare and as-yet unexperienced thrill to his CV when he found himself singing with opera superstar Luciano Pavarotti. 'I loved every minute of it! I soon realised "Nessun Dorma" would be so much fun to sing. It's melodically structured just like a rock ballad. All scales are based on country, Indian, jazz – there's nothing original. It was fantastic.'

The summer of 2001, was spent touring the States with fellow veterans Lynyrd Skynyrd and self-styled wild-man of rock Ted Nugent. Needless to say, it meant much to the band's only American... even though it failed to bring them nearer than 800 miles from his home. Curiously, it had the effect of making him realise what playing to European audiences meant to the band, crediting them with 'the heart and soul that crosses all borders – they're not afraid to love music.'

If the second departure of Ritchie Blackmore had rocked the band and their long-time fans, then Jon Lord's decision to opt out, announced in March 2002, was even more of a landmark event. Ian Gillan later announced that it was 'the most friendly leave-taking in the history of the band', while Lord confirmed that, 'They're my best friends and they'll be my friends for life.'

Such had been the magnitude of the decision that Lord, fearful of being talked round, put his reasons in a letter and faxed it simultaneously to his fellow band members and the management. In point of fact, he might well have stayed, he later hinted, had they been prepared to take a year off to let him concentrate on his own material, but the suggestion was knocked back in friendly fashion. Lord made the valid point that the emphasis of the band had changed and, possibly due to declining sales and/or critical acclaim for their albums, touring was now the number one priority, while he enjoyed creating new material, either for the band or himself.

But the man who'd seen it through still understandably felt a proprietorial twinge. 'It was difficult because Purple was my band... me and Ritchie started it.' Like Blackmore, he was destined to produce more 'serious' fare as a solo artist, which would inevitably polarise Purple's following much as the band's orchestral projects he'd instigated had in times past. Solo albums like 1981's *Before I Forget* had proved unsatisfactory, rushed affairs ('very patchy, I didn't join the dots') but now he could join as many dots as he wanted.

There were, however, precedents for Purple playing on without Jon. The previous summer, when he'd been unavailable for festival dates due to a knee operation, an eminently suitable replacement had been available then as now, in the capable form of Don Airey – ironically, of course, an ex-Rainbow man. Sunderland-born Airey had been all but born to do the job, claiming the first rock concert he'd had the pleasure of attending, in Manchester in 1972, was Deep Purple. He even credited Jon Lord, whose Hammond-bashing he had witnessed that fateful night, with dispelling any thoughts of a classical music career. 'I said to myself that's what I want to do.'

Despite this early rock initiation, Don learned his craft on the cabaret and cruise-ship circuit before joining Cozy Powell's Hammer in 1974. The band had been formed as a vehicle for drummer Powell to promote studio-created hits like 'Dance With the Devil' and 'Na Na Na'. When Hammer inevitably folded, Don used his contacts to make an impact on the session scene.

His next port of call was Jon Hiseman's revamped jazz-rock outfit Colosseum II in May 1975, joining his guitarist brother Keith who had replaced Gary Moore. They cut three albums between mid 1975 and December 1978, and also cooperated with the Lloyd Webbers, Andrew and Julian, to produce 'Variations', theme to the UK's long-running TV arts programme *The South Bank Show*.

Unfortunately Colosseum II was a band in the wrong place at the wrong time, the late 1970s being an era scarcely conducive to jazz-rock of any kind. But Don, who contributed to Gary Moore's 1978 solo *Back On The Streets* and Black Sabbath's *Never Say Die*, provided keyboards or musical arrangements (live and in the studio) for a veritable multitude of acts throughout the 1980s, including Bernie Marsden's Alaska, UFO, Gilbert O'Sullivan, Jethro Tull, Gary Moore, Fastway, Irish rockers Mama's Boys, ELO and Brian May. Studio sessions included, most significantly, Whitesnake's multi-million seller *1987*, while he arranged the winning 1997 Eurovision song 'Love Shine A Light' for Katrina and the Waves, conducting the orchestra in Dublin with aplomb. He also set up Don Airey Music, providing corporate ID and soundtracks for commercial companies.

A solo concept comprising orchestral pieces and instrumentals called *K2* was also released, and featured Colin Blunstone and Gary Moore, with Cozy Powell on drums. In mid 1996, Don collaborated on Tony Iommi's eponymous solo album (released in 2000) and the reformed Quatermass II CD release *Hard Road*. Don toured in 1999 as part of Blunstone's band, and with Moody, Murray and Marsden's Company of Snakes, parting company with them in June 2001. The turn of the century saw Airey assisting British melodic rockers Ten with their highly successful *Babylon* album, shifting 300,000 units worldwide. In a bizarre move, he then turned Rainbow tribute artist when he linked up with ex-vocalist Graham Bonnet to tour a Blackmore-based set around Europe and the UK in 2001.

Jon Lord, for his part, had been scheduled to end 2001 with the last of a final leg of a tour that, let it be remembered, had begun on 1 June 1998 in Istanbul. Bob Dylan's 'Never-Ending Tour' surely had a rival. By its end, it was reckoned Purple would have played more than 240 concerts in 39 countries as diverse as Argentina, Malaysia, Turkey, South Africa, Latvia and, Gillan's perennial favourite, the Lebanon. It wasn't surprising that Lord, who turned 60 that year, felt he needed a break from the road.

The decision was announced while Purple still had unfinished business, as the February 2002 UK leg of the tour had been interrupted when Ian Gillan lost his voice. To assuage any disappointment felt by those who'd had to wait to enjoy their dose of Purple, it was decided that Jon would rejoin for the rescheduled dates – with the result that, at the Hammersmith Apollo in September, the lights went out during Jon's solo spot only for Don to 'magically' take his place. It was both symbolic and entertaining, though the final numbers saw honours inevitably shared by the duo.

The generous seventeen-song set list for the 2001-2002 UK leg of the tour looked back to the *Fireball* and *Who Do We Think We Are* era, offering a chance for their audience to appreciate some rarely heard gems. Steve Morse used 'Fools' as the showcase for some impressive guitar harmonics, Gillan claiming the opportunity to take a break and return to the stage clad in white. His general level of energy, whether scatting along with the guitar, flailing on his congas or hitting the high notes (well, most of them) was astonishing for a man now approaching his late fifties.

Visually, the mood was dark, Roger cutting the biggest dash in a tie-die T-shirt and bandana, Steve Morse remaining restrained in denim. Steve Morse followed 'When A Blind Man Cries' with snatches of some classic rock riffs, the likes of Skynyrd's 'Sweet Home Alabama', the Who's 'Won't Get Fooled Again', Hendrix's 'Voodoo Chile' and Zep's 'Whole Lotta Love' preceding the daddy of them all – 'Smoke On The Water'. He described it in the tour programme as 'a little jokey thing to try and stump the band. Music is supposed to be fun and I don't want to lose my sense of humour.'

As ever, the problem for Purple had been which of the classics to leave out. 'We change the songs from time to time,' said Gillan. 'We put the classics in from the EMI days that everyone knows. Also we have to please the Steve Morse fans whose age can be as young as seventeen–eighteen. So we have to play "Ted The Mechanic" and "Aviator". We're looking at "Child In Time", "Black Night" and "Smoke On The Water". We don't play "Strange Kind Of Woman" and "Black Night" in the same set because they're both shuffles. We'll do two and a half hours.' When it came to playing the oldies, he likened the songs to 'kids –

you gotta like them, whether they're bad or good. It's not a matter if I like them or loathe them, more a question of their relevance or difficulty.'

The final encore trio of 'Black Night', 'Hush' and 'Highway Star' was the icing on the proverbial cake for audiences ranging in age from seven to seventy. Perhaps the nicest thing about the tour was the ability to see the band in smaller venues than had often been the case – a band decision, Gillan revealed. 'When the promoters sent through a list of half a dozen large venues I said I didn't wanna do it. Let's put in some theatres and city halls. Let's get back to playing. We've got a month – let's play every night! The English don't want to see bands in large venues. It's strange. Maybe it's 'cos people get treated like crap at [big] arenas, a dehumanising experience.'

While Gillan clearly still found world touring enjoyable, Jon Lord opened up three years later to *Record Collector*'s Tim Jones and Joel McIver as he prepared to promote new solo album *Beyond The Notes* – released appropriately, given its content, by EMI Classics. He cited the 'incessant touring' as his reason for departure, adding that he was 'getting tired of playing the same-old same-old. I felt that I wasn't fulfilling my role in Purple as well as I should've been though, of course, I'm a professional and there's a level beyond which I won't go.' He could now, he explained, concentrate on getting his own music out – and at the age of 60, it was true that 'If I didn't get on and do it, then I'd never do it. Something had to give.' For the record, Lord played his last Purple date at Ipswich on 19 September 2002.

Beyond The Notes featured guest vocalists Sam Brown, Frida from Abba and Miller Anderson, and was notable for two tracks that paid homage to departed friends: 'I'll Send You A Postcard' (subtitled 'Pavane For Tony [Ashton]') and 'A Smile When I Shook His Hand' ('in memoriam George Harrison'). He also paid tribute to 'the chaps in DP' in his sleeve notes for 'those terrific times we had, their ever more valuable friendship and all the wonderful music. Also – good on yer, Don!'

An interesting but totally unscheduled sideline in early 2003 took Lord back to his blues roots on the other side of the world. He'd agreed to fly over to Australia to play some classical dates, but while there managed to injure his hand. This didn't stop him playing Hammond organ, however, so he turned the time to good use by uniting with bassist Bob Daisley, singer Jimmy Barnes and others to play club dates as blues covers band the Hoochie Coochie Men. The result was later unleashed on the public by EMI in both double CD and DVD formats – arguably a little too lavish for what was effectively a time-filling exercise – but did include a version of 'When A Blind Man Cries'. Jon and pals had also made a TV appearance, and this was also represented in video form.

Meanwhile, back at the band, Deep Purple had faced their first post-Lord studio album in November 2002 in fine form. They even engaged an outside producer in Michael Bradford to liven up their ideas. His track record in hip-hop and rap might have worried fans, but as Ian Gillan related to the author in a pre-recording interview, change was necessary.

'We have been recording in barns, basements, sheds and garages for years. It's something that began with *Machine Head* back in the 1970s. We've never used a major recording studio. So I think we're going to do our writing and then go into an Abbey Road or Power Station. The sort of studio that would make a band sound important right away and give a sense of occasion. I'd also like us to use a producer. Roger Glover has been our in-house producer, but it's time for some objectivity. Roger feels the same way. We want to broaden the spectrum of our music and feel confident enough to augment. If we need bagpipes or a brass section we should go for it!'

He inferred strongly that such an approach would have been impossible without a switch of guitarist. 'Having Steve in the band meant we could come to terms with our age. When I first got into Ray Charles and Ella Fitzgerald, these artists were fifty years old and just reaching their peak. So instead of looking over our shoulders and trying to recreate what we did as kids, we should concentrate on the music. We should think in terms of being competent rather than who sings highest or plays fastest. We still do rock 'n' roll, but we can expand our music. We've got a big audience and I'm sure they're ready for new and different things.'

Bananas was released in August 2003 and indeed proved the shot in the arm (or should that be kick up the ass?) Gillan had hoped it would be. Four of the songs shouldered their way into a set packed with classics. Seasoned Purple-watchers were looking for signs of Don Airey contributing to the songwriting process. Roger Glover saw him as a 'modifying voice', helping them choose between different feels and musical directions rather than contributing 'original starts' in terms of riffs or rhythms.

Fourteen songs were committed to digital hard drive, a dozen making the final cut. The title came from Gillan, who described Morse as 'having gone bananas' when he engaged in a mid-song duel with Don Airey that spiralled out of control. This could well have been on the opening 'House Of Pain', a song that exhibited considerable instrumental interplay.

Gillan raved about *Bananas*' accessibility, but bemoaned the way it had come together between live dates. 'It's interesting how we do things in dribs and drabs. The missing element in the equation is time. It's a year later than it was planned to be – usually we release an album every eighteen months. The last record, the *Concerto*, we went all over the world promoting.'

13. Colours to Come

The first Ritchie Blackmore biography, *Rainbow Rising*, was published by Helter Skelter in 2002. Written by long-time fan Roy Davies and unauthorised by Ritchie or his management, it centred, as the title suggested, on the Man in Black's post-Purple career. A fanzine, *More Black Than Purple*, dedicated to the band's former Strat-wielder, was founded by Jerry Bloom in 1996. It made for essential reading for anyone remotely interested in the man's exploits, but only the man's biggest fans were finding Blackmore's Night anything but mildly interesting.

Deep Purple Y2K was clearly still a major concert draw the world over, record sales were inevitably not of the scale they once were. Yet, for many die-hard fans, the situation in 2005 was just as it was in 1985: the Holy Grail was the 'classic' line-up reunited. While Jon Lord would undoubtedly have been up for it, the black sheep was, as ever, Ritchie.

When questioned by *Record Collector*'s assiduous Jones and McIver in late 2004, he was at pains not to rule it out – and even ruled it in on a temporary, live-only basis. 'I'm the bad boy aren't I, the bad little doggie who left the band. But I would do it, for nostalgic reason, for a week or two, for the fans, for old times' sake. Just as I'd like to see a band that I liked reform. But I wouldn't go into a studio…'

With live CDs and DVDs proliferating as rock's giants scored a last big payday, the odds were that it would happen at some point in the future, Gillan permitting. Curiously, Ian had proclaimed himself a fan of his old adversary's new direction. 'Ritchie's shown he's stuck to his new project,' he said in 2001, 'and I'm very pleased he has. It's intriguing – and I see no reason why we shouldn't have a Scotch together at some time in the future.'

It remained the case that Purple's new releases were having to compete with their classic back catalogue. EMI remastered the first three Purple Mark I albums, compiling their highlights as *The*

Early Years, but topped this in 2002 with an epic six-CD box set portentously titled *Listen Learn Read On* after the opening track from *Book Of Taliesyn*. The set was a worthwhile investment, even more so because the basis of the accompanying booklet was extracted from Chris Charlesworth's long out of print biography from 1983. Musically, it offered some twenty previously unissued live performances, radio sessions and alternate takes – a high percentage of the seventy-four featured – while much other material showed up in crisply remastered form.

The man behind the box set, Sheffield's Simon Robinson, could claim to have done most to keep the band's name and legend in the public eye. Having founded the Deep Purple Appreciation Society and disseminated much information in printed form, he was quick to venture into cyberspace. He'd also revived the Purple Records label, having previously re-released much related material under the RPM imprint: the slogan 'Classic hard rock from the 1970s' said it all.

Even Universal got in on the act, coming up with three compilations – *Knocking At Your Back Door: The Best Of Deep Purple In The 80s*, *Under The Gun* and *Universal Masters* with the material under their control, not to mention straight reissues of *House Of Blue Light* and *Perfect Strangers*.

Purple's winter 2004 tour of Britain and Europe was as headliners on an impressive-looking bill that included Peter Frampton and Thunder. The latter, Brit-rockers of a decidedly younger vintage than either of their tour-mates, had reformed especially for the purpose of opening the show, while Frampton had curtailed his most recent European jaunt on the death of long-time keyboardist/rhythm guitarist Bob Mayo, a fixture since *Comes Alive* days.

Roger Glover had, amazingly, never met the former 'Face of '68', who'd been riding high in the UK charts with the Herd when the bass man had been plying his trade with Episode Six, but he'd 'built up great admiration for him. I like the way he handles himself. I like people who are down to earth and don't get sucked into believing their own greatness.' (Incidentally, Frampton enjoyed booking into hotels under assumed identities – just like Glover, who used the handle of long-dead British comic Wilfred Pickles as his name of choice.)

The dream for Glover was 'a massive hit single' which, he explained, would break the mould and ensure Purple were played on 'active' US radio stations and not just classic rock ones. He felt Britain and America were the two markets 'in which our profile is most damaged' due to a decade of 'in-fighting and decline'. Gillan agreed, but believed that 'Anyone over thirty in terms of singles is either distant mainstream or forget it. We have a song called "The Well Dressed Guitar" that Steve Morse wrote. We played it on the orchestral tour… I was so excited when I first heard this song – I thought it wasn't just something I loved to sing, but leapt out as a commercial track. It nutted me right between the eyes. I could even hear it on the radio. But [record company] reaction was complete apathy.'

In spring 2005, Deep Purple prepared to enter the studio with producer Bradford once more. The EMI contract having run its course, they were once more free agents in control of their own destiny.

The early years of the new millennium had seen a number of side projects emerge. *The Guilty Party* was, amazingly, only Roger Glover's fourth solo album in a run that began in 1974 with *The Butterfly Ball*. The catalyst was American singer-songwriter Randall Bramblett, who fronted the effort. As with all Purple-related product, it would sell a certain number by word of mouth.

Albums from drummers are rare, listenable ones even rarer (don't sue, Phil Collins), but Ian Paice's first ever solo release was not a record but a DVD. *Not For The Pros* combined drumming tips, live footage from Purple's 2001 US tour, two tracks filmed at Abbey Road studios in August that year and, as a bonus, a drum clinic. Paice was just delighted to still be in the game: 'It's a hobby that I still get well paid for, and it doesn't get much better than

that. Empty hotel rooms are the price you pay for the fun
you have!'

And that seemed to be the key to Purple's longevity. Maybe Jon
Lord should have the last word on the subject: 'We don't stop
playing because we grow old – we grow old because we stop
playing.' If the Rolling Stones could reach their fortieth
anniversary, then why not Deep Purple?

PART two

The Studio Albums

shades of deep Purple

The May 1968 recording sessions at Pye Studios at ATV House, Great Cumberland Place, London, were Purple's first as a band. The results, *Shades Of Deep Purple*, appeared that July and would be their only LP to bear EMI's Beatles-related Parlophone label.

Producer Derek Lawrence recalls that 'the album had all been done in rehearsal so we could record it very fast. We did the recording on the Saturday and Sunday and I mixed it the following Monday. The only real input from me was to curb the tendencies of Jon and Ritchie to solo for too long.' Blackmore for his part recalls: 'We took two takes on everything... one and another try in case we made a mistake.' Little wonder the producer boasted the whole album 'cost just £1,500 in studio time' – a bargain even at 1968 prices.

'We were forced into the studios, get in there and do it, and we did,' Nick Simper recalls. When rehearsals started, Ian Paice had only been in the group a few days and, because the management didn't want the rest of former band the Maze to know in case they sued, there was even a question of whether he could get hold of his drum kit.

Paice himself now feels a lack of direction was evident. 'The playing was very good, but the band had no idea what it wanted to be. The influence of Vanilla Fudge was to make music that was a little more interesting. That's why the first record had all those long arrangements. We didn't make any great compromise for the fact it was a studio. We played it with the same energy as if there were people in front of us. I think that comes through on the early records. Okay, they are not perfect tracks, but you can feel when people are bouncing off each other, and I think that's their charm.'

The band had come back from Denmark, to find a studio booked for them to do an album – so chose eight or nine numbers from their stage act. 'People say to me the group didn't sound together,' Nick Simper remarked, 'but we'd only been together as a group for ten days (as a proper group) and yet we came out with an LP like that. It sold bloody millions! I'd only ever played bass finger-style, and Derek Lawrence said "You've got to use a plectrum." So if you listen to the bass lines there's a clicky, slappy sort of sound.'

Simper also recalls trouble brewing when a Rod Evans-Jon Lord song, 'One More Rainy Day', was selected as the B-side to 'Hush', earning them extra royalties. 'Ritchie said, "All Rod Evans does is write bloody words.' I said, "Well any idiot can write a guitar riff, you try and write some meaningful lyrics." He wasn't very pleased.' So even the Number 4 US success of the single, which helped the album reach Number 24 there, was a cause of strife...

And The Address

This impressive instrumental opener, plus 'Mandrake Root', were written when Ritchie came to Jon Lord's flat in a snowstorm, carrying an acoustic guitar. 'That night was wonderful,' recalls the keyboardist. 'Right away I felt that he wouldn't suffer fools gladly, but it felt right. Ritchie seemed dark, he always seemed dark.'

Hush

Ritchie Blackmore claims it was his idea to cover Joe South's 'Hush'. 'I heard it in Hamburg, so I mentioned it to the band and we did it. The whole thing was done in two takes. I liked the guitar solo – especially the feedback. That was done with my Gibson ES-335.'

Bassist Simper, however, recalls Ritchie and himself hearing a version by Dutch singer Kris Ife in a Manchester discotheque called the Phonograph. 'I had a friend in a ballroom band who taught us the song. We created our own version without ever really hearing the record.'

Despite being four and a half minutes long and ending with a minute-and-a-half organ solo, it sold over a million in the States as a single. 'Hush' was particularly huge in California as, unknown to the band, there was a very strong, intense type of LSD going around called Deep Purple. 'When we first got the States people we going "Cool band, cool name",' said Jon Lord. 'I'm sure it had a lot to do with that first success.'

One More Rainy Day

With storm effects from a BBC Sound Effects library album spliced in with the music, this was the last song to be finished, hanging around until the Monday morning of the recording weekend. Still sounds rather like an advertising theme... though it made the band's first ever Radio 1 session.

Prelude: Happiness

An organ-led pseudo-classical intro for which all the band members bar Ian Paice received a writing credit then segued into...

I'm So Glad

This blues song was first popularised by its writer, Nehemiah 'Skip' James, and was well known through Cream's rocked-up version, so might have best been avoided. Yet it had been part of the repertoire of Paice and Evans' earlier group, the Maze, so was an obvious inclusion.

'Prelude: Happiness' and 'I'm So Glad' came to seven minutes in total, the longest track on the album.

Mandrake Root

A bluesy six-minute piece in two parts credited to Blackmore and Evans, 'Mandrake Root Part 1' is 'a vocal section about a "love potion",' while part 2 is 'an instrumental about what happens afterwards!'

Mandrake Root was not only Purple's first song but was also the name of Ritchie's last band before joining Purple. In 1997 Blackmore commented: 'I first had that idea in '68 with a friend of mine who wrote a lot of what he writes in fourths. The melody of that was in fourths. In those days I'd never heard of that kind of harmony.' A real Purple fan favourite.

Help
The band's deal with EMI had been cemented by their Vanilla Fudge-style demo of this Beatles classic, devised by singer Rod Evans. 'We thought, "This guy's got ideas",' said bassist Nick Simper, who added that, while Jon Lord had identified the song to cover, it was when Rod came for his audition that the idea to slow it down emerged. 'It worked well. Lennon and McCartney were knocked out by it and wished *they'd* done it that way.'

Love Help Me
'The management had a studio booked as soon as we'd finalised the line-up, before we'd written a song or anything,' said Simper. 'We kicked around "Love Help Me", which Rod later put some words to... we sorted the chords to that out in a couple of days.' An instrumental version was added to the CD remaster.

Hey Joe
A cover of Jimi Hendrix's debut UK release from late 1966, itself a rock version of a folk song usually attributed to Billy Roberts and credited as such here. Though the last song in the running order, it was the first (along with 'And The Address') to be recorded. Its cod-classical intro was based on 'The Miller's Dance' from Manuel de Falla's ballet score *The Three-Cornered Hat*.

The Book Of Taliesyn

Recorded at London's De Lane Lea Studios in August 1968, Purple's second album was released in the States a scant two months later and peaked at Number 54. Home-based fans, however, would have a much longer wait to hear it. The format of elaborately reworked covers and originals exactly replicated *Shades Of Deep Purple*, a lack of adventure necessitated by lack of planning time.

As Nick Simper revealed, 'There was no time to demo stuff, so a lot was written in the studio. As for production, with all due respect to Derek Lawrence, we knew what we wanted to sound like, no one was very happy with the sound. We were big business in America [but] EMI [in Britain] did nothing, they were stupid old guys.'

Jon Lord explained to US reporters on their arrival to promote the album live by touring as opening act to Cream that 'Taliesyn was a medieval bard or, as you Americans say, poet.' He rates album two, in retrospect, as 'One of the most confused albums I've heard in my life. We wanted to be a progressive band but we didn't know how to be.'

Cover artwork was by John Lord, not a misspelling of the musician but an acclaimed children's book illustrator. The sound of the album, if not its content, was superior to its predecessor. Unfortunately, by the time *Taliesyn* gained UK release on Harvest, the band had moved on in more ways than one. Not only had they cut a third, eponymous, album, but personnel changes were looming.

Listen, Learn, Read On

The track that would, three decades later, give its name to a Deep Purple box set began life here. It refers to the book of the title in its lyrics, and starts proceedings in complex style: a more straightforward track might have been less daunting for the listener.

Wring That Neck

Retitled 'Hard Road' in the States, perhaps due to its violent connotations, this instrumental penned by Blackmore and Simper was, Ritchie revealed, 'actually not original. I'd heard a violin piece that was very similar, and that's where I got the idea from… Jon wrote the E-flat run.'

Kentucky Woman
A clear attempt to replicate the successful formula of 'Hush' and, equally logically, a US single which charted there, if not spectacularly, at Number 38. '[Writer] Neil Diamond liked our version,' says Jon, 'and, because he wasn't a big star at the time, was very glad we'd covered it... we made a bit of money for him.'

Exposition
A lengthy guitar, drum and organ introduction that would, together with the Beatles classic that followed, amount to a marathon seven minutes.

We Can Work It Out
Clearly following on from the debut album's heavy version of 'Help' but, in Nick Simper's (and most listeners') view, nothing like as effective. 'It turned out to be a waste of time, not that we couldn't come up with the goods, just that we didn't have the time to develop it.' He was, however, 'pleased with the bass on it'.

Shield
A very impressive and inventive group effort which has been included on several psychedelic compilation albums and doesn't shame the Purple name in doing so. The introduction is hardly typical but very ear-catching, and 'Shield' retains attention for all of six minutes.

Anthem
This track, the first recorded for the album, sees Jon Lord arranging strings in an early indication of his musical thinking that would culminate in the *Concerto*. It also brought the Mellotron into his keyboard armoury: this used tape loops of stringed instruments and was notoriously temperamental, hence was never used by Lord on stage.

River Deep Mountain High

Purple's pretentious take on the Ike and Tina Turner soul epic
unforgivably exceeded the ten-minute mark. It was edited down
for a US Number 53 single, as well as featuring (in all its lengthy
glory) towards the end of their live set.

Deep Purple

Recorded in January 1969 at De Lane Lea Studios, London,
Purple's third album (and their second on EMI's progressive
Harvest imprint) was released in November that year, by which
time the Mark I line-up was no more.

Any album bearing a group's name should generally be regarded
as some kind of definitive statement. *Deep Purple* however turned
out to be the end of the band's somewhat underwhelming first
chapter – at least in comparison to the recordings to come. Ritchie
for one certainly didn't think that what they were coming up with
was in any way original. 'Originally we were copying Vanilla
Fudge. We loved them and Hendrix and a bit of Cream.
We were just blending their elements.'

Yet that's to undervalue what, viewed in isolation, is an
interesting piece of work that has links with both Purple's past and
future. Derek Lawrence, whose last Purple album this would turn
out to be, had perfected his method of working with the band, and
the speed of recording was remarkable – and necessary, as sessions
were being squeezed in between live dates. Apparently one single
day of recording yielded both 'April' and 'Lalena'.

It's an irony that, though the album was released by the ailing
Tetragrammaton in the States in June, *Deep Purple* would not
make its UK bow on Harvest until November – by which time not
only had the Mark II line-up hit its performing stride but the
Concerto for Group And Orchestra had also been recorded: indeed,
this would be released hot on *Deep Purple*'s heels, in January 1970.

It seemed typical of the general air of confusion that the element of Bosch's painting *The Garden Of Earthly Delights* used for the cover was rendered in black and white rather than the intended colour!

'Deep Purple' failed to chart in either the USA or the UK.

Chasing Shadows

The hard-driving opener owed much to a thunderous Ian Paice rhythm pattern, 'a double paradiddle between two tom-toms. If you play that notation it gives you an amazing rhythm. It's just a rudiment, but if you don't know that rudiment you'll never come out with that configuration of notes, because its not an obvious thing to do.' Evans really pours his heart out on this one.

Blind

This kicks off like a heavier relation of the Zombies' 'Time Of The Season' (via Paice's rhythm part) crossed with the harpsichord of the Yardbirds' 'For Your Love', before wending its own way in poppy vein. Lacks anything like a memorable chorus, though, and only comes alive after two and a half minutes thanks to Blackmore's viciously wah'd solo.

Lalena

A radical version of Donovan's beautiful ballad which Purple had customised *à la* Jeff Beck Group by adding pounding percussion and heavy riffs. A BBC recorded version that's a minute and a half shorter than its less radio-friendly sister was added to the remastered CD.

Fault Line

A song apparently inspired by a Californian earthquake that occurred while the band were in Los Angeles.

The Painter

This was one of the album's heavier self-penned numbers, and one they'd previewed on Radio 1's *Top Gear* in January 1969 as 'Hey Bop A Re Bop'.

Why Didn't Rosemary

A song that continued in the psych-pop style of previous efforts and featured lyrics inspired by the controversial recently released Roman Polanski film *Rosemary's Baby*. A rollicking R&B stomper that hints at the future Purple direction while remaining somewhat generic, it nevertheless highlights Rod's shortcomings as a hard-rock vocalist.

Bird Has Flown

A heavier number despite its 'Norwegian Wood'-derived title, this was an attempt, said Nick Simper 'to zap the US with [a hit] single. We wanted to get over there and milk it while we were big.'

April

The album's crowning moment was a twelve-minute *coup de grâce* written by Blackmore and Lord, which finished off the record. The piece started with an instrumental band section, which was followed by a second instrumental passage featuring strings and woodwinds (composed and arranged by Lord, and recorded separately) before a final section featuring the whole band.

Titled after the month of Ritchie Blackmore's birth, 'it was just a little throwaway tune I had.' The guitarist now regards it as 'pretty adventurous for its time, especially [being] in the key of A flat.'

Deep Purple In Rock

Recorded between September 1969 and April 1970 at De Lane
Lea, Abbey Road and IBC Studios, London, *Deep Purple In Rock*
was released in June 1970 in Britain, where it reached Number 4,
and three months later in the States.

The writing of the new album came easily, the love affair
between the three originals and the two newcomers still in its
first flushes. Roger Glover, in particular, was delighted to find his
songwriting skills being appreciated. 'Episode Six had a rather
patronising attitude [to songwriting]. Now I was in a band where,
no matter what I came up with, they were keen to try it. All the
ideas I came up with, they could play them, and usually did!'
Amazed by his new bandmates' musical ability, Glover believes he
probably wrote more for *In Rock* than for any other album he was
involved with, making full use of all the ideas Episode Six had
bottled up for years. 'All the songs were fresh and had so much
fire and aggression... Ritchie said, "If it's not exciting or dramatic,
it shouldn't be on the album".'

Blackmore, for his part, was looking at Led Zeppelin as a role
model, and candidly admitted that *In Rock* was 'sort of a response
to the one we did with the orchestra. I wanted to do a loud, hard-
rock record. And I was thinking, "This had better make it,"
because I was afraid that if it didn't, we were going to be stuck
playing with orchestras for the rest of our lives!' With that in mind,
Purple's axeman ensured the energy level remained high
throughout: 'It hammered along purposefully, every song.
There was no lull...'

Jon Lord saw the band as searching for a group identity. 'Our
previous LPs had been a mess of different styles. It was the first
one we made with a strong direction. *In Rock* was recorded within
very narrow limits – we wanted to make a definite statement – and
we threw an enormous amount of material out.' In his view, the
music they made 'stands up better than the other Purple albums,
even *Machine Head*.'

Ian Paice agreed that Purple had finally found their formula. 'Every track on the album is a powerful statement about one thing or another, whether it's a lyrical statement – anti drugs – or a musical statement about the virtuosity in the band. In a short space of maybe three or four weeks we found that everything was possible.' There would, crucially, be no more cover versions included to bulk up the album. 'It was all contained within ourselves. We didn't have to look outside, and that was really exciting.'

Gillan puts *In Rock*'s success down to 'a good, balanced chemistry, a suitable amount of eccentricity and common sense. Songs just took off, because my entire musical background of Little Richard, Elvis, and Chuck Berry now had a focus. I could put into practice what I'd learnt, and it all began to mean something to me, as would emerge in the lyrics.'

Speed King

A song that started life with a working title of 'Kneel And Pray' and was often performed as such in early shows, 'Speed King' was the first Purple song Roger Glover wrote. 'Ritchie mentioned he wanted something fast, like Jimi Hendrix's "Fire", to open the show with and that riff just came to me. I stood there in the huge echoey gym and apprehensively started playing the first thing that came into my head that would convey a similar feeling... I just made it up on the spot. They all joined in, making it sound great, and a jam ensued which would set the course of the song. It was exhilarating.'

Despite the connotations, 'Speed King' was not, Jon Lord insisted, a song about amphetamine drugs, but 'a song about playing fast. It certainly wasn't about drugs, it was just how fast can Gillan sing?' The lyrics – 'Good Golly, Miss Molly'... 'Tutti Frutti' – consist almost entirely of quotes from old rock 'n' roll songs.

Lord believes early Purple material has proved influential in the metal genre. 'I think you'd find quite a lot of roots for things that happen in hard rock and metal nowadays [there], for example in thrash or speed metal. "Speed King" is speed metal, no question about it.'

Bloodsucker

Not such a typical Purple track, but again an influential one.
'I think it was one which showed the way to a lot of other bands of a certain style of really hard, nasty playing,' said Paice, who called it 'a little gem'.

Child In Time

This unashamedly owed its inspiration to 'Bombay Calling', a track by US West Coast group It's A Beautiful Day. Jon became fascinated with it and started playing around with the intro during rehearsals at Hanwell. Gillan recalls he started singing phrases over Lord's keyboards, 'and it built up to the scream when Ritchie started playing too. It was totally spontaneous and conceived without any storyline... it's just the way we felt about the world at the time.' Jon also admits to another musical 'steal'. 'You might recognise the slight similarity between the last chord of "A Day In The Life" and that of "Child In Time" The similarity is not accidental! We liked the sound of it, so we nicked it.'

Years later, Gillan learned that it had been adopted as an anthem by resistance groups in Eastern Europe under Communism, but found it less fulfilling to sing after the fall of the Berlin Wall 'when it became lyrically irrelevant. Many people have told me about Radio Free Europe playing that song and people in the Warsaw Pact countries hearing it and knowing there were people on the "other side" who understood. Saw the dickheads of leaders as they did. I met a guy who lived in East Berlin who got ten years' imprisonment for owning Deep Purple records. [laughs] Personally, I'd have given him a little longer!'

Back in 1970, even his arch nemesis to be, Mr Blackmore, conceded that 'Ian Gillan is probably the only guy who could sing that. It was done in three stages, sort of like an operatic thing.

That's him at his best. No one else would have attempted that, going up in octaves.'

The Man in Black is harder on his own work. 'I think the guitar solo is relatively average. I did it in two or three takes. Back then, whenever it came to guitar solos, I was given about fifteen minutes. Sometimes on stage I would play it much faster than the record. I'd play it real fast, and Paicey would like it really fast. Only problem was coming to that part at the end of the guitar solo that the band would do in unison. You can only play that so fast– unless you start tapping, which I don't on principle. It's just an A minor arpeggio, but it's all down strokes… that's hard to do.'

Flight Of The Rat

The track began as a joke when Rimsky-Korsakov's 'Flight Of The Bumble Bee' was mentioned in rehearsal and Jon Lord started playing variations around the theme. The 'Rat' part 'was a drug habit,' Gillan would reveal. 'We'd often play with words that way.' The track was one that would not trouble the live set, much to Blackmore's dismay. 'I would love to do that live [but] Paicey hates it. He doesn't hate the song, he just hates the rhythm. We tried it once…'

Into The Fire

'Another drug-associated song,' said Gillan. One of the band's first compositions together, they performed it live well before recording it for *In Rock*.

Livin' Wreck

This featured one of Ian Paice's favourite drum sounds: 'Really live and metallic and hard and nasty. My favourite bit on the whole album is Ritchie's solo, which isn't fast or flashy but just flows and fits in so beautifully.' The song was tried but was then shelved for a while, recalls Glover. 'We listened to it again towards the end of the album, and we suddenly thought, "Actually, it's not that bad is it?"'

Hard Lovin' Man

Glover's favourite track on the album. 'There is so much fire in the playing, and Jon's solo is so close to his performances on stage. The song to me embodies the real character of the band at the time – driving power, oddball writing, experimentation, two great solos, flippant, cocksure lyrics, exuberant attitude.
A monster groove. I loved it.'

The guitar solo of the song was devised by Blackmore to annoy one of the recording engineers, probably at Abbey Road, who, in his opinion 'was a stuffy bloke who didn't like rock 'n' roll music. While I was recording the solo on that song, I got this urge and started rubbing the guitar up and down the doorway of the control room to get all that wild guitar noise. So this bloke looks at me as if I'd lost my mind.'

Fireball

De Lane Lea and Olympic were the venues for an album recorded between September 1970 and May 1971 and released the following September. It gave Purple their first UK Number 1 album, making 32 in the States. The success of the non-album single 'Black Night' had raised the band's profile at home, and sales of *Fireball* certainly benefited from that.

But producer Martin Birch felt the process of creating the album was 'like an after-shock' after all the positives of *In Rock*. 'The group were travelling a lot and had to fit the sessions in whenever they could. That is never a good way to make an album.' Ritchie Blackmore recalls everything being made up in the studio. 'We never had any time to sit back and think... the only time we got a chance to write was when someone was ill... quite often we arrive at the studios with no idea what we are going to do... there is no time to prepare anything anyway, but the fact is that it is the spontaneity of our music which lends it vitality and excitement.

There are only three tracks that I think are good – "No No No", "Fools" and "Fireball" itself.'

While proud of the material, Ian Gillan admits he was 'definitely in the minority on all that, because the others were pretty negative about the album. I was delighted with the album but because it was lyrically and melodically more adventurous, instead of being hard-rock, it confused a lot of people.'

For Roger Glover, the task of following up a phenomenally successful album made Purple too self-conscious. 'Although it has its moments we were over-awed by the success of *In Rock* and I think we tried too hard. We tried to progress, but overstepped the mark. Compared to *In Rock*, *Fireball* is a contrived album… on the whole a bit of a damp squib.'

Ian Paice, like Blackmore, recognised 'three or four good tracks, but there aren't any belters which is what made the good albums stand out,' while Jon Lord simply feels, 'It showed we could make a fairly decent album under stress. Unfortunately it fell between two very good albums and therefore it might seem to pall in comparison.'

Fireball

EMI wanted a single out and selected this track; Purple listened to their record company and a Number 15 hit resulted. The whooshing sound is the studio air conditioning unit being turned on. Paice recalls he could 'get the speed but I couldn't get the power! So I thought, "What are we going to do?" Maybe dub another bass drum on afterwards in the other part. In the studio from the day before the Who's equipment was still lying around, Keith Moon's kit was still there so I just copped the bass drum from his kit, stuck it next to mine, miked it up and played sixteens instead of eights – that fixed it.'

No, No, No

Then influence of bluesman Shuggie Otis can be heard in Blackmore's playing here, Roger Glover believes. 'A lot of it is

understated, it's not flash… very coolly played.' In contrast, the
bassist's own playing is 'just about the most complicated pattern
I've ever used – usually I just plod along and leave it to the others.'

Demon's Eye
A mid-tempo rocker with what Glover rates as 'some of the
best drum sounds I've ever heard'.

Anyone's Daughter
The country and western feel came from Blackmore – 'a spoof',
he claimed – while Gillan's lyrics harked back to 'Early days of
frustration… never forgotten. Two enraptured lovers, rising sap,
chattering teeth and shaky legs. Ah, but then "father" comes into
the equation…'

For Roger Glover, Purple were 'trying to take rock music one
stage further, and I think we overstepped the mark. "Anyone's
Daughter" was a good bit of fun, but it was a mistake. The reason
we left the rubbish on at the beginning was we'd got used to
hearing it on the playbacks so many times it didn't seem right
without it. This is very strange, this track, because it was recorded
the day after we'd had a big discussion about being exciting and
heavy. We were sitting around the studio waiting for inspiration
when Ritchie started tinkling around with that chord thing and
we joined in.'

The Mule
The lyrics are secondary to the mood on a number that caused
much difficulty in the studio. Roger Glover: 'In an effort to
achieve a flanging effect the tape had been reversed but was
in record mode. Halfway through the error was realised and the
engineer shot across the room to hit the stop button. Too late, the
damage had been done… half the drums had been erased from the
middle to the end of the song. The problem was compounded by
the fact that Ian's drums had been packed and were on their way
to Europe. A kit was hastily rented and Ian had to overdub new

drums but it was impossible to make the two kits sound the same and the difference is still there for anyone to hear.'

Fools

Gillan's voice is 'thickened' on this one, a song 'about a guy who dies and he's looking back and can see the world is run by fools.' Roger Glover was delighted with a guitar solo 'we'd been using on stage for some time, we never thought it would work on record, but its great. None of it is worked out, it's just ad-libbed.'

No One Came

Gillan's words echo his fears 'about the ultimate horror of an empty hall' and are, in Roger's opinion, 'the best lyrics Ian has written, they're autobiographical to a certain extent'. The song was played live at the Camden Arts Festival but didn't go down well with an audience expecting more familiar fare.

Machine Head

Having arrived in Montreux in December 1971 but been left with nowhere to record their proposed album following the Casino fire, Purple Mark II found that the Grand Hotel was empty for the winter and hired the whole place for a reasonable price. Martin Birch parked the mobile studio outside and found a suitable corridor for recording that was shaped like a 'T'.

'We put the drums on the T itself,' explained Birch, 'the guitar and organ at one end and the bass at the other facing into a cupboard full of mattresses. To get into the studio from the truck you had to go through the lobby, through a kitchen, then a bathroom, out onto a freezing cold balcony, back into the hotel, through another bathroom, a couple of bedrooms, yet another bathroom, and finally into the corridor!'

Ritchie already had a backing track for 'Smoke On The Water', which had come about after the fire when Claude Nobs moved them into the Pavilion theatre as an alternative venue. The backing track needed a big echoey sound – but, as they worked, Purple realised the hall wasn't soundproofed and, as it was one in the morning, they were keeping the entire town of Montreux awake.

'The roadies were blocking the doors against the police,' remembers Glover. 'It didn't seem like such a big deal at the time but the song went on to become one of our all-time favourites. The song's lasting success is that gloriously simple yet very original riff. Every person I have ever met that ever played guitar has told me it was the first thing they could play. That's quite an honour.'

Blackmore, the man who originated the riff, recalls the police knocking on the studio door. 'We knew that they were going to say "Stop recording!" because they'd had complaints about the noise. So we wouldn't open the door to the police. We asked Martin Birch, "Is that the one?" And he said, "I don't know. I've got to hear the whole thing all the way through to know if it's *the* one." We didn't want to open up until we knew we had got the right take. Finally we got it.' The move to the Grand Hotel followed…

The guitarist believes the whole album to be better than the previous release, explaining, 'I think the ideas are better and the group were playing well when we recorded it. The songs are more interesting too.' Jon Lord is not in total agreement, however, stating 'One's memory of *Machine Head* is very different to the actuality. I went back to it the other day and it's a very dry, dark sort of album, it doesn't sparkle like you remember it doing… it's very serious and down-the-line.' The result was released in April 1972 and was a serious success, giving Purple their second UK chart-topper and a US Top 10 breakthrough.

Highway Star

Glover describes it as 'The perfect opener. It's fast, everyone gets a solo. Ian has a thing about 1950s lyrics… It was written on a bus; just appeared – scribbled-down lyrics and let's try it tonight, see what happens. It evolved on stage, it wasn't written; it evolved.'

The song looked back to go forwards. 'I worked out the solo for that one before I actually recorded it, which I never used to do,' explained Blackmore. 'That run in thirds is an old run I used to play ten years earlier. Johnny Burnette taught me that run and I hadn't used it for years. It isn't original but it is exciting! I like classical chord progressions, like in the solo... B minor to a C... to a G... that's a Bach progression.'

Maybe I'm A Leo
'A personal thing with Ian,' explains Glover. 'His sign is Leo. Ian Paice and myself have similar tastes... we listen to the same albums, have the same influences, and we both appreciate the way some musicians (particularly American) have a laid-back approach to playing without being lazy, which I think shows on this track.'

Never Before
Two weeks' writing produced what the band thought was the most commercial thing they'd ever done. 'All of us were unanimous,' states Gillan, 'the whole band. We put it out and it was the biggest flop we ever had!' Roger Glover recalls 'Never Before' as 'The song we thought was going to get all the attention... I put a lot of time and effort into that one. A couple of days after we recorded it we were all going round singing it – we suddenly realised it was in our heads...'

Pictures Of Home
A song that talks about the mountains and snow, 'although I don't believe we ever saw eagles,' admits Glover. 'We tried "Pictures Of Home" – which I liked a lot on the record – but it never seemed to work out on stage,' Blackmore explains. 'It was that six-eight fill... but we did it and I was watching the audience. They were yawning.'

Smoke On The Water
'This has lasted so long because it's very simple,' says Blackmore, 'very catchy... basically incorporating four notes. It's got tons of

personality!'

'It was a riff Ritchie had put down,' continues Lord. 'Its working title was "Durh Durh Durh"! It's been very kind to us, that song; it's been worth five figures a year [each]… closer to six figures.'

Lazy

Based on an Oscar Brown Junior song called 'Sleepy', this was written mainly as a vehicle for Jon and Ritchie's solos. 'That's a weird solo,' says Blackmore, 'because I did a particular part one day, and I did another part another day; you can hear the difference. I still criticise that solo. I think the song was great; the composition was good, but I could have done better. I was inspired to write that by Eric Clapton's "Steppin' Out".'

Space Truckin'

This includes a drum pattern lifted from the Nice's 'America' according to Paice, and is all about space travel but done in a 1950s lyrical style 'which is really a way of saying nothing!' teases Glover. 'It's full of puns… we just sat around making up stupid little phrases about space.'

Who Do We Think We Are

Early attempts to record an album in a villa near Rome with the Rolling Stones Mobile in July 1972 having proved barren, the venue switched to Waldorf, near Frankfurt, in October. The release date was February 1973. The resulting album would never be promoted live, and only one track would make it – briefly – to the stage set. It's fair to say, then, that *Who Do We Think We Are* ranks as an even greater blip than *Fireball* in Purple Mark II's relentless progress. But with relations in the band at a low ebb and having been worked into the ground by management and record company, was this really any surprise?

The first sign that sessions would not prove fruitful came when the recording studio truck would not fit under the villa's arched gateway. So, as in Montreux, they were back to the situation that the mixing desk was a long way from where the band were playing. Ritchie Blackmore ended up playing his solos in the truck sitting next to producer Martin Birch, who remembers, 'I could sense they weren't working as cohesively as before. If someone had an idea there was not much enthusiasm for it, whereas before they had always gone into ideas with plenty.'

Ian Gillan confirms the making of this album was an unhappy experience, 'basically because Ritchie and I had had enough of one another. Before we went there was a big discussion about the type of album we should be doing. I thought we should maintain our attitudes towards progression and not fall into the trap of just turning out the same old stuff. The adrenalin wasn't there somehow... it had all been brought on by working non-stop.'

The atmosphere in Rome was indeed bad, guitarist Blackmore absenting himself when Gillan was around. 'During the whole session,' the singer recalled, 'all we recorded was a track called "Smelly Botty", "Painted Horse" and a bizarre version of Conway Twitty's "It's Only Make Believe". I dread to think what it cost.' 'Painted Horse' surfaced on the remastered CD in 2000. Gillan: 'Martin Birch and I liked it very much and assumed it was going to be on the album but no one else did, so it got buried in the vaults.'

As the sessions had yielded nothing, and the band were due to tour Japan and the States before embarking on another British tour, Purple's management booked them in at a German studio in October to salvage the project. This second session seems to have been conducted totally professionally, doubtless partly due to Gillan remaining out of Blackmore's way and adding his vocals to the finished backing tracks.

Purple were finding it harder and harder to come up with the necessary inspiration and, as Ian Paice reflects, 'At the time the success you've been working for is happening you don't realise how much you're draining yourself. Ritchie had been ill and he couldn't come up with the guitar riffs that made the earlier albums… It was a bad, confusing time, and the management were no help, they were lost. They were asked for the first time to do what show business managers do – keep control. They had lucked into success, but knowing what to do in a crisis? Not one idea.'

Despite all the problems, *Who Do We Think We Are* made Number 4 in Britain and 15 in the States.

Woman From Tokyo

To a riff Blackmore self-confessedly stole from 'Cat's Squirrel', Gillan added words anticipating 'the excitement of our first trip to Japan… a pioneering journey, never to be forgotten'. The resulting song was selected as the album's single.

The first middle section was deemed too weak, while another point of interest is the lyrical reference to an earlier composition, 'Black Night'. 'This odd way of occasionally referring to earlier work is something that became a career-long idiosyncrasy,' remarks Roger Glover who, with Jon Lord, put in a rare backing vocal performance on the outro.

Mary Long

Inspired by newspaper accounts of the activities of self-appointed moral crusaders Mary Whitehouse and Lord Longford, 'Mary Long' was clearly a composite name. 'These people would rail against anything which might be considered "untoward",' Gillan explained. 'They were the publicity-conscious PC fascists of their day; nothing much changes except that the currently self-righteous use the *bon mot* "inappropriate". Roger and I clearly were not suggesting that either Whitehouse or Longford would stoop to drowning kittens or drawing a piece of graffiti on a toilet wall, but there is and always has been a sinister whiff of hypocrisy emanating from the pulpit of the pious.'

The song would be the only one to make the live set in 1973, and was again played in the early twenty-first-century set when both protagonists were gone and forgotten – but not by Gillan, whose performance was as self-righteous as ever!

Super Trouper
Roger Glover was thinking of bluesman Freddie King's 'Going Down' when he wrote this song, titled after a stage spotlight and long before Abba thought of doing likewise. (The resemblance, however, is slim.) The bassist described it as 'a soul-baring song about a performer singing to a spotlight, and [we were] also having some fun with tape flanging.'

Smooth Dancer
There's a message to Ritchie Blackmore barely hidden in the lyrics of 'Smooth Dancer', with its frequent reference to black suede, his favourite clothing. Roger Glover found it 'very illuminating to read those lyrics and then realise what was going on in Ian's mind at the time. He wasn't going to take what Ritchie was handing out but at the same time he wanted to be friends again.'

Rat Bat Blue
Roger Glover's favourite track on the album, 'A song based around a drum fill… about picking up a loose chick for the night.'

Place In Line
Inspired by a sci-fi story, this was in Roger's view 'an attempt to create a vehicle for the soloists along the lines of "Lazy".'

Our Lady
Titled by Ritchie after he'd seen it outside a church, 'Our Lady' was, in Jon Lord's opinion, 'quite surprising – for a start it's very slow and concentrates more on the tune and the lyrics and there are no solos. It's just a song, which is not normally the way Deep Purple seems to work.'

Burn

The first album by the Mark III Purple line-up took shape in the same environment that had produced *Machine Head*. Recorded in November 1973 in Montreux with the aid of the Rolling Stones mobile, it was released the following February. Despite the controversial personnel changes that had taken place, it performed better than its Mark II predecessor, *Who Do We Think We Are*, in both Britain (where it made Number 3) and the States (9).

Rehearsals at Clearwell Castle had helped, as had the break from the road which had aided the writing process. Blackmore, his nemesis Gillan now departed, felt 'such a relief that we had some new blood… It was a rock 'n' roll band having a great time and playing well,' while Jon Lord was impressed that 'Ritchie said it was "not bad" … by anyone else's standards that meant wonderful!'

Lord enjoyed the 'different vocal approach' exhibited by David Coverdale. 'It's much freer and looser, a progression.' He saw no evidence of the newcomer, with no studio experience to speak of, being overawed to be working with Purple – or at least if he was 'it only showed when we were talking between ourselves over a beer, never during the actual recording.'

Producer Martin Birch agreed that there was a really good feeling in the band. 'Everyone just wanted to get down and work together and they produced a good rock album rather than let Glenn's funk influences creep in.' Bassist Glenn Hughes agreed that *Burn* was 'basic rock – too basic for me. I wasn't into that kind of material… I had to work with Jon and Ritchie to really get into that kind of music.'

Whatever, it was a success on both commercial and creative levels: these heights would rarely be hit again.

Burn
The guitar riff is remarkably similar to George Gershwin's 'Fascinating Rhythm' but, according to Ritchie Blackmore, was

'exactly how I wanted the band to sound like… It was done very quickly too – in about five takes. Some of the solos hit… I played with Jon, and Jon' s part is very good. I thought the riff was very good. It's "Fascinating Rhythm", although I didn't know until Jon Lord told me!'

Musically, Jon Lord's classical keyboard progression is the magic touch. The riff came first and got David Coverdale 'very excited'… but then he had to write lyrics to fit it! 'I wanted them to have a modern setting yet give a surrealist flavour.' Ian Paice summed them up thus: 'It's all about a medieval theme – witches and people burning towns and things…'

Listen carefully and you'll hear a mistake from Blackmore right at the end, 'a big "klonk" on my guitar. At the time I'd wanted to overdub it – it sounded like I'd caught my fingers in the strings – but everyone said it sounded natural, so it was left on there.'

Might Just Take Your Life

One of Jon Lord's ideas and, in David Coverdale's view, 'a perfect marriage between keyboards and guitar… Lordy heard Ritchie's original backing, thought it too ordinary, and added the organ riff as a contrast.'

Lay Down Stay Down

'It's just a funky piece of rock 'n' roll,' insisted Ian Paice of this somewhat misogynistic song; 'you can't really say it means anything. Musically, he believed it 'harks back a bit rhythmically to Mark II. It had some of that rock 'n' roll fire in it while some of the other songs on *Burn* were slowly moving in another direction.' He concluded it would, with a different lyric, have fitted just as easily on *In Rock* as on *Burn*.

Sail Away

Blackmore had been experimenting with a guitar synthesiser, and the aggressive, unique, growling tone of 'Sail Away' was the result. David Coverdale was up all night writing the lyric and was particularly pleased with the result. 'But, when I was recording the song, I started to panic that the key was too low. I felt like I was doing a monologue instead of singing!' Fortunately he was reassured and the result was 'one of the best songs we ever did – a very intelligent track with lots of feel. It would have made a good single.'

You Fool No One

This was based on a complex and relentless drum pattern created by Ian Paice. When a take was aborted due to something amusing to the rest of the band, the drummer, in Coverdale's words, 'threw down his sticks and stormed off the drum kit... "Hey, this is fucking hard to play... Get it right or I'm off!" He was dripping wet from playing the song perfectly for the last three or four takes-so, needless to say we got the song on the next pass.'

Glenn Hughes felt this betrayed the influence of Led Zeppelin, while Paice himself recalls 'messing around with a rudiment involving the cowbell and the bass drum and as I was playing Ritchie came in with his riff and they just went together. Basically it's a drum paradiddle between the cowbell and the bass drum and the snare, buts it's a wonderful four-four metre you can play this rudiment in.'

What's Goin' On Here?

Inspired by a Jimi Hendrix song, probably 'Highway Chile', this, for Purple's vocalist, 'gave a great opportunity to stretch out a little... It's a story of someone having too much drink. Jon does some fantastic piano, lovely jazz feel interpreting the lolloping, drunk character.' His co-vocalist Glenn Hughes had fun singing it. 'It's just a twelve-bar blues song, very simple, very live.'

Mistreated

A track with a very heavy blues feel that presented a challenge to the singer. 'I had to get right inside it and get myself in the appropriate emotional condition, a very heavy physical thing... That track means so much to me, I tried hard because I knew it was essential to get the emotive qualities the song needed.'

Ritchie Blackmore reveals the song was influenced by 'Heartbreaker', title track of a 1973 album by Free. The riff was only three notes, 'but with them you can express yourself. And if you have nothing to say, you'll fall into a hole, because there's no melody, nothing you can hang your head on... you have to improvise.' He'd invited Glenn to his home in South London and the pair started jamming. 'We got into this half-time groove in F sharp,' recalled the bassist who thought it 'a real blast to have just the two of us face-to-face creating this fine song.'

A200

The only song on *Burn* that wasn't worked on beforehand in rehearsals, this got its name from a lotion to get rid of crabs from sensitive bodily areas! Jon Lord insisted an instrumental appear on the album 'because I wanted to utilise a synthesiser... we just jammed until a song arrived,' while the track contains David Coverdale's favourite guitar solo on the album: 'It's coming from his soul, it's great.'

Stormbringer

Started at Munich Musicland studio and completed at Los Angeles' Record Plant in the summer of 1974 for release that December, the sessions for *Stormbringer*, producer Martin Birch recalls, had 'a strange atmosphere. It wasn't going the way Ritchie wanted and by the time it came to the mixing stage he'd lost interest completely. There was also a bit of strain between Glenn and David about who should sing and where.'

David and Jon had written a lot of material at Clearwell that didn't make it onto the album, while Ritchie was producing fewer good ideas than in the past. This left a gap for Glenn Hughes to fill, which he did, to Blackmore's chagrin in particular. The result, for Lord, was 'a band struggling to look for somewhere else to go but trapped by its own identity'.

Blackmore put the lack of guitar input down to the fact that he was going through some personal problems, notably a divorce. 'I was thinking about other things when I should have been thinking about the music… Glenn was really pushing for the R&B bit, and David had become much more into it too. Those two were taking Jon with them, because they could use funky organ, and of course Paicey was in there 'cause he could play funky too. Everybody except for me! We had become five egotistical maniacs… not a team. *Stormbringer* was crap… I didn't like the album at all.'

Ian Paice sided with Lord in feeling it would have been rated a good album if it had been recorded by anyone but Purple. 'But because people expect certain things out of you they think, well that's weird. I think everyone was a bit confused!'

As open war had developed between Blackmore and the rest of the band, it's no surprise that *Stormbringer* – a Number 6 success in Britain, 20 in the States – would be the swansong for Purple Mark III.

Stormbringer
David Coverdale claims to have written the title track lyric 'to keep Ritchie happy [with one of] those kind of sci-fi poems'.

Love Don't Mean A Thing
Though band-credited, Blackmore curiously attributed the inspiration to 'some coloured guy [who] came up to me at a party and said, "I've got a song for you"… He started snapping his fingers and it sounded great. I figured if it sounds this good just with him snapping his fingers, then its got to be a good tune for the band. We rearranged it, added some parts, and recorded it.' The result surprised many Purple fans.

Holy Man
A Coverdale/Hughes/Lord collaboration which summed up the album's 'black-centric' direction for Ritchie. When Glenn asked him to play some slide guitar, 'He just looked at me strangely, used a screwdriver to play the part and left the room.'

Hold On

A song that was Jon Lord's idea, but still failed to please Ritchie who did his solo sitting in the control room with the speakers on. 'He played it so casually, said he couldn't be bothered, but it was fantastic!' said Coverdale. 'I only played this number under protest,' Ritchie confirms. 'I played up to the solo only with my thumb… it was my way of rebelling. The band gave me black looks, but I said, "Okay, I don't like the song but look, I'm playing it. But don't tell me how to play it".'

Lady Double Dealer

A blues-rock type stomp, with a typical Coverdale lyric of the time. Succinct, punchy, no-nonsense delivery, the commercial sound of which showed a further departure from the Purple sound of old. Featured in the live 1974–1975 shows and resurrected by Glenn Hughes for his solo 1995 tour.

You Can't Do It Right

One of Glenn Hughes' favourite Deep Purple songs and one the visiting Stevie Wonder enjoyed – even though by Hughes' own admission 'I ripped him off [vocally] so bad. He came up to me and could not believe I was white. He touched my face and said, "I can't believe you're not a brother." He took me under his wing. I stayed and hung out with him for two days. I sat on his organ bench while he was playing some keyboards and we became real good friends. He called me his favourite white singer, which I thought was brilliant.'

Highball Shooter

Though he received one fifth of the songwriting credit, Blackmore didn't stick around to find out the title of the song, 'although I recall its in the key of A. I don't like black funk music… it bores me.'

Gypsy

Blackmore's riff and chord progression plus Coverdale's lyrics made up a studio creation that became something of a fan favourite despite a preponderance of synthesiser.

Soldier of Fortune

A Blackmore/Coverdale track with 'middle-ages chords' the guitarist unsurprisingly rates as one of his few favourites on the album. It took a lot of effort to persuade the others to do it,' he claimed. 'Glenn hated it. Ian was fed up after two takes with nothing to do. David would occasionally come up with a song like this, but I felt there was a lack of input on the whole.'

The pair had cut a demo with a multi-tracked Ritchie playing guitars and bass, which persuaded the rest of the band to participate on. Vindicated, Coverdale and Blackmore considered leaving it as it was but in the end redid it.

Come Taste The Band

The first ever Deep Purple album cut *sans* Ritchie Blackmore came together at Munich's Musicland Studios in August 1975 and was released that December. American Tommy Bolin had been selected over ex-Humble Pie guitarist Clem Clempson whose style had failed to gel with the band, and was considered to bring 'something to the table'. Unfortunately, he would bring personal issues too, but that would become more apparent later.

The newcomer had a very different style of playing but, according to producer Martin Birch, 'didn't know what he was doing half the time. He played totally on feel.' Bassist Glenn Hughes locked into Bolin's style most closely, leading to an extra funky feel as Birch states: 'The funk thing now came from both of them.' Given Blackmore had allegedly forbidden Hughes to venture to his side of the stage, the idea of an ally in the band must have appealed.

For Jon Lord, Bolin was 'even more fluid than Ritchie had been, especially on blues things, but he wasn't as accomplished technically.' He made up for it, however, in mastery of effects. 'Tommy bought along Echoplexes and octave dividers and he was great at using them.' Evidence has survived in the shape of some jams from June 1975 which suggest Bolin, unlike Clem Clempson, was not about to be overawed by his predecessor's reputation. Of assistance in that regard was the fact that all the American knew of Purple's repertoire was two numbers – 'Smoke' and one other!

Bolin, who continued his solo career in parallel with Purple as a condition of his recruitment, didn't think his new bandmates would be 'as good as they are at all, or as funky'. He decided to test them, 'to see where they were at. I started playing something very funky, and they immediately caught on. After half an hour jamming I walked over and got a drink, and they sat around talking. Jon, who knows every song in the book, started playing *Cabaret* and I was really drunk and I started singing by mistake, "Come see the band, come taste the band," so that's how the title of the album came about. If Jon hadn't laid back in the studio and let me do all the things I ended up doing, I don't think it would have turned out as well as it did.'

That tale, of course, hints at the lack of self-control around drink and drugs that would bring the guitarist's life to a premature end in late 1976. He was also, notes Ian Paice, unable to handle 'an audience of more than 200 people. A nice record came out of it, but the tour was hell.' Initially though, for Jon Lord, he 'made the band a different place to be'. *Come Taste The Band* reflected both that happiness and that difference. Feelings from fans that this was a bridge too far, however, were reflected in disappointing chart showings of Number 19 in Britain and 43 in the States.

Comin' Home

A storming album opener, with hindsight a taste of things to come with Whitesnake. Great 'effects' solo from Bolin, who played both guitar and bass, as Glenn was (by his own admission) 'out of it' for the initial sessions.

Lady Luck

Tommy had collaborated with a singer-songwriter (and former bandmate in American Standard) called Jeff Cook for many of the songs that appeared on his solo album *Teaser*, released around the same time as *Come Taste The Band*, so when Purple were throwing ideas together it wasn't surprising he'd remember one Cook had written which hadn't been recorded. 'He played the tune, but couldn't recall the lyrics,' Coverdale said. 'We decided to do it anyway, and I wrote new lyrics to go with the tune.'

Gettin' Tighter

Like 'Mistreated' before it, this gained in stature in a live context, and the studio version now seems just a pale imitation. A funk-orientated track dominated by Hughes and Bolin perhaps best sampled in the February 1976 Long Beach performance – all thirteen minutes of it.

Dealer

'This was David's song to me, I guess,' said Glenn Hughes of one of several songs on the album that featured drug references. 'He cared for me a lot and always had his head screwed on.'

I Need Love

Bolin and Coverdale hog the credits again in a rocky song that heralds a trio of songs that were perhaps nearest to Purple's classic Mark III incarnation.

Drifter

A very early product of Mark IV Purple, this was written by the new guitarist, and vocalist Coverdale and lays down a very Free-like blues groove. (Free spin-offs Bad Company were very big around this time.) A line from this gave the title to the *Days May Come, Days May Go* official bootleg.

Love Child

Again credited to Bolin and Coverdale, this Zep-esque rocker was based around a recycled riff from a Joe Walsh song Tommy had performed during his short spell in the James Gang. Something of 'Into The Fire' about this...

This Time Around

One of the few examples of a Glenn Hughes solo vocal, and impressive it is too, with minimal Stevie Wonder impressions for once. A sparse, sorrowful piano backing adds an attractive haunting feel to a song that segues into...

Owed To G

Although Tommy Bolin's technique is totally different to Blackmore's, this is the closest to Mark III in spirit he ever got. A nice melodic instrumental that attempts to continue the theme that 'This Time Around' started.

You Keep On Moving

The original idea for this number had surfaced back in 1974 'when Jon Lord wrote the chords around the "where angels fear to tread" bit', said Coverdale – who, with Hughes, was credited with the track. An acknowledged highlight of the album.

Perfect Strangers

The first recorded fruit of the Deep Purple Mark II reunion, cut in the summer of 1984 at Stowe, Vermont with Le Mobile Studio, and released that November was, in Ian Paice's view, 'a natural progression from the earlier records, but with ten years' growth in-between'. Relations within the band were cautiously friendly: 'Everyone knew it was a rocky boat, so nobody rocked it.'

For Ian Gillan, 'The magic was back... I couldn't keep this

stupid grin off my face.' Indeed, everything came together so easily that recording only took a month. Gillan believed 'the chemistry of what Roger had referred to once as "an old love affair, where love can be very close to hate" existed in *Perfect Strangers*. It felt wrapped in warmth, care and love, which is how our best work has always happened.'

Despite finding chart success with Rainbow in-between times, Ritchie Blackmore was keen to resist producing anything overtly commercial. 'We had to carry on with the same type of Purple music, even though it might fall on deaf ears. We did think about various producers, but in the end we said, "No, let's get Roger to do it." You can't start thinking of glossy production, calling in people like Mutt Lange and doing a Def Leppard or something… we knew we had to stick to our guns and go down with the ship if need be. Luckily it paid off.'

Blackmore came up with most of the musical ideas from a stockpile of material he'd been saving. 'Anything I had didn't come up to that [standard],' said Jon Lord, 'so I didn't put it forward. *Perfect Strangers* had Purple reaching out with one hand across the ten years or whatever and trying to drag that into the future. I thought the title track was fairly current, and the opening to "Knockin'…" was good too… but overall it was a pretty safe album. In fact it was almost impossible to make any other sort of album at that time.'

Purple fans, merely delighted to see their heroes happily back together, sent *Perfect Strangers* into the UK Top 5 and to the US Number 17 position.

Knockin' At Your Back Door

Another Rainbow reject riff that sparked Purple to life and yielded a minor transatlantic hit single to boot.

Under The Gun

Containing Blackmore's favourite guitar solo of the album, this was

Purple at their aggressive best – or as near as they were going to get.

Nobody's Home

A mid-tempo track, with more prominent Lord organ touches, and aggressive, confident singing from Ian. A touch workmanlike in execution overall though, with nothing to lift it out of the ordinary.

Mean Streak

A rather uninspired muddy-sounding backing coupled with a very clichéd (even for Ian Gillan!) lyrical theme makes this filler.

Perfect Strangers

Built around a riff intended for Rainbow that they could never make work. 'It just wouldn't fit,' reflected Roger Glover. 'Then, just for laughs, when Purple were rehearsing up in Vermont, Ritchie dug it out, and what do you know it worked!'

For Ian Gillan, the words he sang referred to the band's uncertainties about themselves and the reaction from the public. 'A recognition that the days of gay abandon had passed and that a new phase was being entered. And so, from my point of view, the loneliness and singularity of all these vulnerabilities being put under a spotlight, a strand of silver for the first time.'

A Gypsy's Kiss

An up-tempo, driving number featuring a impressively precise country-picking solo from Ritchie, and Ian's enjoyment with the nonsensical lyrics is obvious. A pleasant solo from Jon Lord, too.

Wasted Sunsets

Roger Glover wrote most of the lyrics one night. 'I showed them to Ian the next day. He liked them, made a few changes, and that was that.'

Hungry Daze

The autobiographical nature of much the album's lyrics is never more apparent than on this song: 'The stinking hippy' and 'We all went out to Montreux' being the most obvious references to the past. A simple repeated riff comprises the main musical theme. Backward keyboards and phased guitars feature on the rather strange and experimental outro, a highpoint of the song.

Not Responsible

A departure from the obvious commercial sound of the rest of the album (hence its inclusion on CD format only). Some adroit bass touches from Roger underpin the tune, and Paice shines with several attractive changes in tempo and dynamics throughout course of the song. A little more 1970s in feel than the other tracks but an underrated reunion classic.

The House Of Blue Light

The recording of the reunited band's second album, named after a line from 'Speed King', exactly followed the pattern of the first – in Stowe, Vermont with Le Mobile Studio, but two years later in the autumn of 1986.

'We started recording in Massachusetts,' Ian Paice later revealed, 'but the place we were working at was a little too rural for us.' Released in January 1987, *The House Of Blue Light* was not to repeat the glory of the comeback effort. 'None of us got it right,' Gillan now reflects. 'There was no spirit in the group and I was appalled by some of this record.'

The fact that Purple spent three and a half months in the studio this time around as opposed to a month for *Perfect Strangers* was, Jon Lord reflected, because the material assembled a year previously hadn't stood up to the test of time, 'so we had to start from scratch'. Glover had wanted to do 'some gigs in small clubs and "play" the songs in, because we always seem to write material that, once we try to perform live, there's a problem. I really tried to convince the band, but we went the usual studio way.' The result was 'a disappointing album; a rather wooden mess.'

The return to Stowe had been made with reluctance, said drummer Paice, 'because we didn't want the ghosts of the last album hanging over our heads'. Sadly, that was exactly the result. The album's UK Number 10 position (34 in the States) would never be regained by any future version of the band.

Bad Attitude
'An American expression,' explained Gillan, 'and I *hate* posy expressions. I wish people could talk properly.' Apparently deriving from a row between Gillan and Blackmore on the football pitch, 'which ended with me telling him to piss off', the theme developed into the song.

The Unwritten Law
A complex riff from Blackmore – 'the most difficult one I've ever had to write [lyrics] for!' claimed Gillan – this was in Glover's view 'the most progressive thing we've done in years. It's a very modal type riff using sequencers and it sure ain't traditional Deep Purple.' The subject matter uses the subject of venereal disease – a rock musician's occupational hazard – as 'a general comment on how people should have a little more responsibility.'

Call Of The Wild
When presented to the record company, this was immediately marked out as 'an obvious single.' The band, especially Gillan, had considered it 'too sloppy at first, but when it was finished it had a nice edge to it. It sounds like some of the more accessible songs we've done in the past.' For Roger Glover, it was 'our sort of nod of respect to 1950s rock 'n' roll… Chuck Berry's "Memphis Tennessee", that sort of thing.'

Mad Dog

'Just good fun,' said Gillan of another track whose lyrics may have been aimed at someone close to home.

Black And White

No plea for racial tolerance but a light-hearted attack on the press and people's attitude towards it. 'Some people believe that if they see something in black and white it must be true, although very often it's not true at all. It is difficult to tell people that what they read in the newspapers isn't necessarily true.'

Roger Glover recalls the band reading the tabloids while rehearsing and talking about abuses of freedom. 'I said to Ritchie, "Let's channel this anger into a song, since it's something we feel strongly about".'

Hard Lovin' Woman

Having recorded a song called 'Hard Lovin' Man' in their early days, Purple thought 'Hard Lovin' Woman' 'would be a laugh,' recalled Gillan. 'Roger and I wrote a whole list of potential titles up on the wall of this little room in Stowe, and that was one of them. We wanted a hard rock 'n' roll song with tight harmonies, that kind of thing... and the title fitted the bill.'

Spanish Archer

Ian Gillan didn't think this song should have been included on the album at all. 'It isn't properly arranged... just a series of verses with jamming in between, and it wears on me. But everyone else disagrees with me, which is par for the course! If you give someone the "Spanish Archer",' he continued, 'you give them the elbow... so this song is all about giving some lump the heave-ho.' For Jon Lord, the track's saving grace was 'some incredible guitar playing... Ritchie at his finest.'

Strangeways
Gillan's favourite song on the album, thanks largely to the vocal harmonies on the intro. For Jon Lord, this was 'a long and intense number which we spent a long time on'.

Mitzi Dupree
A song inspired by a chance encounter Gillan made on a flight to Salt Lake City while he was briefly in Black Sabbath. 'I saw this amazing boiler sat in my seat. I went over to talk to her and she said, "Hi, I'm Mitzi... Mitzi Dupree." It turned out she was going to a mining town in Canada to do a show. I asked her what she did and she told me she did an act with ping-pong balls...! The song came out of a live jam and we recorded it for reference. I played it back afterwards and thought it was great... I couldn't stop playing it, so I said to Roger, "We've got to do something with it." He said, "Well, we can write on it, but we can't play it again because everyone else hates it." So we wrote the lyric, I sang it to the jam tape, and left it at that... so natural and spontaneous.'

Dead Or Alive
Another song 'everyone else likes but I don't', though even the protesting Gillan could see 'It's going to be good on-stage.' Ritchie felt it was 'much too fast for the audience to relate to'.

Slaves And Masters

After the disaster of *House Of Blue Light*, distanced by the *Nobody's Perfect* live album that followed it, Purple made a conscious effort to start making records like they had twenty years earlier. 'All be in a room, play it together and try and get it right!' said Ian Paice, who concluded: 'I think we got about fifty per cent of that back.' The room(s) in question was Greg Rike Studios, Orlando and the Power Station, New York early in 1990, the album being released in October of that year.

The first major difference was the presence of Joe Lynn Turner in place of Ian Gillan. This showed not only in the vocal style but also in the lyrics. 'Ian tended to write in a surreal vein,' Jon Lord noted, 'while Joe's a bit further down the body. Roger and Joe spent an enormous amount of time together working on the lyrics to this album and I think they really bonded.'

Indeed there were many parallels with the early 1980s Rainbow albums, with Turner singing, Blackmore soloing and bassist Glover producing. But for the new boy, 'this album is dirtier and nastier [than Rainbow]. Everyone was anxious to be Deep Purple but also be a bit up to date. Some may say it's not as aggressive but I think the album has drama, and lots of different grooves... It incorporates drama and excitement... We had the Purplesque attitude, but we also had some Rainbow styles... it still sounds, to me, closer to the truth of Deep Purple than what's been coming out lately!'

With its UK Number 45 chart placing, this was Purple's least successful album on home soil since Mark I days, while American audiences bought enough to send it to Number 87. The ultimate verdict was delivered by Jon Lord at the launch of follow-up album *The Battle Rages On*, by which time of course Ian Gillan had been reinstated. 'We want to show we can deliver better things than *Slaves And Masters*, which was not really a Deep Purple album at all. It carried the name, but the sleeve was deceiving.'

King Of Dreams

After an unproductive couple of days in the studio, Ritchie started playing a new riff. 'He played it only once,' said Glover, 'and when we'd done it I said, "That's really good, let's work on it." But Ritchie wouldn't! We came back to it a couple of weeks later, did some overdubs, Joe got to work on a set of lyrics I'd got, then by the time the rest of the band came in we had a song.'

The lyrical reference to 'Real smooth dancer' by Joe Lynn Turner refers to Ritchie, who wanted his solo 'to evoke a certain mood. It isn't meant to be a pointless exercise in speed that's why it's very sparse.'

The Cut Runs Deep

For once the band sound like they mean it. A sharp metallic opening riff and Joe performs with a sense of urgency. A superb flowing Lord solo, with some great organ flourishes as JLT leads the outro. A tight, well-constructed contemporary track hinting at what the line-up could achieve.

Fire In The Basement

The emphasis on Lord's Hammond in this song drives it along – plus there's a great solo from Ritchie who, says Jon, 'plays like a demon'.

Truth Hurts

This power ballad of the type so beloved of American radio comes across as a plodding, lacklustre affair, although a good break from Blackmore momentarily lifts the mood. Gained more majesty when performed live.

Breakfast In Bed

A promising guitar run opens a song which quickly turns into another rather bland AOR track that could be a latter-day Rainbow composition. Some attractive Blackmore doodling throughout.

Love Conquers All

Co-writer Lord has suggested this had the potential to 'When A Blind Man Cries', 'Child In Time' (the quiet parts) or 'Wasted Sunsets', describing it as 'a ballad of the kind we sometimes play, a blues ballad. But then Joe appeared and turned it into some sort of cabaret song I continuously said, "No, no, no – what are you doing?" I really tried to steer the piece into a different direction. I have for example put in a string quartet... I used a Hammond Emulator II for the string section... I wanted it to sound a little more sour and not so sweet.' Turner 'sang it like it was a real kitsch ballad!'

Roger Glover felt there was 'a Motown influence' in that his bass outlined where the chords are, the guitar keeping basic time.

Fortuneteller
The basic riff idea surfaced on a couple of occasions during live shows in 1988. Once given the JLT treatment, it becomes one of the more Rainbow-esque songs on the album.

Too Much Is Not Enough
A song Turner had prepared for his next solo album, but hadn't recorded, co-written with Al Greenwood, once of Foreigner. 'I didn't really think the song was for Purple, but Ritchie liked it so much he wanted to include it. We did a good version of it back then, but I don't think it should have been on the record.' (He re-recorded it for a subsequent album, *Hurry Up & Wait*.)

Wicked Ways
Contains Ritchie's best moments on the album, with the latter third of the song taken up with a lengthy twisting solo that soars into the stratosphere, well supported by the rest of the band. A good groove rhythm-wise too, perhaps one of the better all-round performances on the album.

The Battle Rages On

Two sets of recording sessions gave birth to this most uneasy of albums, the last to feature the combined talents of Ian Gillan and Ritchie Blackmore. The instrumental backing tracks were recorded prior to Gillan's return at Red Rooster, Tutzing, near Munich in November and December 1991, and Greg Rike Studios, Orlando, Florida, in February–March 1992 and Connecticut May–June 1992. The vocals were added at Greg Rike at the beginning of 1993 and the album finally released that July.

The songs were, of course, written with Joe Lynn Turner in mind, but the rest of the band (bar one) wanted Ian Gillan back to sing them. 'I wanted to bring someone else in,' said Blackmore, 'but I was outvoted, so I said, "I'll go along with that".' He also wanted to do much longer solos, 'but the management wouldn't let me'.

While Blackmore described his 'adversary' as 'like glue, he brings things together, and he has identity. We're not the best of friends but we make some good music', Gillan admits, 'Things worked better on this album because I totally ignored Ritchie... the only way to make this record was for that to have happened.' He also described the making of the album as 'a job, not a labour of love'.

Gillan and Glover came up with tunes and words for ten complete backing tracks over a period of some seven to eight weeks. The quality of the results can be gauged by the fact that no fewer than four songs from *Battle*... made it into the stage set. 'That says a lot about the album,' Glover confirms. 'Since *Machine Head*, we've been lucky to get two or three songs that work live from an album.'

The album had been overseen for the first time since the Mark I era, by an outsider. Thom Panunzio, though not a big-name producer, had engineered for John Lennon and Bruce Springsteen, and helped bring the troubled project to some sort of completion. The result was very nearly a UK Top 20 album, even though it only made Number 192 in the States. Another live album, *Come Hell Or High Water*, would be next.

The Battle Rages On

In Gillan's view, this is 'archetypal Purple, but very 1990s with it, very impressive. It flows very naturally and is one of the few tunes where you feel Jon Lord was involved in the writing. Roger's lyrical idea was that when the Berlin Wall came down everyone felt it was the end of trouble. Yet at the last count there were twenty-six wars going on around the world.'

Lick It Up

The singer's favourite track on the album. Why? 'It just felt dirty to me!'

Anya

Similar in structure to 'Woman From Tokyo' , where you take the spirit of a people and a country and turn it into a girl. This time, 'It's the spirit of freedom that existed behind the Iron Curtain before it came down, the overwhelming desire in every culture to have freedom of expression. It's the spirit of Hungary actually, the people who were almost destroyed by the regime, but who always fought back.'

Roger Glover explained how the intro came about, 'We had written the song but didn't have an intro. One afternoon Jon played an intro and when Ritchie walked in that night he asked, "What's that?" "That's the intro." "Nah, shit." What now I thought? "Is there an acoustic guitar nearby?" Ritchie asked. There was. The studio belonged to Peter Maffay and there was an acoustic guitar. Ritchie doodled around and I said I liked it and why didn't he go ahead and we'd see what the result would be. We installed him with a mic. He played and played, at least for forty minutes and no words were exchanged in the control room. He played whatever entered his mind, stopped, thought about it, went on playing and meanwhile the tape kept rolling.

'The next day in the studio Jon asked me what Ritchie thought of his intro. "He didn't want to have anything to do with it, but he did some guitar parts and now I have this idea." For four hours I went through all the things Ritchie had done in those forty minutes and chose three or four pieces. Those I fed into the computer in a distinct order and proposed Jon work around his intro from the previous day and to fit it in the guitar parts. That's the story of the "Anya" intro, which cost me almost a complete day of work. It was cutting and pasting instead of live, but I think it turned out very well.'

Blackmore, for his part, 'always felt that "Anya" was ruined by Gillan's singing'.

Talk About Love

A funky, tongue-in-cheek number with distinctly Zeppelin-esque overtones, but one some Purple fans feel should never have made it to the live set over 'Time To Kill', probably due to Blackmore's reservations about the latter.

Time To Kill

A poem of Ian Gillan's set to existing music. 'When you've time to kill you can think about trying to resolve some problems. The meanings of the songs are always secondary to the music, but there's some interesting stuff there anyway. It seemed to work pretty well, and everyone liked it except Ritchie... who didn't like the words, the tune, or the title, he'd rather I'd have used Joe's tune and lyrics.'

Ramshackle Man

'A biographical lyric that could have been written in the early 1970s overlays a 'Green Onions' Stax-style backing. 'I used to be a friend but now I'm second hand' has parallels to 'Is there someone waiting in the wings to take my place' from 'Spanish Archer'.

A Twist In The Tale

An intense song that took on an almost country feel. 'I started singing a "Fireball" thing, but then I thought better of it,' Gillan explained of a song some have compared to Rainbow's 'Spotlight Kid' and which, with 'Anya', made it to the live set.

Nasty Piece Of Work

A Roger Glover composition: 'I've no idea about who,' says Gillan.

Solitaire

When he first heard the haunting backing track, it reminded Gillan of the Shadows' instrumental 'Man Of Mystery'. Initial vocal lines didn't gel well with the backing, but when he tried singing the words an octave lower and it was accidentally left on the track 'a startling effect' resulted. 'They left it that way and it works really great.'

One Man's Meat A melodic way to end the album, with a proverbial lyric. Almost! 'I deliberately don't say "is another man's poison" anywhere, although I did write "One man's meat is another man's aching butt." A cheap shot, but that's rock 'n' roll!'

Purpendicular

With Ian Gillan back on board and a new guitarist in Steve Morse, Purple were in high spirits when they entered Greg Rike Studios in Orlando, Florida between June and August 1995. The album appeared in February 1996. Jon Lord was delighted to report that 'the music is as aggressive and discordant as everything we ever made. Almost like grunge. Even if I am older than anybody who would buy it, I'm really in love with [this] album.' He regarded it as 'a turning point in our band'.

Gillan regarded the sessions as 'basically like going to work every day. We'd start at noon and work until seven o'clock. Hard work for a bunch of musicians who've got that creative bug back...' They took a break and went off and did a couple of tours in Korea, Africa and India 'to try out some of the material we had been writing and when we came back from that we started recording... we had something like sixteen songs or more, so we were in pretty good shape.'

New boy Morse wanted to bring lots of ideas to the songwriting sessions, 'but didn't want to change the group too much. I told them I would keep bringing in ideas and if they could find anything useful we would use it. If they thought something was too strange, I wanted them to tell me and we wouldn't use it.' He sensibly deferred to four of the original five members in a room when deciding if something sounded like Deep Purple.

From Ian Paice's point of view, 'Some of the understandings that you have when you've been playing with somebody a long time haven't really quite blossomed.' Even so, *Purpendicular* is a real fan favourite that made many a fan swallow their scepticism on the replacement of Ritchie Blackmore. For others, though, it was good… but it wasn't Purple, a fact reflected by a disappointing Number 58 UK chart placing.

Vavoom: Ted The Mechanic

When Purple were writing *The House Of Blue Light*, Gillan ran into 'one of the kind of guys who wants to talk… over the next hour or so he told me his life story and I managed to scribble it all down on a few napkins, which I put into my exercise book and promptly forgot until some years later when they fell to the floor as I was moving my stuff. I was intrigued that it was possible to encapsulate an entire life onto a few napkins. His name wasn't Ted – but it is now – and he wasn't a mechanic either. I'd never heard the word "Vavoom" used in dialogue until a friend of mine used it to describe the sort of thing a girl should have if she wanted to get on in life.' Musically, this is a Steve Morse showcase.

Loosen My Strings

Again, it's Morse's guitar work rather than the Gillan vocal that catches the ear, especially towards the end.

Soon Forgotten

Unusually, Gillan already had the words to this song written before he came to the studio. The song hits the spot, with key changes and dissonance between guitar, keyboards and vocals adding spice to proceedings.

Sometimes I Feel Like Screaming

A ballad made for Gillan to showcase (what else but) his scream – which he does at the end, even though his vocal contributions could do with being higher in the mix.

The Aviator

Steve Morse's love of Led Zeppelin fused with Irish folk
influences and came to the fore here in a track that differed
deliberately from Deep Purple's archetypal sound. 'I thought they
could use some of that feel to get along with all that heavy stuff…
they've been open-minded about everything, that's a key element
of this album.' He used a Music Man mini-guitar in place of a mandolin.

Gillan had wanted to write something about Morse's skills as a
pilot. 'Finding this somewhat difficult, without embracing the
banal, Roger and I turned to imagery. We started in the second
verse with the kind of flying that took place in childhood dreams
and travelled laterally in both directions from there.'

Cascades: I'm Not Your Lover

Morse pushed Jon Lord to play the organ 'with more distortion the
way he used to. I brought one of my guitar effects units and put it
into his organ rig… programmed some effects for him. "Cascades"
has a heavy organ and guitar lines like in the old days when
Ritchie and Jon played a lot of triplet lines together.'

Rosa's Cantina

A demo that felt so good Steve Morse thought, 'Hey, are we gonna
do it again just for the sake of it? If it feels right, leave it.'
Glover's bass line echoes the Beck Bogert Appice treatment of
Stevie Wonder's 'Superstition'.

Castle Full Of Rascals

Gillan's jaundiced take on contemporary politics. 'The Houses of
Parliament, in fact Westminster/Whitehall, like so many other
governments, are no longer relevant – more of a nuisance really.'
Good upfront vocals help him make his point.

A Touch Away

A song on which Morse played a 12-string Steinberger,
but it's the keyboards that catch the ear.

Hey Cisco

An old-school Purple rocker inspired by reports that Clayton Moore, the actor who used to play the Lone Ranger on TV, was being refused permission to open supermarkets because the studio owned the intellectual rights to the image/character. Gillan: 'The situation was transferred, using artistic license, to another couple of heroes of the day, the Cisco Kid and his sidekick Pancho – the message remains the same.'

Ian Paice's one-off use of a double bass drum is also noteworthy.

Somebody Stole My Guitar

A Gillan road trip in Texas with erstwhile tour manager Al Dutton saw them happen across an old Ghost Town called Calico. 'I took some of the ghosts with me when I left Calico... you will too if you ever go there.'

Purpendicular Waltz

The first Morse-era composition that obviously benefited from a live evolution in the stage show prior to recording. A darker vibe to this than the rest of the album, with Paice playing anything but a straight 4/4.

Abandon

The band repaired to Greg Rike Studios, now relocated to Altamonte Springs, Florida, in late 1997 to cut their sixteenth studio effort. The resulting album, Gillan announced, was to be called *Abandon*. 'The definition I favour, from my Oxford dictionary, is, to yield oneself completely to a passion or impulse, [show] lack of inhibition or restraint; reckless freedom of manner. In simple terms, it's fuck-off rock 'n' roll.'

For Roger Glover, *Abandon* 'started out with the unspoken intention of being a harder album... an unconscious desire on

behalf of all of us to echo our road experience in the studio.'
That's as may be, but only a quarter of the tracks were cut live, the
rest built up in much more of a studio fashion.

Nothing outstayed its welcome, only two tracks breaking the
five-minute barrier. Some tracks like 'Seventh Heaven' would
become part of the live repertoire, yet as an album *Abandon* is still
seen as the *Fireball* to *Purpendicular*'s *In Rock* status. As Glover
said, 'I have a theory that every time you do a great album, the
next one's tough.'

Abandon made it into stores in May 1998 but failed to make a
chart impression on either side of the Atlantic.

Any Fule Kno That

The spelling came from a series of *Molesworth* books written by
Geoffrey Williams in the 1950s when Ian Gillan grew up, the
music almost an Aerosmith homage in 'Walk This Way' style.

Almost Human

A great beat from Paice sets up what Gillan labels a drinking song:
'At the beginning of the first verse I am talking to my whisky,' he
says – and 'Afore ye go' is indeed taken straight off a Bell's label.

Don't Make Me Happy

This throwback to 'When A Blind Man Cries' was released in
mono because the stereo version of the song Purple wanted to use
had a problem; the sound on one side was out of sync with the
other. 'Thinking that this was a computer malfunction,' Glover
explained, 'we manipulated the data so that it was back in sync, no
easy task. However, it was now in mono, not stereo. We could
have rectified the problem by remixing the track from the original
multi-tracks but that would have meant delaying the album by
about two months, thereby postponing the tour by at least the same
amount of time. Or we could release in mono... Maybe in twenty-
five years we'll put out the stereo version.'

Seventh Heaven

A song created during an early writing session, but when it came to recording it the spontaneity and live feel was absent. So they salvaged the demo recording and the result is, for Roger, 'one of the best songs on the album. I think it exemplifies the spirit of Deep Purple more than any other song, It doesn't sound like anything else we've ever done, but it does have that raging spirit.'

Watching The Sky

Abandon engineer Darren Schneider enjoyed the part he played in creating 'a certain atmosphere. There's something for everybody in "Watching The Sky" – it's got a spacey, almost psychedelic verse, it's got the real hard chorus, it has a lot of elements that could reach a lot of different people.'

Fingers To The Bone

The highlight of the album to some, this is not really typical Purple but boasts a soulful Gillan vocal in the guise of a man hitting hard times. A thoughtful piano, rather than organ, solo from Jon Lord increases the distance from the well-known trademark sound of old.

Jack Ruby

This began life just after the 1980s reunion when, during a rehearsal, Glover and Paice started playing 'an odd sort of riff in 6/4 time. I liked what it sounded like and so we continued, with Jon joining in. Ian started singing something unintelligible (it was a normal day) and our engineer, at my signal, recorded the whole thing on a cassette. One day, years later I found that cassette in my basement studio, edited it and added some synth horn parts. Because the recording had been in a room, the sound was pretty fat and the drums had a character approaching Bonham's Zeppelin sound. Nothing happened to this idea until a lot later, when I played the tape to the rest of the band. They liked it, we all worked on it, and it ended up as "Jack Ruby".'

She Was

A mid-tempo song that, like the following 'Whatsername', is probably not one of Purple's most memorable moments. The riff didn't inspire, and any Purple song without a decent riff was doomed from the outset.

Whatsername

Continuing the move from metal towards classic rock, and arguably further from Purple as we knew and loved it, this came straight in and, with its 'here we go again' chorus, went straight out again.

69

A road song inspired, reveals Gillan, by memories of 1969. 'All the places mentioned in the second verse are real venues from that era. "The Speak" is the Speakeasy Club in the West End of London, where we spent many an hour with other musicians, girls and liggers. The Marquee is probably London's most famous club and was run by Jack Barry. The Paradiso is a club in Amsterdam where the audience was always stoned and oblivious. The Boat House at Kew Bridge on the River Thames was a rock/blues/jazz venue. The last verse touches on a cheap motel in LA and "Hallelujah!" was the first song Roger and I recorded with Deep Purple.'

Evil Louie

For Ian Paice, this was 'one of the hardest things' to record. 'There's a middle-eight section that I just couldn't get. It was one of those slow ones, and even with a click track I couldn't find a part that would work with it. And it took almost two weeks of going in for a couple of hours every day at the end of the sessions just to try and get this bloody eight bars. Eventually I found it just by playing a sixteenth-note part with a straight backbeat, but instead of playing the sixteenth notes on only the hi-hat or ride cymbal, I played them between the two. And for some reason the motion of my arms doing that made that part fit right in with the click and it felt great. It's a very weird feeling when you know that what you are being asked to do is so simple but you can't find the right way to do it.'

Bludsucker

A re-recording of the *In Rock* classic (albeit with a modernised, phonetic spelling) was the major surprise of the album. 'We were jamming in the studio and it got taped,' said Gillan. 'I think it was Bruce Payne our manager who said it sounded as good today as it did when it was originally recorded, so it kind of sneaked on to the record, with an attitude!'

The band had been playing it on their last world tour in 1997–1998 and, drummer Paice revealed, 'a lot of younger people who were coming to the shows were saying, "What's that great new song you've been playing?" They didn't know it was from an old record. So we thought, well, it's got so much interest let's do it again and try to revitalise it.'

Bananas

Recorded in early 2003 in Los Angeles and released that August, *Bananas* marked the Deep Purple recording debut of Don Airey, kicking off the post-Jon Lord period and leaving the band with just one original member in drummer Ian Paice.

The bulk of the writing had happened in over four weeks in LA, the recording coming about over a similar period – 'a little too quickly for my liking,' observed Glover. I wanted to do another couple of days of jamming and maybe a couple of songs in the pipeline.'

Not that Roger was cracking the production whip this time round. For the first time since *The Battle Rages On*, Purple had opted to use a producer from outside the band. Michael Bradford

had made his name producing the likes of rap meets rock star Kid
Rock, but was a long-time Purple fan. He first met the members of
the band in 2002 after a gig and Glover admits his first thought was
'My God, he's this huge black guy, what's going to happen here?
Are we going to turn into Run DMC meets Aerosmith or what?'
Once convinced he wasn't out to change their musical direction,
even the suspicious bass player was happy to go along with things.

Far from trying to turn them into something they weren't,
Bradford insisted the band embrace their musical trademarks and
get the guitar and organ interplay that once made Purple such a
vital band going again. The result was impressive.

House Of Pain

Written by producer Bradford with 'a few words here and there, as
well as the title' contributed by Gillan, who adds, 'It sounds like a
tribute to the management, although the true derivation is
something I can never reveal.'

Bradford felt the best way of starting the album was 'with a big
guitar riff and Ian screaming… [that] would be a great way to say,
"Wake up everybody! We are back!"'

Sun Goes Down

'That one was developed in rehearsal,' said Bradford. 'The band
really wrote that one as a team. It was the first song where we did
background vocals on the chorus that we knew wouldn't be
doubled live, but that's why albums are different. The song had lots
of great parts; it was a matter of putting them in the right sequence.'

Haunted

This conjures up the classic 1960s rock sound of Procol Harum or
Traffic more than anything contemporary. Michael Bradford added
strings and backing vocals after the band had disappeared, making
it arguably as much his creation as theirs.

Roger Glover had come up with the chord sequence but not the
title, yet was cautious of introducing it until 'after about a week or

so of nailing the ones we knew were going to be obvious and maybe some of the lesser ones, I plucked up enough courage again to pick up an acoustic guitar and play what is essentially a non-hard rock song, it's just a song.

'I worried that it was just too non-Purple, but Michael embraced it, he loved it. He is really into radio and he just thought it was a smash. "We could put this in a film, put this on radio, anywhere, it's a great song" … we were led by that.'

Razzle Dazzle

'This could well be a true story,' said Gillan, 'although conveniently I don't remember a thing… it's a real fine line between an orgy of destruction and a wonderful time.'

Silver Tongue

A jam to which Gillan added cryptic lyrics, producer Bradford processing Don Airey's clavinet 'to give the song a little bit of a mechanised feel'.

Walk On

Presented to the band by Bradford, Gillan rewrote the lyrics. 'I changed a few words to personalise the character, but really I felt good with the song from the moment I heard it. He was generous enough to put my name on the credits.' The solo that Steve Morse played was a first-take shot from the original rhythm track.

Picture Of Innocence

In similar fashion to 'Woman From Tokyo' two decades earlier, this was, said Gillan, 'a figurative representation of the EU idiocracy or the PC Mafia; I'm happy to attack both.'

It started as a jam between Ian Paice and Steve Morse in Greg Rike Studios some three or four years earlier. Glover recorded it on a DAT, 'took bits and pieces and spliced them together to form the arrangement pretty much as it now exists, adding some bass guitar.' In 2001 he played the finished result to the band.

I Got Your Number

One of the first songs to be written for *Bananas*, this was originally performed under the title 'Up The Wall' but 'always felt unfinished' to Glover and it was only when Michael Bradford suggested that it needed a chorus that it took final shape. 'I thought I heard Ian sing the words "I got your number", although he probably didn't – he kind of sings words that aren't words but sound like they are. Anyway I sang them back to him and it clicked. Jon wrote with us but Don played on the record.'

Never A Word

A song Glover says 'doesn't sound anything like Purple, but felt right' was brought into the studio by Steve Morse. 'I think we've explored most emotions,' said the bass player, 'which is so refreshing because most bands only have one emotion, and that's anger; I'm fed up with anger. I'm fed up with negative... I don't know, I'm still living in '67.'

Bananas

A 7/4 riff from Steve Morse inspired a song which, Roger Glover confesses, 'is the same chords as in one of the *Spinal Tap* songs, "Big Bottom" I think it is. But of course, it's in 5/4 so we got away with it.'

Ian Gillan 'couldn't stop laughing as I worked out where to count seven and where to count five in this unusual arrangement. It proved to be very difficult for an old blues singer like me. So, I ignored the time signatures entirely and sang the tune as if it was a straight 8/4. I just tapped my foot to every beat, and developed a psycho-twitch as I ignored the missing last beat of each bar, and then drew inspiration from the harmonica. Fortunately with a blues harp you have to suck in order to bend the notes...'

Doing It Tonight

A song about a girl who is desirable but unattainable – so, says its singer, 'the last verse is pure sour grapes and the word imagine takes on a different meaning.'

Contact Lost

With cello from Elton John associate Paul Buckmaster as a counterpoint to Steve Morse's guitar melody, 'Contact Lost' pays its final respects to the crew members lost on the tragic final flight of the space shuttle Columbia. 'In particular Kalpana Chawla was a friend, a Deep Purple aficionado,' Ian Gillan explained. 'She arranged to carry some Deep Purple CDs during the mission and one of her wake-up selections to commence another twelve-hour shift was "Space Truckin'" … Music doesn't need words to be lyrical and Steve Morse was able to speak with his guitar when we were all speechless.'

Bibliography

All of the below proved helpful to the author, and can be recommended.
The long-unavailable but at the time definitive Chris Charlesworth book
was incorporated, with permission, into the Simon Robinson book that
came with *Listen, Learn, Read On.*

Books
Rainbow Rising by Roy Davies (Helter Skelter, 2002)
Child In Time by Ian Gillan (Smith Gryphon, 1993)
Smoke On The Water: The Deep Purple Story by Dave Thompson (ECW
Press [Canada], 2004)
Deep Purple: The Illustrated Biography by Chris Charlesworth
(Omnibus, 1983)
Pete Frame's Rock Family Trees (Omnibus, 1984)

Records
Sleeve notes of the EMI CD reissues and the *Listen, Learn, Read On* box
set.
Websites consulted include deep-purple.com (the band's official site),
deep-purple.net (Deep Purple Appreciation Society site),
thehighwaystar.com and others. Rarely has a band been so well served
on the internet!

Publications
*Sounds, New Musical Express, Melody Maker, Disc & Music Echo,
Kerrang!, Metal Hammer, Record Collector, Record Buyer, Classic Rock.*
Darker Than Blue (DPAS magazine, contact via deep-purple.net) and
interview reprints.
Tour programmes.
More Black Than Purple (Ritchie Blackmore magazine,
jerry@mbtp.freeserve.co.uk)

Others
Author's interviews with Ian Gillan and Roger Glover.

Index